DEMOCRACY AS HUMAN RIGHTS

Freedom and Equality in the Age of Globalization

Michael Goodhart

Routledge
Taylor & Francis Group
New York   London

Published in 2005 by
Routledge
Taylor & Francis Group
270 Madison Avenue
New York, NY 10016

Published in Great Britain by
Routledge
Taylor & Francis Group
2 Park Square
Milton Park, Abingdon
Oxon OX14 4RN

International Standard Book Number-10: 0-415-95177-1 (Hardcover) 0-415-95178-X (Softcover)
International Standard Book Number-13: 978-0-415-95177-7 (Hardcover) 978-0-415-95178-4 (Softcover)
Library of Congress Card Number 2005003045

Library of Congress Cataloging-in-Publication Data

Goodhart, Michael E., 1969-
    Democracy as human rights : freedom and equality in the age of globalization / Michael Goodhart.
      p. cm.
    Includes bibliographical references and index.
    ISBN 0-415-95177-1 (hb : alk. paper) -- ISBN 0-415-95178-X (pb : alk. paper)
    1. Democracy. 2. Human rights. 3. Globalization. I. Title.

JC423.G63355 2005
321.8--dc22
                                                                          2005003045

Taylor & Francis Group
is the Academic Division of T&F Informa plc.

Visit the Taylor & Francis Web site at
http://www.taylorandfrancis.com

and the Routledge Web site at
http://www.routledge-ny.com

For Susan

Contents

Acknowledgments

This book began as my doctoral dissertation at the University of California, Los Angeles; both the University and its Department of Political Science provided generous funding in support of research and writing. Brian Walker was always supportive and encouraging despite his reservations about certain aspects of the argument. Mick Mann and Ron Rogowski provided numerous helpful and insightful comments on successive drafts and somehow always found the time for engaging conversations about many of the topics covered here (and others as well). Carole Pateman's dedication and loyalty as a reader, critic, mentor, and friend have proven invaluable at every stage of the project's evolution, and her example of scholarly achievement continues to humble and inspire me. The revision and editing of the manuscript have been undertaken at the University of Pittsburgh, whose own Department of Political Science provides a congenial atmosphere for research; I am especially grateful to Fred Whelan and John Markoff for their comments and suggestions on several chapters.

Joan Tronto generously read the entire manuscript and offered enthusiastic support along with her incisive comments; Brooke Ackerly and Susanna Wing have read chapters—sometimes on quite short notice—with sharp eyes and good cheer, and my collaborations with Brooke over the past few years have been challenging and fun. Andrew Lister and Dan O'Neill have read, and more importantly, argued with me on innumerable occasions about some of the central claims in the book, pushing me to clarify and deepen my argument in ways that make it stronger than it could ever have been without their (insistent) probing. Susanna, Andrew, and Dan have also commiserated with me over a range of anxieties, professional and otherwise; I am grateful for their friendship as well as their expertise. Rob Tempio at Routledge has been an enthusiastic advocate from the beginning, and the entire production staff has performed with great efficiency and effectiveness. My parents and sister have been supportive throughout this project (and all of my others), as has Deric Gerlach. Finally, Jamie Mayerfield undertook a careful, detailed, constructive, and remarkably insightful critique of the entire manuscript that has improved it from front to back.

Numerous other colleagues, many of them discussants and co-panelists, have read and commented on various chapters or otherwise supported this effort, including George Andreopoulos, Shelley Angelo, Zehra Arat, Daniele Archibugi, Roland Axtmann, Chuck Beitz, Fred Dallmayr, Amanda Dickins, Jack Donnelly, Steve Elkin, Michael Freeman, Lew Friedland, Mark Gibney, David Held, Peter Juviler, Stephen Kobrin, Nancy Kokaz, Andrew Kuper, Jane Mansbridge, and Henry Shue. Numerous valuable suggestions have come from audiences over several years; participants in the international conference "Democracy, Community, and Social Justice in an Era of Globalization," held at the University of Denver in April 1998, and in the Democracy Collaborative Affiliates' Conference on the State of Democratic Practice, held at the University of Maryland in January 2002, deserve special mention.

Portions of chapter 1 were originally published in an article that appeared in *Polity*; portions of chapter 5 appeared in an article published in *Democratization*. Though they are included here in substantially revised form, I thank those journals for permission to reuse that material. I have also received support from the Richard D. and Mary Jane Edwards Endowed Publication Fund at the University of Pittsburgh, which I gratefully acknowledge here.

Finally, Susan Hoppe has been a keen editor, trenchant critic, and unwavering friend. The debts I owe her can be acknowledged but never adequately expressed.

Introduction

The Tacoma Narrows Bridge opened in July 1940, linking the city of Tacoma to Washington's Olympic Peninsula.[1] The bridge gained immediate renown for the undulating motion of its deck, which earned it the nickname "Galloping Gertie"; people came from near and far to "ride the bridge." Engineers determined that unanticipated wind conditions in the Narrows, combined with certain design features of the bridge itself, were responsible for the wavelike movements. While no one seemed to doubt that the bridge was safe, studies were made into possible ways of mitigating the wind effects through structural modifications. But on November 7 of that same year high winds created unusual pressure on the structure, causing one of the main cables to shift slightly and allowing the bridge deck to move laterally as well as vertically. At around 11:00 a.m., several spans of the deck collapsed; images of the falling roadway and snapping suspension cables have been made familiar to generations of physics students through films shot by a University of Washington engineering professor who was studying the bridge's movements. Subsequent structural analysis showed that tensions generated by the wind pressure had compromised the entire superstructure, which had to be torn down.

The story of the Tacoma Narrows Bridge is a good metaphor for democracy in the age of globalization, because globalization exacerbates previously unrecognized structural tensions within modern democratic theory and practice; while few observers predict imminent collapse, many agree that democracy's coherence and integrity have been severely tested, perhaps compromised.

Many people—scholars and protesters, citizens and government officials—understandably see globalization as a serious threat to democracy. Globalization means many things: it is associated with a variety of ills, such as poverty,

1

inequality, insecurity, terrorism, and a race to the bottom in wages and environmental protection, as well as with a variety of goods, from information and communication technologies to cultural interchange and democratization. This diversity of meanings makes it difficult to pin down exactly how globalization is supposed to threaten democracy and difficult to work out a clear, democratic response to it. Many people find retreat and disengagement as undesirable as they find the prospect of a global state. We want a more democratic global order with meaningful guarantees of basic human rights, but we don't want a global government; we want global democratic norms and decision making without global armies and parliaments.

This apparent dilemma reflects a failure of the democratic imagination, a failure stemming from an ossified understanding of democracy itself. We have become too committed to defending democracy as we currently conceive it, either by seeking to extend existing models of democracy into the global arena or to buttress state-based democracy against the storms of globalization. Both approaches emphasize the nature of the threat globalization poses; neither subjects democracy itself to adequate critical scrutiny. It is a mistake to conceive globalization as a threat from the outset; doing so sets up whatever it happens to be threatening as something to be defended. Many of the values called into question by globalization are among our most important and most cherished—values such as freedom, equality, community, democracy, and human rights—but in presuming that globalization threatens these values we squander the invaluable opportunity it offers us for reassessing and revitalizing them.

This study differs from many others, then, in that it does not defend existing democratic theories or institutions against the purported threat of globalization. Instead, it places democracy in the analytic foreground, investigating its conceptual foundations in light of the challenges globalization presents. My hope is to understand better democracy's present confusions and to find better remedies for them. So while the book is occasioned by globalization and the questions it raises for modern democratic theory and practice, it is not a book *about* globalization. Rather, globalization serves as a lens, a way of magnifying and clarifying the tensions besetting modern democracy. This approach requires a number of important simplifying assumptions that emphasize globalization's broad transformative impact on the configuration of rule in the global political system and downplay its ideological character. These assumptions bring certain problems within modern democracy into sharp focus, but they also place some of globalization's nastier aspects outside our narrowed field of vision.

The nastier side of globalization is probably familiar to most readers. There is a lot wrong with globalization so far, and a lot more that could go wrong with it if certain fundamental changes to do with democratic priorities are not made soon. Like much else, however, globalization presents both threats and opportunities; it is neither the end of history nor the end of civilization, as its defenders and opponents would have us believe. The trick is to keep our analytic focus tightly on democracy; once we have reached some conclusions about what democracy means and what it requires in the age of globalization, it will be possible to consider how globalization itself can be democratized.

My approach resembles the sociologically oriented one adopted by the nineteenth-century French liberals, who identified and assessed the theoretical implications of social change.[2] In particular, my argument has a certain affinity with Benjamin Constant's analysis of the French Revolution and its aftermath.[3] Constant identified in the Revolution an ideology and politics grounded in what he saw as ancient and anachronistic modes of liberty. He believed that revolutionary excesses grew from a sincere though misguided fascination with these modes of liberty—misguided because it denied the practical impossibility of realizing these ancient liberties in modern times.[4] While himself deeply sympathetic with the ideals and aspirations animating the ancient ideal of liberty, Constant saw the error in pursuing a political project subverted by radically transformed social, economic, and cultural conditions.[*] Like Constant, I am fiercely committed to the values democracy represents; like him, I am also persuaded that political ideals must change with the times. If, as I shall argue here, globalization does seriously challenge not just the practice of modern democracy but also its conceptual coherence, only bold, imaginative thinking will allow us to envision a more democratic future. Modern democratic theory is full of insight and inspiration, but its basic assumptions no longer provide an adequate framework for democracy in the age of globalization.

This book attempts to rethink democracy, to work out what its core principles of freedom and equality for all might mean and what they might require. The argument is informed by a critical conjectural history of the origins and development of modern democratic theory, tracing its conceptual entanglement with sovereignty. This history seeks to uncover the assumptions that earlier theorists in the democratic tradition took for granted so that we can grapple with the legacy of those assumptions in our own thinking about democracy. This approach differs from that of the increasingly dominant Cambridge School, which emphasizes recovering theorists' intentions or reconstructing what the discursive paradigms of their day would have allowed

---

[*] Critics have chided Constant for overstating the break between past and present; his understanding of the modern form of liberty, defined in opposition to the ancient, rests on the supposition that the rise of commercial society represents a thoroughgoing transformation of social, political, and economic mores. The critics point out, rightly enough, that such a totalistic vision blinds Constant to important continuities; postulating complete rupture renders continuity insignificant or invisible. Still, I think Constant's approach and insights remain instructive.

them to argue. One of the intuitions underlying the Cambridge approach is that past political theorists were concerned with their own problems and therefore cannot provide us with solutions to ours.

I certainly agree that we should not simply rummage around in the history of political thought for ready-made solutions to contemporary problems; but if we hope to understand why and how globalization affects democracy and what might be done about it, it will not suffice to understand what the early theorists of sovereignty and democracy were doing or thought they were doing.[5] We must interrogate modern political thought, asking of it questions it could never have been concerned with because such questions obviously had not and could not have been formulated in the past. In my view, the past is not merely a story to get straight; it is a place of origins, a place to which we must return repeatedly with new questions as we begin the search for new answers. Old ideas are not simply objects to be studied, like the ruins of ancient temples, as historical artifacts; they are sometimes also the deeply buried foundations of our contemporary intellectual edifices. We need to dig up and expose these foundations so that we can comprehend our own conceptual architecture, understanding what remains sound and what must be built anew.

The book is divided into two very different but complementary parts. Part I comprises the conjectural history of sovereignty and democracy, a history designed to clarify the challenge globalization poses for democracy and to establish the conceptual and practical limits of modern democratic theory. Part II offers a reinterpretation of democratic theory, an account called *democracy as human rights*, that responds to this challenge. Part II is primarily normative and constructive, though the normative theory builds on the historical and analytical conclusions of part I. Because the argument is cumulative in this way, its centerpiece—the defense of democracy as human rights—appears somewhat later than might be expected. To make clear how the argument develops and provide some orientation for readers, the remainder of this introduction presents a broad overview of the book.

In the first chapter I attempt to cut through the confusion surrounding current debates on globalization and democracy. I demonstrate that pervasive conceptual problems plague these debates, problems that obfuscate important questions about why globalization should affect democracy in the first place. By introducing some simplifying assumptions about globalization, I show that the answer to why and how globalization affects democracy lies in understanding democracy's complicated relationship with the sovereign state. Despite a recent resurgence in scholarly interest in and attention to sovereignty, political theorists have been slow to recognize and appreciate its complex combination of normative and empirical assumptions in a unique discourse about the territoriality of rightful rule. This discourse, I argue in chapter 2, explained and justified a significant transformation in the configuration of rule in early modern Europe and profoundly shaped subsequent political thinking.

In chapter 3 I argue that modern democracy was deeply and directly influenced by this discourse of rightful rule. Theories of popular sovereignty and social contract, I contend, establish the theoretical idiom in which modern democratic theory develops. I advance this claim through close readings of Locke and Rousseau, thinkers representing the dominant currents in modern democratic theory. Once this link between democracy and sovereignty is established, I consider in the next chapter why and how globalization affects democracy. I argue that it does so *through* its impact on sovereignty. Globalization is again transforming the configuration of rule, dissipating sovereignty in the process. This transformation exposes a paradox in modern democracy: it seems simultaneously to require and to rule out supranational governance. This paradox reflects a long-submerged tension between democracy's universal premises and its restriction within the conceptual and territorial limits of sovereignty.

Chapter 5 briefly considers recent cosmopolitan and communitarian democratic responses to globalization in light of the foregoing analysis. Ironically, from this perspective it becomes apparent that both make similar mistakes, failing to recognize the interdependence of modern democracy's normative and empirical (territorial) dimensions. Contemporary efforts to rethink democracy in the age of globalization do not go far enough, I conclude: they remain wedded to theories of democratic legitimacy or to particular institutions and procedures that no longer make sense once unmoored from their conceptual anchor in sovereignty.

In the second part of the book I articulate and defend a reinterpretation of democratic theory informed by the conjectural history and analysis presented in part I. This reinterpretation, democracy as human rights (DHR), begins from the core democratic principles of freedom and equality and attempts to work out what their universal promise might require once disentangled from sovereignty. DHR defines democracy as a political commitment to universal emancipation through securing the equal enjoyment of fundamental human rights for everyone. It might seem odd to think of democracy as human rights, but, in chapter 6, I establish that there is a long tradition of doing just that. Since the seventeenth century, emancipatory democrats have understood democracy as a political promise of freedom from domination and unwarranted interference for all, and they have employed human rights as the language of democratic empowerment. I briefly sketch the contours and central concepts of this tradition, which provides important historical resources on which DHR draws.

The final three chapters develop the theory of DHR. In chapter 7, I lay out and defend the theory itself, stressing that it is a critical reconstruction or reinterpretation—a claim not about what democracy *is* but rather about what democracy *might be*. I explain the theory's key propositions and answer a range of anticipated objections. Chapter 8 focuses on DHR's institutional requirements, with a particular emphasis on its most novel and distinctive proposals, those most relevant to resolving the puzzles typically associated with global democracy and globalization. The final chapter discusses problems of implementation—how DHR might come about and how it might work. In a brief conclusion, I return to consider those nastier aspects of globalization bracketed throughout my analysis.

My argument engages four important areas of contemporary debate among scholars of political theory and human rights. The first and most obvious is democratic theory. In addition to its clear relevance to ongoing debates about democracy and globalization, my argument offers the first fully developed account of democracy's conceptual dependence upon sovereignty, an account that challenges some of the deepest assumptions about democracy's meaning and practice. Second, my argument suggests that the now widely accepted division of the democratic tradition into neatly opposed liberal and republican variants risks obscuring an important strand of emancipatory thinking about democracy. The third debate to which the book contributes concerns the theory of human rights. Most of the literature on this subject focuses on the origins of human rights and their philosophical grounding or foundations. My argument strikes out in a different direction, providing a rigorous analytic account of the political, and specifically democratic, nature of human rights. Finally, my argument suggests a possible new direction for the contemporary human rights movement. Critics have recently suggested that human rights is facing a "midlife crisis," that "the precarious triumph of human rights" might be coming to an end.[6] These critics lament that the human rights movement has never been transformed into a political force capable of mobilizing democratic citizens and shaping democratic politics. DHR provides a model for a democratic politics of human rights and a framework for understanding human rights and democratization as crucial elements in a broader emancipatory politics.

Studies completed after the collapse of the Tacoma Narrows Bridge attributed its failure to the "improper shape and not improper strength" of the bridge. Although stress from the winds and from the collapse itself did compromise the bridge's superstructure, its piers remained undamaged. Nearly eight years later, workers began construction of a new bridge on those same foundations. Modern democracy's core principles remain sound; this book is an attempt to reconstruct it on those foundations.

PART I

The Limits
of Modern Democracy

CHAPTER 1

States of Confusion

Many scholars, activists, politicians, and citizens perceive that globalization poses an imminent and serious threat to democracy. Impressionistic evidence of this threat is certainly powerful: transnational corporations (TNCs) seem ever more able to evade the reach of state regulation. The policies and activities of the IMF and WTO frequently interfere in what many regard as the sovereign affairs of states, constraining states' autonomy in promoting a global corporate or free-trade agenda. Some critics even allege that these and other institutions are actively antidemocratic, either designed or destined to undermine democratic rule.[1] Financial turmoil in Southeast Asia and Latin America at the turn of the twenty-first century, which many observers attribute to speculative short-term capital flows and reckless private lending, and the devastating effects of IMF-backed structural adjustment programs in much of the developing world, seem to confirm that the will of the people is increasingly subject to the whim of the market. Nowhere is this impression more firmly held, ironically, than in the rich countries of the West. Fears of capital flight and low-wage job competition, and of the declining standards of living, lax environmental protection, and curtailed social provision linked with them, fuel a backlash against free trade and encourage growing hostility toward immigrants. The irony is that while much of the world sees globalization as the new face of Western capitalism and imperialism, citizens of the Western democracies nonetheless feel themselves terribly aggrieved by it.

While the view that globalization threatens democracy is widely shared, scholars have had a hard time establishing the nature and extent of the threat on firm empirical grounds. Much of the evidence is ambiguous or controversial; numerous skeptics reject the entire debate as "globaloney" while others suspect that globalization is little more than rhetorical or ideological cover for a neoliberal economic agenda. Our seeming inability to make sense of globalization's empirical realities perpetuates this controversy, and the high degree of uncertainty surrounding the entire debate has led some prominent scholars of democracy to suggest that political theorists can probably contribute little of use to the debate on globalization.[2]

I am not convinced that this view is correct. I shall argue in this chapter that much of the confusion arises because we are asking the wrong question, at least with respect to democracy and globalization. The usual question—how does globalization affect democracy?—requires that we quantify globalization's effects and measure them against some (invariably controversial) historical baseline, inviting precisely the sort of empirical uncertainty just described. Framing the inquiry this way makes it a question about globalization; democracy apparently becomes a dependent variable. Upon closer inspection, however, democracy drops out altogether. Most contemporary arguments purporting to analyze how globalization affects democracy actually study globalization's effects on *states*. I shall argue that this conceptual slippage reflects an unquestioned assumption that the state is democracy's natural and appropriate container, that they fit together unproblematically. Although the close historical connection between state and democracy enjoys the warrant of history, conflating them leads to analytic confusion and contradiction, crippling efforts to understand globalization's consequences for states and for democracy.

This conceptual confusion, I contend, suggests that we need to ask a different question: *Why* does globalization affect democracy? This question concentrates our critical attention on democracy rather than on globalization, generating a wide range of further puzzles and problems much more within the bailiwick of political theory. Most significantly, it forces us to interrogate the presumed natural fit between democracy and the state. Once we challenge this presumption, it becomes plain that the relationship is much more complex and much more problematic than we are wont to realize.

How Does Globalization Affect Democracy?

There are probably as many definitions of globalization as there are students of it; the term "can refer to anything from the Internet to a hamburger."[3] Scholars cannot even agree whether globalization exists, much less what it might mean or imply. Though globalization is most frequently discussed in economic terms, it is also described as a postmodern development, a socio-cultural process, a political transformation, and an ideological construct. We can identify eight themes or commonplaces that recur throughout the vast literature on the subject (remembering that critics disagree about them adamantly).

1. *Market integration*: the integration and expansion of markets in goods and capital, sometimes described as interpenetration of markets. Trade has expanded tremendously, and the opening of financial markets and unleashing of vast flows of capital initiated by this expansion are often described as new or unprecedented.

2. *Technological developments*: the advances in technology, especially information and communications technology, that facilitate rapid movement of capital, people, and ideas. The Internet, satellite communications and cellular telephony, and continuing innovations and efficiencies in transportation are often mentioned.

3. *Expansion/internationalization of governance and regulatory capacities*: the growing role of international governance organizations (IGOs) and TNCs in governance activities in a variety of policy areas. Critics complain that this expansion and internationalization of governance place it beyond public and democratic control, undermines sovereignty, and weakens and delegitimizes states.

4. *Declining policy and regulatory role of the state*: the diminishing policy autonomy of states and their inability to remain effective actors in international political and economic affairs. Markets constrain or dictate state policy, especially fiscal and economic policy; rapid capital flows and speculation against currencies can destabilize and even wreck national economies.

5. *Homogenization of global culture/cultural imperialism*: the spread of a single (American) popular culture, primarily through the mass media. Many worry that this process destroys local/indigenous cultures, reducing culture to just another commodity for sale in the global marketplace.

6. *Shrinking/accelerating world*: the acceleration and intensification of various transnational ties and interactions help to "shrink" the planet, minimizing the importance of distance as relations deepen and multiply across borders, largely through faster and easier communication. Enhanced communication strengthens ties among tribal, familial, and ethnic groups scattered across continents and facilitates the development of transnational classes of professionals and bureaucrats. Social, cultural, economic, and political boundaries become more fluid. These connections are sometimes described as an emerging global civil society (GCS).

7. *Fragmentation or localization*: the trend toward ethnic revivalism, reinvigorated nationalism, religious fundamentalism, and other local patterns of identification and organization. Fragmentation is the flip side of global integration; terms like *fragmegration* or *glocalization* indicate

this dialectical relationship. Localization might reflect increasing cultural assertiveness in societies emerging from the shadow of colonialism or nascent resistance to changing cultural or economic imperatives.

8. *Neoliberalism*: ideologically, the conviction that capitalist markets and market forces are natural, efficient, and adequate mechanisms for allocating and redistributing resources, wealth, and income and that an economic system governed by market forces constitutes human freedom. Politically, neoliberalism refers to a set of policies including privatization, deregulation, lowering corporate taxes, interest rate liberalization, competitive exchange rates, decreased capital controls, and secure property rights—the so-called Washington Consensus.[4]

No neat typology of these claims, trends, and developments is possible; many overlap or intersect, and each may contain a mix of empirical, normative, and ideological claims. Moreover, there is a good deal of disagreement about just how new and significant globalization really is. First, flows of people, capital, goods, and ideas among societies are as ancient as societies themselves.[5] Similarly, as colonial monopolies like the Dutch and British East India Companies demonstrate, transfers of capital and resources among societies under corporate auspices are themselves centuries-old phenomena; powerful corporations are no newcomers to the sphere of global governance. Moreover, technological innovation in transport and communication—from Roman highways to steam railways—has long fostered social and economic integration. When considered with the history of cooperation and coordination among political authorities in almost every imaginable area of human endeavor, the "changes" associated with globalization hardly seem new, much less revolutionary. Many critics reach precisely this conclusion, intimating that much of the uproar about globalization is hyperbole. Second, critics also maintain that existing levels of economic integration (variously measured) may only now be approaching levels seen at the beginning of the twentieth century.[6] They also cite the continued strength of states, including their active role in shaping and controlling emergent IGOs, as evidence that claims about integration and the erosion of sovereignty are vastly exaggerated. On this view, commonly associated with the neorealist school of international relations theory, the continued preeminence of states in international politics shows that no fundamental change has (yet) occurred. Taken together, these objections prompt us to question whether there is any such thing as globalization.

Ongoing disagreement about what globalization is has not preempted a wide-ranging discussion of its effects on democracy; if anything, the disagreement has intensified debate on this subject. The most frequently cited threats to democracy include: decreasing policy autonomy, especially economic policy; increasing demands for policies to counter the adverse effects of open trade, coupled with states' increasing inability to provide such a safety net; erosion of sovereignty, mainly through ongoing shifts of legal, regulatory, and governance authority to IGOs; declining living standards and reduced social and economic rights; and, corporate capital's growing ability to elude government control and regulation. That many of these "effects" of globalization are nearly indistinguishable from the most common definitions of it attests to the high degree of confusion reigning in the field.

Globalization's purported effects on democracy are often conceived as democratic deficits or disjunctures. Global governance appears increasingly undemocratic as nonstate agencies like IGOs and TNCs assume greater roles and state autonomy and sovereignty decline. There are really two distinct but closely related hypotheses here. First, there is a claim about the limited competence of the popular or democratic will as realized and executed through state-based democratic institutions. This is mainly a claim about the scope of global political problems relative to state jurisdiction. I prefer to use the term *disjunctures* exclusively for this kind of problem. David Held describes these disjunctures as occurring "between the idea of the state as in principle capable of determining its own future, and the world economy, international organization, regional and global institutions, international law, and military alliances which operate to shape and constrain the options of individual nation-states."[7] In short, global politics and state-based political institutions do not "match up," and the resulting disjunctures represent areas in which states have incomplete or inadequate political control. These disjunctures limit the effective reach of democratic decision making; IGOs created to remedy these disjunctures seem to drain control and authority from democratic institutions.

The second claim involves the growing number of governance functions performed by such international actors as IGOs and TNCs, which are not subject to traditional democratic controls. I prefer to use the term *democratic deficit* to describe such cases.[8] The worry here is that a larger and larger share of the important decisions impacting citizens of democratic states are made by institutions that are opaque, unaccountable, and unrepresentative, or even, as in the case of the European Union, insufficiently transparent, accountable, and representative.* Democratic deficits, then, describe shortcomings in existing governance institutions, while disjunctures refer to shortcomings in the scope and effectiveness of existing democratic institutions; deficits are

---

*Democratic deficits are discussed almost exclusively in connection with international governance, though the critique of existing institutions seems equally relevant in domestic contexts.

normative claims about the (il)legitimacy of existing governance regimes, while disjunctures identify the empirical and conceptual limits of state-based democratic governance.

To recapitulate: scholars analyzing democracy and globalization typically concentrate on *how* globalization affects democracy. The usual answers include restrictions on policy autonomy, erosion of sovereignty, destabilizing flows of transnational capital, and the activities of unaccountable corporations and governance agencies, among others. All of these claims are contestable and contested: whether and to what degree policy is really limited (or more limited than it has been historically) by international financial concerns; whether sovereignty really is eroding and what the mechanism of that erosion might be; how important and how unprecedented current flows of global capital are; how powerful corporations and international agencies really are vis-à-vis states; and how permanent we should consider any recent trends and developments, are all fiercely debated.

States of Confusion

These controversies aside, there is something odd about the entire debate —or at least, about the parameters within which the debate takes place. Of all the alleged effects of globalization on democracy, none clearly has anything directly to do with democracy. They are really claims about how globalization affects the state (and citizens or groups of citizens within states). Each of the threats discussed above concerns a diminution of state authority or capacity, usually involving pressures imposed or exacerbated by a highly fluid and integrated world economy; it is taken to follow that these developments threaten democracy. Sometimes the gap between assertions about the various ills globalization visits upon states and the conclusions drawn about democracy is acknowledged in brief statements about constraints on democratic decision making or legitimacy or violations of the social compact; more often the disconnect goes unaddressed or, one suspects, unnoticed.

Arguments about democracy's dependence upon and imbrication with the modern state are simply left out of most discussions of globalization. This oversight reflects a widespread assumption that the relation between states and democracy is too obvious to mention. Readers reflexively complete the implied syllogism: globalization affects the state; democracy is embedded in the state; thus, globalization affects democracy (through the state). The syllogism undoubtedly reflects important elements of truth about the close historical and theoretical links between states and democracy (more below). My concern is that despite its formal adequacy, the logical interpolation of the state between globalization and democracy obscures more than it clarifies.

Specifically, at least five analytic confusions result from efforts to understand globalization's effects on democracy mediately through the state:

1. *Our analytic focus slips from democracy to globalization.* In the standard account, how globalization affects democracy is a function of how and to what extent it influences the state, so a great deal of effort gets channeled into quantifying trends, measuring integration, comparing statistics, contesting definitions and indicators, and assessing the novelty of various patterns of interaction. Since reliable conclusions about the fate of states and, indirectly, democracy are contingent upon reliable evaluations of globalization, the tremendous complexity and uncertainty surrounding globalization itself becomes an issue; suggestions for reforming or strengthening democracy will stand or fall with the credibility of the accounts of globalization informing them. I do not mean to suggest that understanding globalization is unimportant; rather, my point is that this task is so vast and so difficult that it tends to postpone direct questions about democracy indefinitely.

2. *It is unclear how we should assess democracy's vitality.* This problem hearkens back to the old debates between normative and empirical theorists of democracy.[9] Empirically there can be little doubt that globalization is correlated with a rapid spread in liberal–democratic forms and procedures. By some recent counts there were as many as 119 democracies in 2004, 62 percent of all states, as compared to 41 (just over a quarter of the total) in 1974.[10] Yet as we have seen, critics worry that globalization is undermining democracy, and fears are growing that the liberal model of democracy exported to the developing world as part of the process of globalization is more formal than real.* Moreover, fears that globalization weakens or undermines democracy dampen the enthusiasm we would otherwise certainly ascribe to this democratic trend. If globalization decreases the capacities of states and limits their sovereignty and autonomy in ways that undercut the effectiveness of democratic institutions, the proliferation of formal democracy might mask a secular decline in substantive democracy. More states are democratic, but states themselves are said to be less able to enact or protect the popular will.

Some critics attribute the paradox of democracy's simultaneous success and crisis to a contradiction between democratization and globalization:

---

*This exportation often occurs through conditions attached to various forms of aid and to membership in elite clubs like the European Union; the Cold War's end has emboldened Western democracies to use "conditionality" much more aggressively. Not surprisingly, states seeking political or economic favor (and favors) with the West are eager to adopt democratic forms to placate Western critics. Thus it remains unclear just what the correlation between globalization and democratization reflects about democracy.

although the formal elements of liberal democracy are proliferating, huge increases in social inequality and the erosion of welfare states are destroying the material foundation of political equality on which democracy depends.[11] This leaves us in the odd position of opposing globalization because it promotes and extends liberal democracy and because it undermines liberal democracy. The real difficulty is that when we conflate states with democracy, it is hard to decide whether globalization fortifies or eviscerates democracy, harder to account for the fact that it seems to do both.

3. *What is good for states might not be good for democracy.* The conventional wisdom seems to be that what is good for the state is good for democracy; this wisdom to some degree reflects and acknowledges democracy's long containment within the state. If states are eroding, weakening, or even dying, democracy is directly threatened. Inversely, if states remain strong, this logic suggests that democracy must likewise be robust. We should be able to infer from the lamentations of democracy's sorry condition that states must be getting weaker. Are they?

At one level this is an impossible question; asking whether globalization strengthens or weakens states as a group makes little sense. Not all states are alike: some are strong and others weak, some democratic and others not.* States are situated differently in the global political economy and are impacted differently by globalization. Such distinctions get lost easily, however, when our focus vacillates between states and democracy. States have adapted to recent economic and political developments by creating a wide range of cooperation and coordination mechanisms that allows them to assert collective control in global affairs. Many states are rapidly adopting forms of economic and political organization ("the competition state") that have proven particularly successful in recent years.[12] Further, deregulation and privatization, while associated with laissez-faire economics, actually require states strong enough to reshape markets and redistribute wealth on a comprehensive scale (and many democrats would worry, in the wrong direction). Technology heightens state internal regulatory and monitoring capacities, as exemplified in police and border control activities. Global events, such as the terrorist attacks on the United States in 2001, provide the pretext for tremendous expansions of state powers in areas like surveillance and detention. Other states, however, have collapsed or imploded.

The conventional wisdom obfuscates that what is good for states might not, after all, be good for democracy. Consider the growing role of IGOs in international politics: many scholars see their rise as a direct threat to democracy

---

*What constitutes strong and weak states is poorly understood. Many states deemed too weak to achieve social, economic, and political liberalization are strong enough to commit systemic human rights violations in the pursuit of wealth and power for the ruling elite.

and democratic governance, as we have seen. But students of international regimes remind us that they are the creatures of states struggling to retain some measure of control in issue domains where complex global economic forces diminish the utility of unilateral action. These regimes "are political creations set up to overcome perceived problems arising from inadequately regulated or insufficiently coordinated national action."[13] The passive voice sometimes disguises the vital role of states here; international regimes are set up *by states* to address a complex range of global phenomena. The institutions and organizations to which states have allegedly lost sovereignty and autonomy, such as the WTO, can also be understood as mechanisms through which states—especially the most powerful ones—find solutions to long-term governance problems.[14] This is why Cerny describes globalization as "a process of political *structuration*"; states create new political institutions to meet their changing needs.[15] The thickening web of IGOs is not some trap waiting to ensnare unsuspecting states; it is states themselves that spin its threads. The web is designed to catch, through collective action, issues that elude unilateral competence.

International regimes do not necessarily weaken states,* but it does not follow that they are good for democracy. Few abide by traditional democratic norms, which is to say that they suffer from democratic deficits. Typically IGOs are staffed by technocrats, appointees of powerful states. They hold few if any public discussions of their policies or programs, are unaccountable (except nominally to the national leaders who appoint them), and often operate in tightly guarded secrecy. This example shows that we cannot simply assume that what is good for states is good for democracy; matters are much more complicated. In fact, it is increasingly difficult even to say what is good for democracy in the first place: the weakening of the state is considered a serious threat, yet the measures states take to increase their power and efficacy in an interdependent world also seem to undermine democracy.

4. *Processes that affect states similarly do not necessarily affect democracy within states similarly.* Take as an example here that, as we just noted, changes in the global political economy are leading many states to adopt policies designed to enhance the competitiveness of national enterprises; firms must be leaner, the thinking goes, government debts and corporate taxes lower, market regulation less intrusive and more business friendly. As a result, many states are converging around the model of the "competition state." In developed states this convergence takes the form of Thatcherite deregulation

---

*Of course, they do not necessarily strengthen states either. Within any particular regime, we would expect to see powerful states dominate; see Robert O. Keohane and Joseph S. Nye, *Power and Interdependence: World Politics in Transition* (Boston: Little, Brown, 1977). Much also depends on the location of a state in the geopolitical order; see Andrew Hurrell and Ngaire Woods, "Globalization and Inequality," *Millennium: Journal of International Studies* 24, no. 3 (1995).

and privatization, while in developing states it is enforced through strict IMF conditionality and broader structural adjustment programs as well as by demands made by individual donor governments. To orthodox neoliberals, the competition state is a one-size-fits-all model for states coping with the pressures of economic integration.*

Convergence around this model has entailed paring back welfare states in the West, and to the extent that generous social provision is considered a vital part of the social contract in contemporary liberal-democratic states, this seems to represent an assault on democracy. Three points, however, demand attention: first, many democratically elected governments—originally those in the Thatcherite mold, more recently those of the (erstwhile?) left—have actively promoted this transition. Widespread dissatisfaction with welfare in the American sense and a strong dose of tax revolt have been powerful popular stimulants of such reforms.[16] This revolt is also linked to growing resentment directed against immigrants and minorities who are suspected, often wrongly, of being the disproportionate beneficiaries of social security programs. In some respects, the postwar social–democratic consensus seems to be breaking down, no doubt in part because of pressures and perceptions of globalization, but not solely because of them, and not solely because of the nefarious machinations of sinister global capitalist forces.

The second point to keep in mind is that for some societies the move toward a competition state and the pressures associated with the global economy can initiate improvements in political and economic conditions that can in turn enable or enhance democracy (though there is no guarantee they will do so). Insistence on "good governance" and the rule of law, which is frequently denounced as democracy lite in the West, represents significant democratic progress for many states. External pressures can also promote democracy more directly: it is hard to imagine Suharto being deposed so easily without the economic collapse brought on by the Asian financial crisis and the accompanying anger and resentment it unleashed. More constructively, states hoping to gain admission to the European Union have undertaken important political and economic reforms in pursuit of that goal, some of which—greater governmental transparency and accountability, guarantees for the rights of minorities—can plausibly be seen as enhancing democracy.[17]

---

*The Western gloating that marked the early phases of the Southeast Asian economic crisis of 1997–98 exemplifies this orthodoxy. Before the West realized how much money it would lose, its leaders and economic policy-makers touted the troubles as proof that "crony capitalism" was inferior to the Western model (quite a contrast with popular fears of "Japan, Inc." and the "Asian Tigers" in the 1980s). The singular faith in this model among IMF and United States Treasury officials is also clear in their hostile treatment of unorthodox alternatives; for instance, Russia's interest (lately cooled) in using inflationary monetary policies and other interventionist measures and Malaysia's decision to impose capital controls in the wake of the 1997 financial collapse; see Joseph E. Stiglitz, *Globalization and Its Discontents* (New York: W.W. Norton, 2002), passim.

Moreover, theorists on the left and the right have argued that a market society brings a certain degree of respect for some rights and freedoms and for the rule of law that is necessary for democracy to flourish.[18] Most basically, economic growth, despite its drawbacks and inequities, can lift many people in developing countries out of poverty. The point is not that convergence is *inherently* good or bad for democracy but rather that a lot depends on where states are converging from and how the process is managed politically, facts that are easy to overlook from the perspective of developed countries.

Third, the process of convergence itself must be seen as more or less democratic depending in part upon a state's geopolitical position. If the United States or the United Kingdom undertakes liberal market reforms, it must answer to its electorate; developing countries often answer first to rich donor countries and their institutional proxies at the IMF and World Bank. Even though reform might strengthen democracy or prospects for democracy over the long term, the reform process itself is fundamentally undemocratic, with consequences that are rarely considered by economic policy-makers. New or transitional democratic governments often wind up between a rock and a hard place. Much of their appeal lies in the hope that they can deliver economic growth and improvements in the standard of living. Achieving these gains requires aid, however, which is typically conditioned upon structural reform. Often this reform actually entails reductions in social programs, inflicting pain on citizens that compromises the government's legitimacy by making it seem more concerned with the interests of bankers and corporate elites than with those of the people. In short, it is far too simplistic to assume, as most analyses do, that similar trends in states have similar implications for democracy.

5. *What is good for democracy in some states might hurt it in others.* Conflating states and democracy leads to the presumption that processes strengthening (weakening) democracy in one state will strengthen (weaken) it in all states. This confusion is clear in much of the literature on globalization, which, while purporting to describe global or worldwide processes, really reflects Western experiences with globalization. Many perceived threats to democracy and the state are relevant only to developed countries. The notorious "race to the bottom" is an excellent example: many people in the rich world worry that low-wage competition brought on by increased trade with poorer countries forebodes a precipitous drop in real earnings. Because wages and workplace and environmental standards are lower in many developing countries, the reasoning goes, competitive pressures resulting from freer trade will undermine equality and standards of living and threaten democracy.

From the vantage-point of developing countries, however, the higher wages, growth, and standards of living associated with increasing trade are crucial to stability and can in fact strengthen democracy.[19] The dissatisfaction of many developing world trade ministers with the present WTO regime is often cited, without elaboration, by WTO opponents in the West as an example of solidarity against a corporate or neoliberal agenda. The truth is that most developing world critics of the existing trade regime argue that it is not open enough—in agricultural goods and textiles especially—and that the system at present favors rich countries at the expense of developing ones.[20] Similarly, the erosion of the welfare state brought on by increased international competition can hardly seem undemocratic to poorer countries long suffering within a global system of inequality and domination in which generous social provision (built on the backbone of conquest and empire) is seen as democratic entitlements only for citizens of wealthy Western states. If one exchanges the perspective of rich, established democracies for that of developing countries and emerging democracies, it becomes unclear exactly who it is that is racing to the bottom, whose prosperity is being threatened, whose rights and welfare imperiled, whose ox otherwise gored. One of the signal failures of contemporary Western democratic thinking about globalization has been its inability (or unwillingness) to address the rather awkward problem of inequalities in the global distribution of and entitlement to wealth and social justice.[21] Specifically, there is an almost hypocritical silence about how measures needed to protect Western levels of benefit and standards of living ("democracy") conflict with steps crucial for improving conditions in the developing world ("race to the bottom"). It is parochialism of the worst kind to maintain that declining standards of living at home amount to an assault on democracy and in the next breath to reject the goal of economic development abroad as part of a capitalist agenda anathema to democracy. Again, the point is not that globalization is always good for developing countries; it is not. The point is that existing inequalities in wealth and power among states make it dangerous and misleading to generalize about democracy from the experience of Western democracies.

As these examples illustrate, most attempts to understand globalization's effects on democracy through the state end up mired in deep analytic confusion. Yet the conflation of states and democracy is not simply an analytic error or oversight; it reflects much more deeply held views about the nature and study of politics. The sovereign state anchors the spatial ontology of the social sciences and structures their epistemology.[22] Modern political theorists have long taken for granted that the sovereign state is the site of politics and thus the natural starting point for political inquiry and analysis; this assumption extends to most thinking about democracy as well.[23] Although democratic principles do not specify the framework in which they should operate, many theorists hold that democracy is probably impossible without the state, which defines the political community and supplies the institutional apparatus through which democracy works.[24] Moreover, democracy has deep historical, theoretical, and institutional ties with the state, ties whose importance seems to be confirmed empirically: democratic accountability isn't guaranteed by state sovereignty, but it has only been achieved within the framework of sovereignty.[25]

As this discussion suggests, the confusion arising from lumping states and democracy together in studies of globalization does not mean that the connection between them is unimportant. On the contrary, it indicates that their relationship is more complex and problematic than we have typically recognized.

Democratic Responses

Democratic theorists have reacted to globalization in markedly different ways. Some, whom I shall loosely call *cosmopolitans*, hold that the numerous social, cultural, economic, political, and environmental challenges posed by globalization can only be adequately addressed through common integrated structures for democratic action at the regional and global levels. Others, whom I shall even more loosely call *communitarians*, believe that democracy cannot be meaningfully dissociated from the state. I shall revisit these two democratic responses to globalization in chapter 5; here, I merely want to specify what I take to be the main point at issue between them.*

Communitarian responses comprise liberal nationalist and neorepublican viewpoints. I am not too concerned with the communitarian label; we might alternatively choose "statist" or "particularist," though both seem to me to have pejorative shadings. Moreover, these subcategories should be seen as representative and overlapping. What unifies this family of views is its treatment of the link between states and democracy as necessary and appropriate; in this sense communitarian views are less responses to globalization than reaffirmations of state-based democracy in spite of it. Communitarians see the link between states and democracy primarily in terms of communal solidarity. While most liberal nationalists agree that national self-determination need not mean state sovereignty for national communities, most also agree that nation, nationality, or nationalism provide a necessary community foundation for democratic politics. Nationality fosters and sustains a common sense of belonging, a shared social bond that underwrites the social sacrifices democracy requires.[26] Kymlicka has argued that a shared linguistic framework is also required for democracy to flourish.[27] Nationalism, appropriately reconciled with rights and special protections for ethnic, national, and cultural minorities, can satisfy liberal

---

*In the following discussion and throughout the book I shall focus on the debate concerning *democracy*. There is a wide-ranging debate about the requirements of *justice* that pits cosmopolitan against various particularist viewpoints, but consideration of that debate lies beyond my scope here.

demands for freedom and autonomy without attenuating the bonds of community.[28] On this view, while the link between democracy and nationalism is not necessary, "the historical link between ideas of democracy and ideas of national self-determination is hardly accidental."[29] Nationality seems to be taken for granted by liberal theories of popular sovereignty, which are otherwise circular or underdetermined.[30] Increasing global interdependence, whatever its implications for more robust global governance, cannot change democracy's dependence on a strong community.

The neorepublican position is in many respects similar to the liberal nationalist view; in particular, it emphasizes that citizenship entails "[playing] an active role in shaping the future direction of ... society through political debate and decision making."[31] A citizen, on this conception, is "someone who thinks and behaves in a certain way": she identifies with her political community and is committed to promoting its common good through active participation in politics.[32] Active participation in the neorepublican view includes deliberation; members of the community shape their common fate through deliberation culminating in authoritative collective decision making. This deliberative ideal differs from the liberal nationalist ideal of democratic citizenship in that it adds to the citizens' sense of rights and duties an active willingness to defend the rights of fellow citizens and a willingness to take part in both formal and informal political activities.[33] It is nonetheless consonant with the nationalist ideal insofar as republican citizenship is "feasible only where it can call upon the ethical resources of a national community."[34] While the modern state might be too large to maintain genuine republican ties among citizens, nationality can provide an alternative glue. In response to globalization, which threatens social solidarity, neorepublicans seek to reassert the core values of republican citizenship by strengthening state democratic institutions and bolstering national political identities. Whatever the merits of cosmopolitan thinking, it is a mistake to think that citizenship can be detached from the bounded communities that anchor it.[35]

Communitarian democrats do not necessarily share one view of globalization. Liberal nationalists and neorepublicans might accept globalization as real and significant or might see it primarily in terms of ideology. They might take seriously the questions it raises about international and universal moral obligations and how best to conceive and fulfill them or reject such questions as so much loose talk about globalization. Yet it is certain that communitarian democrats do not see globalization as changing in any fundamental way the bases or dynamics of democracy and citizenship. What communitarians do share, again, is the belief that democracy is necessarily—ethically, politically—something about states. To try to extend democracy beyond the national state is fundamentally to misapprehend citizens' obligations to one another, obligations which are crucial to, even constitutive of, democracy itself. Whatever challenges globalization might present to state-based forms of democracy must be met by reasserting the primacy and potency of democracy within states.

Cosmopolitan theorists hold that numerous social, cultural, economic, political, and environmental issues and problems can only be adequately addressed through common, integrated structures for democratic action at the regional and global levels. Cosmopolitan democrats are united in holding that the connection between democracy and the nation-state is empirical rather than normatively compulsory.[36] On this view there is no principled reason why the link cannot be broken, democracy scaled up, to address democratic deficits and disjunctures. In fact, there are good reasons—related to freedom and autonomy, to democratic norms of participation, and rule by those affected—for extending democracy in just this way. Only by doing so can effective popular control be realized in conditions of globalization. Cosmopolitan approaches would remedy disjunctures by extending democracy globally through these new institutions; deficits would then be eliminated by subjecting global governance regimes to democratic norms and control.

Cosmopolitan democrats also fall into three general subcategories: champions of institutional reform and innovation, advocates of GCS, and proponents of a global democratic constitutional framework. The first category, of institutional reformers, is something of a catch-all for those favoring reform of existing global institutions and the creation of new ones. These proposals are typically not comprehensive but rather emphasize the potential democratic contribution of a range of institutions from People's Assemblies and ambitious UN reform to universal compulsory jurisdiction for the International Court of Justice (the World Court) and support for and defense of the International Criminal Court.[37]

To its proponents, GCS overlays the existing political spaces of states and international politics, allowing for new political spaces populated by new actors—networks, movements, and organizations—tied together transnationally by shared social and political purposes.[38] GCS creates channels for information, learning, dialogue, and influence in the international sphere. Moreover, global groups and networks also represent "the most promising source of enhanced democratic participation in the emerging global polity."[39] Participation in GCS organizations "helps enfranchise individuals and groups that are formally excluded from participation in international institutions. It strengthens the global public sphere by mobilizing this disenfranchised public into discussions of global issues, thereby democratizing the global political process."[40] Participation thus serves a representative function that widens discussion of the global public good and expands both the agenda and the range of policy options considered. Proponents claim that GCS can provide democratic legitimacy to the emerging system of global governance.

As increasingly dense transnational discourses develop into networks that shape global opinion, they provide "the most appropriate available institutional expression of a dispersed capacity to engage in deliberation" that promotes democratic legitimacy.[41] Seen in this broader context, one aim of GCS is to reconnect politics with the moral purpose and values associated with democracy.[42] In certain respects, the deliberative logic underlying much of this argument closely resembles the neorepublican variant of communitarian theory, with the obvious difference being how far such networks can be meaningfully (democratically) extended beyond existing nation-states.

Perhaps the best-known model for cosmopolitan democracy, however, is David Held's cosmopolitan democratic constitutionalism.[43] Held's proposals for cosmopolitan democracy begin from an appreciation of the state's democratic limits in the emerging global order. He recognizes that the state's important democratic functions are constrained by their embeddedness in the sovereign nation–state and concludes that cosmopolitan democracy requires an alternative framework of empowerment based in a global democratic constitutional confederation. Only such a framework allows the pursuit of individual and collective projects required by democratic autonomy. "In a highly interconnected world, 'others' include not just those found in the immediate community," Held writes, "but all those whose fates are interlocked in networks of economic, political, and environmental interaction." This condition is not met if "the quality of life of others is shaped and determined in near or far-off lands without their participation, agreement or consent."[44] The obligation to ensure everyone's participation, agreement, and consent in an era of heightened global interdependence means that a community of all democratic communities must be among the highest priorities of all democrats. Such a community, akin to Kant's pacific federation but somewhere between a federation and a confederation, could eventually hope to embrace the whole planet. It would entail the enjoyment by all individuals of multiple citizenships in each of the diverse communities that significantly affects their lives.[45]

Cosmopolitan democrats (like communitarian democrats) do not necessarily agree about globalization; they might regard it as the cancerous spread of neoliberal ideology, as a complex and ambiguous development, or even embrace it wholeheartedly. What unites cosmopolitans is their shared acknowledgment that some form of global political framework is an indispensable part of any democratic response to globalization. Cosmopolitan and communitarian democrats differ mainly in how they conceive the link between democracy and the state: communitarian democrats see it as normatively compulsory, while cosmopolitans consider it empirical and thus contingent. As this discussion makes clear, communitarian and cosmopolitan democrats disagree less about what democracy is than about the conditions necessary for its realization and the way globalization bears on those conditions. Both views share understandings of democracy based in freedom, autonomy, and republican forms of deliberation, yet they reach radically different conclusions about what these ideals require in the age of globalization. In part this uncertainty reflects the difficulties involved in assessing globalization, but it also points to a fundamental ambiguity at the heart of modern democratic theory: both its universal and particularist facets are central to its contemporary meaning and practice. The question is not whether democracy requires exclusive citizenship within a bounded community or whether it instead requires a global constitutional framework; the question is how to make sense of the fact that democracy seems to require both.

Reassessing the Problem

By challenging the familiar boundaries of modern politics and political thinking, globalization upsets the conventional wisdom regarding democracy's natural fit with the sovereign state. This conventional wisdom, upon further scrutiny, appears to rest on two closely interrelated assumptions, one spatial, one normative. The spatial assumption, as we have seen, is that the state contains politics, and thus democracy as well. This assumption, taken alone, is primarily empirical; it is a statement about where politics takes place. On this assumption, changes prompted by globalization seem to indicate the need for extending democratic procedures and institutions to the global scale as a way of resolving deficits and disjunctures. But there is also a normative assumption underlying the conventional wisdom about states and democracy: that the state is the natural and appropriate container of and vehicle for democracy. On this view, democratic deficits necessarily exist whenever there is supranational governance because legitimate *democratic* governance can only transpire at the level of the state. Thus what is needed is resistance to and reversal of globalization and the invigoration of democracy at the state level.

Ultimately, cosmopolitans and communitarians pay insufficient attention to the interdependence of these two assumptions. Neither adequately addresses questions about whether and how the specific spatial configuration of modern democracy bears on the realization of its core principles. Discussions of deficits and disjunctures do not adequately comprehend such questions, which have to do with how democracy's entanglement with the state and with the modern discourse of sovereignty affect its meaning and justification. We cannot simply extend democratic institutions to the global level without understanding whether and how their legitimacy depends upon their conceptual relationship with the political units in which they originally evolved, nor can we simply attempt to strengthen existing democratic institutions at the state level when the empirical assumption underpinning their legitimacy is increasingly suspect. Comprehending the prospects for democracy in the age of globalization demands that we find a way to bring the complex relationship between democracy and the sovereign state into sharper focus.

To achieve this focus, I propose using globalization as a lens. We have already seen that globalization reveals tensions in the link between democracy and the state, tensions manifest in the spatial incongruity of disjunctures and the normative deficits created by global governance regimes. By making some simplifying assumptions about globalization, it might be possible to isolate and analyze the source of these tensions. To begin, we need a definition of globalization that emphasizes its impact on the spatial configuration of modern democracy. Michael Mann has argued that social activity in the broadest sense, including economic, political, and cultural activity, can be analyzed at five levels: local, national, international, transnational, and global (I shall refer hereafter to the latter three levels together as *supranational*).[46] We can think of globalization as the trend toward increasing social activity and interaction at the latter three levels—that is, toward the supranational.* This trend includes the creation of new forms of social activity and interaction (such as the World Wide Web) as well as the supranationalization of established forms through new and deepening cross-border linkages. Globalization also encompasses the process(es) through which this trend operates. I propose, then, a very simple definition of globalization: *supranationalization* or *universalization*.† On this view there is nothing particularly new about globalization; the same processes that initiate and extend ties among clans, tribes, villages, and city–states—war, art, love, trade, greed, power, music, religion, technology, curiosity, happenstance—continue to impel social relations upward or outward toward the supranational.‡ These forces are undeniably ancient, though they have almost certainly intensified recently, in large part, as they always have, through new means of communication and new technology.

Two further simplifying assumptions can now be introduced. The first is that we are currently experiencing such a shift; globalization is happening.[47] The second assumption is that we should treat the (notionally) sovereign state as the relevant baseline in making assessments of globalization; it is the dominant contemporary arrangement of social activity and interaction.

---

*This definition uses Mann's framework in a way he might not wholly endorse; I shall return to this problem below. Taylor ("Embedded Statism") adapts Mann's position in a similar way.

†I shall prefer *universalization* as perhaps the less unlovely of these two unlovely words, but it should always be understood to include all three supranational levels, not just the global.

‡This same definition could apply to almost any era of globalization, though in earlier ones the shift might be most pronounced from the local to what becomes the national level.

Mann and others would probably object, arguing that networks of social power and interaction are constantly shifting, making concepts like state and society inherently suspect.[48] I agree. But as we have seen, modern political analysis takes for granted that the sovereign state does contain social activity and interaction. By beginning with the assumptions held by modern political thinkers, accurate or not, we will be able to see how globalization affects those assumptions and the theories built upon them. Because globalization upsets the conventional wisdom about an unproblematic fit between democracy and the state, this approach will let us get at the difficult nexus between the empirical or material processes of globalization and their normative effects.

My definition and assumptions are certainly contestable; given the lack of consensus about what globalization is or even whether it exists, *any* definition will be. I am not claiming that mine is the only or the best way to conceptualize globalization; those interested in different questions will find different definitions more productive. But my definition is plausible and useful for pursuing the questions in which I am interested. Understanding globalization broadly and simply as a universalizing trend lets us sidestep fruitless debates about novelty and historical thresholds. It also lets us dispense with further quantitative specification, providing a conceptual definition broadly consistent with those surveyed earlier and familiar for the political theorist. Most importantly, this definition captures something very basic about globalization: its tendency to push, stretch, transcend, penetrate, or just overrun all kinds of established conceptual and institutional boundaries. As Rosenau puts it, "any technological, psychological, social, economic, or political developments that foster the expansion of interests and practices beyond established boundaries are both sources and expressions of the processes of globalization."[49] It is this tendency or aspect of globalization that I shall stress here, because it directly touches globalization's effects on our established notions, both empirical and normative, of the boundaries of democratic politics.

Viewing the link between states and democracy through the lens of globalization provides a way of getting clear on the nature of their interconnection. Is it necessary, as communitarian democrats insist? Is it merely empirical and contingent, as cosmopolitan democrats suppose? What is it about the trend in social activity and interaction toward the supranational that attenuates this link? To get at these questions, we need a better understanding of sovereignty's empirical configuration and normative dimensions. Only once these have been established can we begin to untangle democracy's complex relationship with sovereignty and to reckon globalization's impact and consequences.

CHAPTER 2

Sovereignty and the Modern Configuration of Rule

A rancorous debate about the future of sovereignty is underway. This debate is remarkable merely for taking place, given that for a long time "scholars treated the concept of sovereignty with indifference, their eyes glazing at the very mention of it."[1] Recently, globalization has breathed new life and new controversy into the subject: whether sovereignty is intact or eroding, dying or transmogrifying, is now hotly contested, no doubt because sovereignty represents much of the old in a conflict driven by fierce disagreement about what is new.

Many scholars today are ready to abandon sovereignty as hopelessly contentious or ultimately indefinable;[2] others insist that it remains or should remain the dominant organizing principle of international politics.[3] Still others argue that sovereignty is being dramatically transformed, refashioned in the crucible of globalization.[4] Such profound disagreement points to the concept's importance and to the confusion in which it is presently mired. Oddly, however, the relevance and intensity of present debates might actually be contributing to our confusion about what sovereignty is and why it matters. We have only resumed caring about sovereignty now that it is in question, and in our rush to fathom its uncertain future we barely pause to consider its past significance. The current hand-wringing about sovereignty resembles the strange emotion people sometimes feel upon hearing of the death of a forgotten uncle; we mourn his passing even though we barely knew him.

One prominent scholar has attempted to cut the Gordian knot of sovereignty through careful analysis of its various senses. According to Krasner, our confusions about sovereignty stem from its use in describing four logically distinct characteristics of states: their exclusivity, their international legal status (independence), their ability to control cross-border flows, and their domestic authority structures.[5] These "analytically distinct" characteristics do not necessarily covary, Krasner claims, so blanket statements about sovereignty can be dangerous and misleading. He holds that disaggregating these characteristics should dispel much of the confusion and imprecision surrounding sovereignty. Yet, pace Krasner, I shall argue that our contemporary puzzlement about sovereignty is due less to its designating too many things than to a failure to appreciate the underlying unity among the things it designates. Like the proverbial blind sages who encounter the elephant, our perceptive analysis of the parts deceives us about the whole. We need to look at the big picture; contemporary debates prove frustrating precisely because they do not do so.[6]

In contemporary debates "the *essence* of sovereignty is rarely defined; while legitimate authority and territoriality are the key concepts in understanding sovereignty," few scholars pay attention to how these concepts change over time or to their interdependence.[7] We care about sovereignty, I contend, because it implies control, independence, exclusivity, and domestic authority all at once. The trick, then, is not to disaggregate these seemingly disparate elements but to understand what holds them together. I shall argue that sovereignty is at bottom a normative concept and that this normative dimension is the glue binding its component parts together in a coherent (if problematic) whole. My aims in this chapter are to recover this normative dimension of sovereignty, to show how it is linked empirically to a particular configuration of rule, and to suggest a partial answer to why sovereignty matters again today.

Recovering sovereignty's normative dimension requires revisiting the historical moment of its crystallization; its significance can best be apprehended in connection with its role in explaining and justifying what came to be called the Westphalian states system in early modern Europe. Yet contemporary historical and analytic accounts of sovereignty overlook or ignore its normative dimension. After briefly reviewing these accounts, I undertake a history of my own, one emphasizing sovereignty's crucial role in the normative reappraisal of politics in early modern Europe. Sovereignty was forged in the crucible of the long and sometimes bloody transition from the medieval to the modern European political system. It explained and justified a new configuration of rule in Europe and provided a normative account of political life and political subjectivity that made sense of the new empirical realities of politics. Three crucial changes apparent in this transition help to fill in the big picture: a shift from a nonterritorial to a territorial configuration of rule, a related shift from functional differentiation of authority to consolidation of all public authority within a particular territory, and a shift in the explanation and justification of this configuration of rule. Sovereignty consists in this third shift, I contend; it justifies these spatial and empirical changes, weaving them into an account of rightful rule that locates supreme political authority within an exclusive territorial state. By conjoining territoriality with rightful rule, sovereignty posits a strangely particularistic argument for the political universality of the modern state—with important implications for the structure of international politics.

This historical account shows that sovereignty's normative significance lies precisely in its justification of territorial political authority. Moreover, it demonstrates that this justification is predicated upon a historically contingent configuration rule; its persuasiveness depends upon the plausibility of its underlying empirical assumptions. This connection, I conclude, explains how sovereignty helped to stabilize the Westphalian system in its early days and indicates why questions about sovereignty are once again contentious.

The Trouble with History

Recovering sovereignty's normative dimension is, I have suggested, a necessarily historical task: understanding how and why sovereignty came to matter in the way that it does in modernity requires that we understand the political context in which it emerged. Unfortunately, most historical treatments of the concept do not address these normative and political questions. Hinsley's classic study traces sovereignty's emergence from antiquity to modern times, focusing on the history of the idea itself.[8] It has a Whiggish tone, describing the concept's historical development as if its contemporary meaning somehow governed its emergence and transformation.[9] Philpott's constructivist account tries to show how and why sovereignty was taken up by various political actors;[10] Murphy, another constructivist, focuses on how the sovereign territorial ideal shaped European thinking and ideology in the modern era.[11] Krasner uses history to falsify sovereignty as a general descriptive account, showing that its various elements are so often violated in practice that the idea of sovereignty amounts to a form of "organized hypocrisy."[12] Bartelson's genealogical approach treats sovereignty primarily as a form of knowledge, or as an epistemological principle governing other forms of knowledge in modernity.[13] In short, the few historical studies of sovereignty available do not deal with its normative dimension.*

This omission results in part from the dominance of neorealism in contemporary international relations theory. While early realist theorists regarded the Westphalian system of sovereign states as the outcome of a historical process,[14] neorealists today treat sovereignty as a logical abstraction, a

---

*This is not to say they do not regard sovereignty as a norm; by normative dimension I mean the substantive content of its justificatory claims (as opposed to their structure).

starting point for political analysis rather than a contingent feature of world politics. For Kenneth Waltz, neorealism's leading proponent, there is little to be explained by history: "the enduring anarchic character of international politics accounts for the striking sameness in the quality of international life through the millennia."[15] In anarchic systems, units are differentiated territorially and each unit performs the same functions as the others. Territorial differentiation is equivalent with anarchy: basically similar territorial units claim authority within their own boundaries (sovereignty), ruling out central authority by definition. Thus territory implies anarchy implies sovereignty; Waltz sees this tautology as a description of permanent and unchanging features of the international system. Hierarchic systems, where the units stand in relations of subordination and superordination with each other and perform a limited number of specialized functions, exist in principle, but the "striking sameness in the quality of international life" obviates this possibility in practice. Change in anarchic systems occurs solely at the level of unit capabilities (e.g., unipolar, bipolar, multipolar); change at the level of unit differentiation is impossible because sovereignty implies the sameness of all the units.

Analytically Waltz is right on: anarchy, sovereignty, and territoriality go together; they are a package deal. Yet this analytic fact does not dispatch historical questions. Neorealism's trouble with history, as Ruggie and others have shown, is that because it apotheosizes sovereignty as a permanent and unchanging feature of the international system it cannot "account for, or even … describe, the most important contextual change in international politics in [the last] *millennium*: the shift from the medieval to the modern international system."[16] A systemic theory that cannot explain this quintessential systemic shift, Ruggie maintains, is necessarily deficient. He faults Waltz for missing that all anarchies are not equivalent: "if anarchy tells us *that* the political system is a segmented realm," he contends, "*the principles on the basis of which the constituent units are separated* from one another" can tell us more about the character of particular systems.[17]

Following Giddens, Ruggie defines a system of rule "as comprising legitimate dominion over a spatial extension."[18] Because every system of rule involves a spatial extension, every such system operationalizes boundaries and imbues them with distinctive sociopolitical significance. Luhmann argues that knowing the principle according to which boundaries form is crucial to understanding the system of relations among territorially bounded units.[19] He illustrates this point by comparing two territorial systems, those of ancient China and modern Europe. The ancient Chinese conceived the world as divided into realms of "civilization" (inside, *Chinese* civilization) and "barbarians" (outside, all others). Their perception of the salient boundary as one separating civilization from barbarism emphasized economic and military concerns.[20] In modern Europe, by contrast, frontiers distinguish legal and political systems rather than cultural or civilizational ones. Ruggie maintains that we can understand the medieval–modern transition as a shift in the principle of territorial separation among political units. The modern system is distinctive because "it has differentiated its subject collectivity into territorially defined, fixed, and mutually exclusive enclaves of legitimate dominion"—sovereign stated.[21] In this it marks a change from nonexclusive territorial arrangements of authority in the Middle Ages in which authority was personal and parcelized within and across territorial foundations and in which the basis of legitimacy was inclusive.[22] In Ruggie's view, these changes inaugurate a new mode of legitimation.[23]

Ruggie's critique usefully identifies sovereignty as a principle of legitimation and contextualizes it within the medieval–modern transition. Unfortunately, his account misses the full significance of this history; in holding on to the neorealist assumption that the international system in Europe in the Middle Ages was anarchic, he gets the nature and extent of the transition wrong and thus mistakes the meaning of sovereignty.

From Chaos to Anarchy

Ruggie characterizes the medieval system as one based on a territorial principle of rule; this seems doubtful. Spruyt explains that

> as with all forms of political organization, feudal authorities occupied a geographical space. But such authority over territorial area was neither exclusive nor discrete. Complex networks of rival jurisdictions overlaid territorial space. Church, lords, kings, emperor, and towns often exercised simultaneous claims to jurisdiction. Occupants of a particular territorial space were subject to a multiplicity of higher authorities.[24]

Ruggie himself recognizes that

> the medieval system of rule "reflected a patchwork of overlapping and incomplete rights of government," which were "inextricably superimposed and tangled" and in which "different juridical instances were geographically interwoven and stratified, and plural allegiances, asymmetrical suzerainties and anomalous enclaves abounded."[25]

Yet Ruggie (like Spruyt) insists on interpreting this system as territorial: "this was quintessentially a system of segmented territorial rule; it was an anarchy."[26]

This interpretation flies in the face of Ruggie's own depiction of the medieval system. Its units were related in a complex and geographically overlapping hierarchy of rule. It is not just that the territorial units were nonexclusive;

territory was not the principle according to which they were differentiated and did not provide the basis of their authority. The medieval system, however chaotic, was not anarchic; it seems at least equally plausible to conceive authority in the Middle Ages as a system of structured hierarchies—albeit a chaotic, multipeaked, and highly conflictual one. Ruggie mischaracterizes this system, obscuring the nature and significance of the change sovereignty represents. To appreciate this change, we must focus on three distinct but related aspects of it: the shift from a hierarchic to an anarchic system, the shift from functional to territorial differentiation, and the remaking of the political subjectivity that justified the dominant configuration of rule. In the next section I shall address the first two changes, which are broadly empirical; in subsequent sections I shall trace how this new political subjectivity evolved. Put differently, I first try to figure out what needed justification, then look at how it was justified.

Medieval Europe "had never been composed of a clearly demarcated set of homogenous political units."[27] There were many loci of authority, each of which was embedded in broader, overlapping networks of authority. The system resembled an "ordered universe of fixed hierarchies" based on personal ties.[28] In these nested hierarchies, involvement in a particular relationship involved one in other hierarchies within which that relationship was situated.[29] The resulting web of allegiances or network of hierarchies defined the role, status, and privileges of everyone from the parish priest to the archbishop, from the lowliest peasant to the wealthiest lord. Authority was a function of one's role and place within these hierarchies; it might derive from land ownership, from a position in the church, from familial connections, from services owed by one's liegemen, or from some title or office—which might have been earned, conferred, purchased, or inherited. The systems were often complex: a bishop might be temporal lord of hereditary lands outside his bishopric; a king might, with respect to a particular piece of land, be vassal through a complex chain of enfeoffments to a lord who was elsewhere his subject.

This cartographical complexity was matched by functional complexity. Although unfamiliar today, systems in which several authorities govern simultaneously in one geographical location but in different spheres of activity were once common; most people saw nothing odd in overlapping allegiances and multiple and competing loyalties.[30] Religious, juridical, economic, military, and other functions were carried out by a variety of different agents, or sometimes (as with our bishop) by the same agents acting in different roles. As Ullmann observes, religion, authority, land ownership, and social obligation were so tightly interwoven that it is impossible to speak of distinctly *political* authority in the Middle Ages.[31]

Medieval authority was "inextricably superimposed and tangled," "interwoven and stratified," but this had little to do with the nonexclusivity of territory. Overlapping and conflicting claims of authority were commonplace not because borders were porous or fungible, though they were, but because of a high degree of functional specialization within the system. Numerous functional authorities operated in, cut through, and stretched across the same geographical spaces. Competition among various authorities frequently stemmed from disagreements about the parties' roles or functions and the rights and privileges associated with them. The investiture controversy, for instance, pitted religious authorities against kings and princes in a conflict over who had the authority to appoint bishops. The problem had little to do with territory; it turned on the fraught question of whose proper function it was to select the prelates.* In the medieval system, then, function rather than territory was the basis of authority; units did not claim territorial authority within their domains and did not aspire to perform all the same basic functions, though they did compete to perform some of them. All of this suggests that medieval authority was part of a highly complex system or network of hierarchies.[32] This system was chaotic but it was not anarchic.

Christendom was the central concept justifying this system and its peculiar configuration of rule. Christendom was an organic notion; agents understood themselves as part of a single spiritual community (effectively a single polis, for Aquinas), in which all had particular divinely instituted roles or functions to perform.[33] The earthly order was God's order, and the social inclusivity fostered by this notion of universal religious community anchored and legitimized the tangled intricacies of medieval authority. God delegated authority to his servants on Earth: the emperor, who wielded the sword, and the pope, who held the keys. Which of them possessed superior authority was contested in symbol (e.g., the famous crowning of Charlemagne) and in substance (e.g., wars between imperial and papal forces in northern Italy). Organic conceptions of community do not imply the absence of conflict;

---

*Fischer mistakenly sees such conflicts as rejections of communal norms. They are better seen as struggles to define or interpret norms, to sort out what roles entailed which privileges. Fischer's broader claim, that the behavior of medieval actors can be described in neorealist terms and therefore confirms a neorealist interpretation of the system, is logically flawed. Our description of actors' behavior is unrelated to their subjective understanding of it and unconnected with the intersubjective worldview in which it made sense to them. We can, undoubtedly, describe the behavior of others in any number of ways, but that does not indicate that they understood it in that way. Descriptive "fit" does not amount to evidence of fact; that a shoe fits me does not mean that I am wearing it. See Markus Fischer, "Feudal Europe, 800–1300: Communal Discourse and Conflictual Practices," *International Organization* 46, no. 2 (1992).; cf. Rodney Bruce Hall and Friedrich Kratochwil, "Medieval Tales: Neo-Realist 'Science' and the Abuse of History," *International Organization* 47, no. 3 (1993).

rather, they set the terms and parameters of conflict.* Christendom "provided a universalist ideological matrix for conflicts and decisions, which was the necessary obverse of the extreme particularist heterogeneity of the political units themselves."[34] In other words, Christendom's logic of "universal" legitimacy bound this fractured and fragmented system together.[35]

During the medieval–modern transition, the social, economic, political, and ideational foundations of this worldview, for the most part slowly, though sometimes dramatically, collapsed.[36] By about the fourteenth century a period of sustained economic growth began, ending a long era of stagnation. Prompted by technological change, population growth, geographical exploration and conquest, and rapidly expanding trade, the traditional land-based economy underwent gradual but profound reorganization. Especially in the principal trading and banking towns of Italy and in the manufacturing regions near Flanders and on the south coast of the Baltic, trade and commerce took off thanks to the development of relatively advanced capital markets. New military technology rendered costly mounted knights obsolete, undercutting the logic of the social and economic arrangements, most notably the manor system, that had sustained them.

The broader economic transformation was driven as much by politics as by purely economic forces; ambitious monarchs seeking wealth and power pursued bold and sometimes reckless strategies of territorial expansion while striving to consolidate the disparate elements of power in the domains they controlled. Nascent capitalism was conditioned by the emergence of states, and thus by the needs and interests of rulers, as well as the other way round. Emerging territorial monarchies began to develop effective financial and administrative capabilities directed toward war making. Their need to finance and maintain large armies shaped the development of politics and citizenship across Europe. For instance, the creation and maintenance of modern armies required taxation; effective taxation in turn required a strong economy and the development of certain forms of technical infrastructure like roads and seaports as well as the administrative capacity to collect the tax, build the infrastructure, and run the army. This economic and political transformation initiated social upheavals that destroyed traditional forms of communal organization. The process was vastly complex and varied from region to region, but the enclosure of common lands led to the eventual displacement of peasants, huge migrations to towns, and the creation of a rudimentary wage labor market. Many of these changes were well under way

---

*Again, pace Fischer, conflict can occur within and over any set of rules or principles; it is distinctive neither of sovereign actors nor of neorealist analysis; cf. Ruggie, "Territoriality and Beyond," 150, note 57. The justificatory scheme behind any system of rules tips us off to where conflicts are likely to arise.

in Western Europe by the seventeenth century, and most began much earlier. Together they helped to unravel the webs of feudal allegiance, assistance, and obligation that structured much of medieval life.

Ideational factors were also pivotal in transforming the structure of medieval society. The Reformation shattered the unity and universality of the church and with it the already fractured and fragile notion of a single Christian community. Monarchs like Henry VIII of England seized the opportunity to nationalize churches within their domains, concentrating spiritual and temporal power; with sword and keys in one hand, the absolutist ambitions of monarchs soared. After the "Peace" of Augsburg, many "defenders of the faith" espoused different and politically expedient versions of it. The result was that the organic and spiritual unity of the church exploded in famously brutal and bloody conflagrations that left the European countryside, not to mention European social order, in smoldering ruin. Reformation theology—which invited individuals to interpret scripture for themselves and even to resist their superiors in certain dire circumstances—fomented social unrest and fostered a modern individualism subversive of traditional forms of spiritual and secular authority. An increasingly anthropomorphic worldview cultivated during the humanist revival of the Renaissance, the (re)discovery of much classical learning, especially in the arts, the law, and in philosophy, and the seeds of the scientific rationalism that would later flower during the Enlightenment, all helped to undermine the old ways of thinking, and in particular the dominant cosmology.

As the old hierarchies collapsed, authority began to coalesce in the unified, exclusive structures of the state, signaling that the principle of hierarchical subordination was giving way to an order based in spatial exclusivity. We can glimpse something of this process in the development of the King's Peace, the consolidation in the royal government of all legal jurisdiction within a given territory. In the Middle Ages, kings typically "lived of their own," relying wholly on revenues derived from their private lands or estates. Many of the sovereign's prerogatives derived from his status as the owner (and feudal lord) of these lands. *Dominium*, the right to dispose of one's property and related affairs, was a function of ownership; few kings enjoyed much real authority beyond that typical of the proprietors of large estates. Jurisdiction in most legal matters belonged to the local lord and was linked to ownership as well as to feudal obligations; bishops had jurisdiction in ecclesiastical cases.

Kings worked to expand their personal property holdings, typically through conquest and marriage, and by maneuvering to become liege lords of greater numbers of their nominal subjects. (In France, for example, the story of state building is largely a story of centuries of such maneuvering by a succession of ambitious rulers.) The accompanying growth in their authority was partly a function of bringing more land under their direct control; a king's ownership rights simply stretched across a greater territory. As his power and stature increased, so did his ability to provide security and aid to loyal vassals and subjects. This enhanced ability made enfeoffments more attractive to would-be vassals of the king, further expanding his sphere of control and thus his authority. As their direct control over territory grew, moreover, kings used it to amass authority in new functional domains. In matters of justice, for instance, the royal court's legitimacy was initially wholly feudal: it was based partly in the privileges of ownership, partly in voluntary submission to the king's will by his vassals. But as his territory and feudal authority increased, his position at the apex of a sprawling network of personal allegiance and direct territorial control uniquely situated him as a mediator of disputes cutting across multiple jurisdictions. The royal court's legitimacy became essential to resolving disputes among lesser nobles and gained currency throughout those domains where the king ruled through ownership or allegiance. As his authority expanded in these ways, the ideas of possession, supremacy, and territory began to fuse. This fusion endowed royal authority with a possessive character reflected in the dual meaning of the term *propriety*: ownership and right.[37]

The nationalization of churches, both Protestant and Catholic, further contributed to the king's growing authority, as did the development of those administrative capacities we have already noted and the economic advantages they conferred. Gradually, the king's authority came to encompass all public functions within those territories under his jurisdiction. Supreme will within a territory the king rightfully possessed evolved into the right to make law within that particular territory. Of course, in practice these processes were never as neat or as thorough as this sketch suggests; most notably, kings constantly had to negotiate their authority with parliaments or estates and contend with external threats and rivals. The power to levy taxes, for instance, grew out of the king's demands for greater revenues for the defense of the realm; that this prerogative was almost universally subject to the consent of the estates of the realm stems from feudal liege–lord relations assigning vassals the right and obligation to give counsel to their lords in important matters affecting both.[38] These often violent accommodations were crucial in the historical development of particular states. The larger point, for our purposes, is that over time kings contrived to consolidate functional authority within their exclusive territorial domains. This development marked the culmination of a long transformation from a hierarchical system of functionally differentiated rule to one in which multiple territorial units perform similar functions and compete for wealth and survival. It is this transformation that sovereignty explains and justifies.

Theorizing Change

So far I have emphasized two features of this restructuring: a shift to territorially exclusive political units and the bundling of functional authority within them. The third crucial feature of this transition was its theorization and justification; modern political theory had to create a new subjectivity for these changed conditions.[39] Sovereignty reflects a new way of thinking about territory and authority, one precipitated by the wholesale restructuring of community and authority.

In his penetrating book on international relations and political theory, Walker argues that the idea of state sovereignty can be understood as the "resolution of [the] late medieval and early modern struggle to free accounts of political life from the hierarchical incorporation of particularity into an overarching universalism—while also preserving the possibility that particularity might still be reconciled with a reconceptualization of what universality entails."[40] In other words, it was necessary to find a way to think about politics outside the conceptual limits of Christendom, to give up the idea of a universal community and central Christian authority without giving up on the idea of universality itself. Thinkers like Machiavelli and the Renaissance humanists, Walker claims, tried to construct accounts of political life that could provide an alternative to the universalistic conceptual categories of the medieval world.[41] This is right as far as it goes. Walker is also right, I think, in arguing that Hobbes and Machiavelli occupy places of prominence within political theory and international relations because their work is at once concerned with theorizing the new territorial units of political authority and with justifying their separation from older, universal hierarchies.

Missing from Walker's account, however, is a clear sense of *why* an alternative to the inclusive medieval worldview was necessary in the first place. The answer is that the medieval worldview no longer meaningfully corresponded with the reality confronting the early modern theorists. Medieval social theory was conceptually unequipped to make sense of the numerous problems posed by the profound reconfiguration of rule we have just surveyed. The old ideas of Empire and Christendom, with their divinely sanctioned roles and otherworldly orientation, were losing sway because the world was increasingly difficult to apprehend through them. Inclusion in the universal hierarchies of medieval life became harder to reconcile with newly emergent political forms: territorial states and omnicompetent monarchs. The early modern theorists' development and articulation of sovereignty is not a response to spatial and temporal dilemmas taken up out of some proto-postmodern sense of dissatisfaction with the universal metanarratives of medieval thought, as Walker almost seems to suggest.[42] Rather, these theorists were tackling a very practical and urgent task: the explanation and justification of the new social order emerging across Western Europe.

The idea of a sovereign polity figures so prominently in these accounts because the state and its unique configuration of authority are structural developments in need of explanation and justification. By the fourteenth century in Italy, the term *state* was being used to describe independent political realms and their condition. Advice to rulers of the day included admonitions to maintain the existing character of the regime, to avoid diminution of their territorial holdings, and to assert control over all of the power structures and institutions within the *regnum*. In these examples the ruler or chief magistrate possesses or embodies the institutions of the state. Renaissance republican authors soon articulated a vision of the best regime as autonomous and self-governing. A distinct form of autonomous civil or political authority regulating the public affairs of an independent community and consolidating coercive power emerges in their work.[43] The state thus represents a new kind of association or body politic, one distinguished by the presence of such a power within it.[44]

By the start of the seventeenth century, as Quentin Skinner's magisterial study of Renaissance and Reformation political thought shows, "the concept of the state—its nature, its power, its right to command obedience—had come to be regarded as the most important object of analysis in European political thought."[45] Among the preconditions Skinner identifies for this development is the recovery of the political as a distinct branch of moral philosophy.[46] This "new" theory of political space marked a radical innovation, one aided by the rediscovery of Aristotle's political philosophy. The polis provided an instructive model of an independent, self-governing community. Perhaps more importantly, the recovery of politics as an independent analytic category helped theorists conceive political association as an end in itself. The notion of Christendom as an all-embracing (catholic) community gave way to the idea of the polis or polity as the highest form of human association, one directed toward human ends and governed by a distinctly human law.[47] The universality of this community or association consisted in its centrality to the attainment of those *political* ends. If the nature of human beings is political, the fulfillment of this nature through the state makes the state itself natural, necessary, and in its way, universal. Of course Aristotle's influence did not lead immediately or inexorably to these conclusions.* While the overlapping and conflicting structures of medieval authority endured it was difficult to determine where the polis was, and thus to which particular community

---

*As we have seen, Aquinas had used Aristotelian arguments in a rather different way. Thomas Aquinas, *The Political Ideas of St. Thomas Aquinas*, ed. Dino Bigongiari, trans. Fathers of the English Dominican Province (New York: Hafner Press/Macmillan, 1983).

Aristotle's wisdom pertained.[48] The exigencies of rule dictate that authority has to be located somewhere; for early modern theorists, the state provided a practical answer to where.

Two further aspects of thinking about the state in the early modern period contributed to the evolving notion of sovereignty: the ideas that the "independence of each *regnum* or *civitas* from any external and superior power should be vindicated and assured" and that "supreme authority within each independent *regnum* should be recognized as having no rivals within its own territories as a law-making power and an object of allegiance."[49] Thinkers like Bartolus, Bardus, Marsilius, Machiavelli, and Charles Du Moulin were key figures in this development, which culminates in the theories of sovereignty advanced by Bodin and Hobbes.

"That Mortall God"

For Machiavelli the need for a strong ruler was a purely practical consideration arising in fractious times. In such conditions, order, unity, and the defense of civic virtue and civil interests required independence under the rule of a strong prince. Like Machiavelli, Bodin took the commonwealth and its welfare as the starting points of political analysis, but he took the argument one step further, defining the commonwealth partly *in terms of* sovereignty. This move makes sovereignty virtually a logical extension of the territorial state: if such a community exists, there must be the kind of power necessary for its defense.[50] Bodin makes this logical relationship fairly explicit, describing the commonwealth as "a just government, with sovereign power, of several households and of that which they have in common."[51] Sovereignty is entailed by commonwealth, is part of its very definition. Hobbes calls the sovereign the "essence" of the commonwealth.[52]

In what does this essence consist? For Bodin "sovereignty is absolute and perpetual power"; it is "not limited in power, or in function, or in length of time."[53] All authority within the commonwealth belongs to the sovereign; there is nothing greater on earth, after God, than sovereign princes.[54] Their prerogatives all derive from the right to give law to all in general and to each in particular, without the consent of any other.[55] More specifically, the sovereign is entitled to declare war and peace, to hear final appeals of any magistrate's rulings, to institute and remove officers, impose taxes, grant pardons, coin money, oversee weights and measures, and demand loyalty from all his subjects and liege vassals.[56] Hobbes puts the point with less precision but with characteristic force and eloquence, describing the sovereign as "LEVIATHAN, or rather (to speake more reverently)...that *Mortall God*...[who] hath the use of so much Power and Strength conferred on him, that by terror thereof, he is inabled to forme the wills" of all his subjects.[57]

In Carl Schmitt's view, this image of the sovereign reflects the image of God directly: "all significant concepts were transferred from theology to the theory of the state, whereby, for example, the omnipotent God became the omnipotent lawgiver...."[58] In both arguments we see existing facts on the ground reflected back in theory.

In sovereignty the idea of absolute authority to govern merged with the older notion of sovereignty as individual will.[59] Thus the acts of will of a supreme ruler were legitimate because they emanated from a source whose right and authority within the relevant territory were recognized and long established.* The extensive lists of the sovereign's rights and prerogatives in Hobbes and especially Bodin remind us that the fusion of these various functions is every bit as novel and important as the idea that the sovereign has exclusive authority within a particular territory. This configuration of authority contrasts vividly with the medieval one, wherein authorities were defined mainly by what they did rather than where they did it. The sovereign does everything; what distinguishes him from other sovereigns is where he does it. Consolidation of functional authority in a supreme ruler promotes territorial exclusivity: there can be only one authority within a given territory. This arrangement implies its own strange kind of universality: the sovereign, like God, holds final, absolute, unchanging, and all encompassing authority—but only within the limits of the state.

The justifications for this authority evolve as the theory develops. Sovereignty has conceptual antecedents in *dominium*, as we have seen, as well as in *majestas*, the awe-inspiring dignity and formality of the ruler, in *imperium* or Empire (which also signified rule by rules), and in the idea advanced by church radicals and reformers that the authority of leaders derived ultimately from the people.[60†] This final point is crucial, for while the origins of authority remain vague in the work of Machiavelli and Bodin, who, again, simply take the commonwealth for granted, thinkers like Althusius, Grotius, Hobbes, and others uniformly locate it in contract.[61] Initially this contract was the ancient one between ruler and people, with the inconvenience that it was never evident, and was in fact much disputed, which party ultimately retained sovereignty. The practical necessity of rule being agreed by all, the question turned entirely upon whether the people alienated their right permanently or only temporarily.[62]

---

*This formulation of sovereignty remains with us today in common notions of the sovereign states system: "Since it assumes the state as an actor, the concept of formal sovereignty is linked to the classical conception of sovereignty as will...." Robert O. Keohane, "Sovereignty, Interdependence, and International Institutions," in *Center for Social Theory and Comparative History Colloquium Series* (Los Angeles: 1991), 6.

†This doctrine, central to conciliarism and to certain later Protestant (mainly Calvinist) sects, is sometimes referred to as "popular sovereignty." I avoid that terminology here, as I shall use the term rather differently in the following chapter.

Hobbes resolved the problem by transforming it: he abolished "the people" altogether. In his view, sovereignty unites individual subjects who, until they agree to transfer all their right and power to Leviathan, are locked in a war of all against all in the state of nature. Their contract creates their unity, the commonwealth, and authorizes the sovereign as the embodiment or essence of that unity. The sovereign is a creation of the contract rather than a party to it, and his absolute power merely reflects the complete transfer of all right and authority that rational individuals recognize as offering the only escape from their miserable natural condition. Though most later theorists resisted Hobbes's version of the contract and its rigid absolutist implications, what we might call the general form of his solution survived for centuries. Individuals, by a transfer of their right, create and authorize the sovereign through the social contract. This arrangement is free and consensual, a rational solution to their collective dilemma. Thus the sovereign is not only the supreme authority within the commonwealth but also its embodiment; his authority is tied inextricably to the territory and the political association—to the commonwealth—he rules and represents. Nuances of terminology testify to this complexity: "sovereign" refers to a kind of space, a kind of power (always within that space), the legitimacy of that power, and the person who holds and exercises it.

The eventual triumph of the sovereign state has usually been attributed to its superior military prowess; Spruyt has more recently ascribed it to economic efficiencies and strategic advantages as well as to system externalities generated by them.[63] Critical theorists and constructivists explain sovereignty's success as a function of socialization, arguing that "normative and ideational structures [shape] actors' identities and interests through…imagination, communication and constraint."[64] There are elements of truth in each of these explanations, but they all obscure what for our purposes is the crucial point: sovereignty—as opposed to the territorial state with which it is associated—was formulated, embraced, and expounded by early modern theorists because it provided plausible solutions to the central problems of authority associated with the modern state: territoriality, the functional consolidation of power, and the revaluation of political subjectivity. Without question, this theoretical embrace helped to justify and stabilize the new order it sought to explain.[65]

Anarchy, State, Myopia

This new modern political subjectivity provides an account of rightful rule inside the state that makes politics and authority outside impossible. This impossibility is frequently described by neorealists through an analogy with Hobbes's state of nature. States in the international system are like individuals in nature: both are sovereign and autonomous; both are independent; both possess rights. The agents in these states of nature are roughly equal in power (or at least in their ability to destroy one another) and unable to rely on others to keep their word in the absence of a superior authority to enforce covenants. These conditions describe anarchy and are generally believed to make international morality impossible.[66] Wendt argues that the anarchy Waltz and others describe is better understood in Lockean terms, the key difference being that states recognize the sovereignty of other states as a right possessed by all.[67] In either case it follows that politics, the pursuit of the good life, is only possible within the state; outside lies the world of mere relations, the constant struggle for survival.[68]

Upon closer inspection, however, the individualist analogy is flawed, and the flaw proves quite revealing. It exposes a complex interdependence among sovereignty's normative and empirical, and its internal and external, dimensions and shows this complex configuration of rule to be historically contingent. Inside the state, the uncertainty and instability of anarchy compel sovereign individuals to forge a contract to protect themselves, to secure their rights and interests. When individuals "contract out" of the state of nature, they give up some of their rights in exchange for stability, protection, and other advantages of government.* Their decision to form a political society and escape anarchy is viewed as rational and consistent with their sovereignty and autonomy. Contracting out of nature is among their sovereign prerogatives, a strategic response to the uncertainty of anarchic conditions.[69] For states, however, the possibility of contracting out of anarchy is rejected categorically. Like individuals in the state of nature, states face the instability and uncertainties of anarchy; like individuals, states are held to be rational and to pursue their own self-interest. Yet while anarchy supposedly necessitates and induces the creation of civil authority internally, it creates a permanent and insuperable obstacle to authority externally.

There is little mystery surrounding the source of this theoretical nearsightedness; the world of states looks anarchic in these theories because that is how it had to look to justify sovereign authority inside. By the time the social contract was being worked out in the sixteenth and seventeenth centuries, the modern sovereign state had reached maturity in many parts of Europe, most notably in those countries—France, England, the Netherlands—where the classic theorists lived and worked. When Bodin, Hobbes, and Grotius speculated about the origins of legitimate authority, they saw their task as

---

*Among the classic theorists, Grotius (sometimes), Hobbes, and Rousseau conceive of individuals sacrificing all of their rights to the sovereign, while Locke, Pufendorf, Kant, and others see the transfer as a limited one with individuals retaining most of their rights. This difference traces to their characterizations of the natural condition. In the following discussion, nothing hinges on which version one adopts.

validating authority *within the state.* The state of nature is a conjecture, more prescriptive than descriptive, designed to justify sovereign authority. Contracting out must be an alternative to anarchy inside because *the very idea of inside* presupposes an already-existing political community. If individuals did not contract out of anarchy to create civil society, there could be no political community, no inside, in the first place. The social contract is the solution to a hypothetical problem contrived to yield it, a foregone conclusion. This insight helps to explain a strange omission in most early theories of sovereignty: the territorial origins and limits of the sovereign state are rarely discussed, probably because by the time these theorists were writing they too could be taken for granted.* Tellingly, most of the theorists do describe the conditions of just conquest.

Once authority inside is constituted as sovereign, however, contracting out among states becomes a theoretical impossibility. Sovereignty is a theory of final and absolute authority within a particular territory. If states formed a contract it would undermine their sovereignty, their reason for being.† The impossibility of a contract among states is an artifact of the problem theorists of sovereignty set out to tackle; they were stuck with the contradiction implied in the international (dis)analogy. A few addressed this contradiction head on, if lamely: Hobbes, after describing the "continuall jealousies" of princes that leave them "in the state and posture of Gladiators," remarks that "because [princes] uphold thereby, the Industry of the Subjects; there does not follow from it, that misery, which accompanies the Liberty of particular men."[70] Vattel simply asserted that states had less need of cooperation than individuals.[71]

It is doubtful that the inconsistency much troubled those theorists—perhaps explaining their limited engagement with it. Contractual relations among states must have seemed impossible to them; the brutal wars of religion and the civil war in England had dispelled all illusions of broader unity. Anarchy was a more or less accurate description of the world of European states by the seventeenth century, so we should hardly be surprised that these theorists' ideas fit the world they were trying to explain. As Anthony Giddens remarks,

> reflection on social processes (theories, and observations about them) continually enter into...the universe of events they describe.... Consider, for example, theories of sovereignty formulated by seventeenth century European thinkers. These were the result of reflection upon, and study of, social trends into which they in turn were fed back.[72]

---

*I return to this omission in the next chapter.
†Individual states sometimes formed contracts—England and Scotland in 1707, for instance—but such agreements did not significantly alter the international order and in some respects confirmed it. I am grateful to Fred Whelan for pointing out this example to me.

Because sovereignty's theoretical implications for the international order were broadly consistent with the reality these theorists perceived, there was little difficulty in accepting them. The potential contradiction between a theory of rightful rule within the state and contractual or political relations among states never materialized.

But the potential tension does reveal that anarchy is at once a logical implication of sovereignty and an empirical prerequisite of it—a tautology, much as Waltz claims. Rather than making sovereignty and anarchy time-less analytic truths, however, their tautological character demonstrates their extreme contingency. Sovereignty remains a plausible account of political authority only so long as it remains a plausible description of the international system. Sovereignty and anarchy are no more permanent than the notions of Empire and Christendom they replaced. These normative accounts justify historically contingent configurations of rule; as those configurations change, the conceptions of authority linked to them become increasingly implausible. I am not claiming that sovereignty ever provided an accurate empirical ac-count of political authority or the international system; like all theories, its explanatory power derives from abstraction. My argument is rather that sovereignty's utility and persuasiveness are contingent upon some reason-able fit between these abstractions and the world they purport to describe. Sovereignty remains theoretically useful and politically viable only so long as it clarifies more than it obscures.

Conclusion

In concluding this chapter I want to emphasize two aspects of sovereignty recovered here, its normative dimension and its historical contingency, and to reiterate their interdependence. Sovereignty explains and justifies a particular historical configuration of territorial rule: final and absolute political authority within the political community when no such authority exists elsewhere.[73] This explanation provides a new political subjectivity for early modern Europe, one that makes sense of the shift from a hierarchic and functionally differentiated network of overlapping and entangled medieval authorities notionally subordinate to Church and Empire to an anarchic world of functionally similar, territorially exclusive states concentrating public power within them. Sovereignty's normative function, its validation of this new form of territorial authority, cannot be dissociated from the historical processes that shaped this particular form of authority. Sovereignty replaces the organic Christian cosmology of the Middle Ages with an ontological ac-count of a world comprising natural, independent, and autonomous political units. It is simultaneously a description of political fact, if initially a precocious one, and an argument justifying that fact; its very precocity helped to call the world it described into being.

It is easy enough to see why sovereignty mattered to its early theorists and why it seemingly ceased to matter once no one really questioned that the world was in fact as sovereignty depicts it in theory. It is also plain, I hope, why sovereignty is again generating controversy today: because sovereignty provides an empirically-based justification of what is ultimately a contingent political order, the changes in the international system wrought by globalization raise questions about the system's nature and legitimacy. Among the most important such questions are those concerning democracy, to which we now turn.

CHAPTER 3

Sovereign Democracy

In the previous chapter I argued that sovereignty should be understood primarily as a historically contingent *justification* or *validation* of the Westphalian configuration of political authority. If that were all, however, it would be difficult to imagine why anyone other than academics would care; few people spend their time worrying about the normative foundations of rule in the international political system. Yet all kinds of people *do* care about changes in the international system and about the perceived erosion of sovereignty in particular: not just theorists but politicians, antiglobalization protesters, and everyday citizens. Intuitively these people recognize that threats to sovereignty threaten democracy as well. In this chapter I try to show why this intuition is correct. I shall argue that modern democracy is sovereign democracy: it incorporates the logic of sovereignty, taking over sovereignty's distinctive justification of territorial authority. Democratic legitimacy depends upon this particular configuration of rule; it shares sovereignty's normative and empirical foundations.

At one level few students of democracy would probably object to this claim. The sovereign state was the site of democratic theorization and became the target of democratic political struggle. Popular sovereignty rarely attracts theoretical notice; it is the starting point for arguments about what democracy means and how it should be realized, the idiom in which democratic theory developed.[1] The demos, an exclusive, self-governing body of citizens exercising political authority in a state either directly or through representatives, is fundamental to modern democratic theory;[2] "popular sovereignty is the regnant legitimacy idea of our time."[3] Contemporary political theories cannot do without the notion that the democratic state derives its authority from the consent of these citizens, that authority ultimately resides in the people.[4] So while democratic theorists argue vigorously over the best way to justify rule by the people and to secure citizens' consent, they rarely bother to argue that the people *should* rule within the state; that assumption is so fundamental, and the political questions underlying it so firmly settled, as to no longer require articulation or defense. Despite popular sovereignty's widespread acceptance as the starting point for thinking about democracy, however, it is not taken seriously *as a theory of sovereignty*. It mainly serves as an alternate expression for democracy, a way of summarizing a theory of legitimacy grounded in citizens' consent. With the emphasis thus squarely on the *people*, what popular sovereignty implies about *rule* is routinely ignored.

In this chapter I argue that modern democracy incorporates sovereignty's normative and empirical assumptions in its account of political authority. In doing so, however, it severely limits and circumscribes the universality of freedom and equality, the principles in which democracy is based. I begin by showing how theorists of popular sovereignty used universal freedom and equality to establish political authority in consent. These principles effectively transferred sovereignty to the people, and they opened the door to more thoroughgoing democracy. I show that the theorists checked this democratizing potential by introducing certain assumptions about sovereignty into their arguments. The social contract through which political authority is constituted is, I argue, a sovereign contract. It limits freedom and equality inside the state through a restrictive notion of citizenship and limits them outside by affirming and justifying the boundaries of sovereign states. The contract also constitutes the international system as one in which sovereignty is a right for (some) states. Thus freedom and equality get reconfigured to fit the limits required by sovereignty. The tensions introduced by this reconfiguration remain visible and operative in key features of modern democratic theory that only make sense against the background assumption of sovereignty. Modern democracy is, in a very real sense, sovereign democracy.*

Throughout the chapter I rely, for several reasons, on the arguments of Locke and Rousseau in advancing my own argument. First, their importance in the history of modern thinking about democracy is solidly established. They are widely regarded as foundational figures in the main schools of

---

*My argument concerns *modern* democracy; I do not engage the long-running debate about whether and to what extent classical democracy was "really democratic." This restriction poses no difficulties, however, because "no practical component of ancient democracy has survived intact into the world in which we now live"; John Dunn, ed., *Democracy: The Unfinished Journey 508 B.C to A.D. 1993* (Oxford: Oxford University Press, 1992), 256. Modern democracy, whatever considerable inspiration it has taken from classical sources, is founded on principles of universal freedom and equality that were unknown and probably unthinkable to the classical Greeks. This difference warrants treating modern democracy independently, regardless of the position one takes on Athenian democracy.

modern democratic theory; Locke, of liberal or representative democracy, and Rousseau of participatory and (through Kant) deliberative democracy. Since a comprehensive survey of democratic theory's history and development is impossible here, addressing Locke and Rousseau allows us to address, if indirectly, a wide portion of the field. Second, because these theorists wrote near the start of modern theorizing about democratization, certain problems and assumptions remain visible in their work that later dissolve into the background. In emphasizing that these thinkers similarly reconcile freedom and equality with sovereignty through the social contract, I do not intend to obfuscate the important differences between them. Rather, I mean to establish that reconciling universal freedom and equality with sovereignty was an unavoidable problem for any thinker working within the idiom of popular sovereignty.

Absolutism and its Discontents

The absolutist uses and implications of Bodin's doctrine of sovereignty had been quickly grasped by defenders of monarchy; his argument concerning the necessity and indivisibility of sovereign power fit nicely with divine right and patriarchal theories of monarchy. It also provided a theoretical blueprint for order and stability in states wracked by religious warfare. As sovereignty gained adherents and as Western European monarchs worked to expand their power, their opponents became acutely sensitive to the need for a theory with which to combat them. By the seventeenth century "it was clear that some notion of popular sovereignty provided the only plausible basis on which to challenge the theory and practice of absolutism."[5]

Popular sovereignty was not a new idea. That the people were the ultimate source of authority in religious or secular affairs had been argued in various forms for centuries. William of Ockham and Marsilius of Padua were early and forceful proponents of the idea.[6] Resistance theories (many advocated by Protestant sects) supplied theoretical grounds for opposition to tyrants. The traditional role of parliaments and estates in questions relating to taxation and other important matters—predicated on the dictum that what touches all should be decided/approved by all—offered a precedent for popular consent and approval for royal decisions.[7] None of these resources, however, provided an adequate response to the absolutist claims advanced by followers of Bodin. Among the chief limitations of these older arguments was their reliance on a compact between ruler and people that left unclear whether the people's validation of authority conferred complete or only limited power to their rulers and whether it did so permanently or only for a time. A further insufficiency was that while the supreme authority of the people might be acknowledged in theory, it was normally invoked in support of rulers whose selection was also seen as ordained by God and thus deserving of popular approbation. The practical result was that the people's consent was largely formal and was usually assumed, even when the assumption was unwarranted.

The innovation of the seventeenth-century theorists was to abandon the scriptural and Aristotelian justifications for popular sovereignty favored by medieval theorists like Marsilius, which had been restrictive in their reliance on organic communities and divine will, and instead to derive their doctrine from novel arguments about the natural freedom and equality of all people. Ironically, it was the royalist Thomas Hobbes who first used the freedom and equality of a hypothetical state of nature to locate the origins of authority in consent, even though for Hobbes they led ineluctably to the absolute authority of the sovereign. Hobbes's arguments were criticized by his royalist allies, partly for their extremism, but also because some of them apparently recognized the danger in basing authority on consent. Filmer wrote that while no man "hath so amply and judiciously handled" the rights of sovereignty, "I cannot agree to his means of acquiring it."[8] Bramhall called *Leviathan*, with its doctrines of natural freedom and equality, "the Rebel's Catechism."[9]

Natural freedom and equality found their most lasting expression in the work of John Locke, whose argument for government by consent was put to quite different purposes. Locke designed his theory to aid the radical Whig causes with which he was deeply involved for over twenty years.[10] After demolishing Filmer's arguments for paternal sovereignty, Locke, in his renowned *Second Treatise of Government*, articulated a revolutionary theory of popular sovereignty based on man's natural freedom and equality.

The Logic of Universality

The simple premise that everyone is free and equal undermines justifications for natural authority and subjection: "the doctrine of natural individual freedom and equality was revolutionary precisely because it swept away, in one fell swoop, all the grounds through which the subordination of some individuals, groups or categories of people to others had been justified."[11] If all people are equal and share an equal freedom based in natural and inalienable rights, political authority can no longer be justified through claims of rank, birth, or status. Free, equal individuals are naturally subject to no authority: "Men being...by Nature, all free, equal and independent, no one can be put out of this Estate, and subjected to the Political Power of another, without his own *Consent*."* It follows that if natural freedom and equality make consent

---

*John Locke, *Two Treatises of Government*, ed. Peter Laslett (Cambridge, UK: Cambridge University Press, 1960), II§95. Hereafter when citing the *Two Treatises* I shall enclose the Treatise and Section numbers in parentheses in the text.

a requirement of legitimate rule, final political authority must rest with the people rather than with their rulers: "the *Community* perpetually *retains a Supream Power*" inside the state" (II§149). Clearly, then, the natural freedom and equality of all men is central to Locke's "major task of enunciating a theory of popular sovereignty."[12]

Two logical features of this justification for popular sovereignty, features shared with most later theories, deserve special emphasis here. The first is that both freedom and equality are necessary to make the case for popular sovereignty airtight. Neither principle alone suffices to undercut claims of natural authority and subjection. Individuals might be equal but born into political or other subjection; conversely, they might be born free but manifestly unequal in strength or character, giving the fortuitously endowed among them eminent title to rule. Freedom and equality together eliminate such possibilities. The second important feature of popular sovereignty is that both of its core principles are necessarily universal. If only some individuals are free and equal, they would be likely to rule over the others, again introducing the possibility of a natural foundation for rule and opening the door to patriarchal and divine-right claims. So freedom and equality must be universal to secure popular sovereignty; Locke treats them as innate moral characteristics of all human beings. This is (in part) what he and others meant by calling them natural.[13]

It is sometimes objected that Locke is not a theorist of popular sovereignty or of sovereignty at all.[14] Critics note his careful deployment of "sovereignty" in the *Second Treatise*, where he reserves it for descriptions of God's powers and glosses of Filmer's texts. Locke prefers "supreme" to describe the political authority he envisions; his division of power between the executive and legislative leaves neither sovereign and makes an "appeal to heaven" the only recourse in cases of intractable conflict. Moreover, God's proprietorship over men can be read as precluding human sovereignty altogether (see II§6).[15] The most parsimonious explanation of Locke's terminological preferences, however, is his desire to contrast the limited government he proposes with the absolute and unlimited power that royalists like Hobbes and Filmer consistently called sovereignty. While sovereignty is "final and absolute political authority" it need not be absolutist, as Hobbes and Filmer (but not Bodin) assumed; "absolute" means something close to "supreme" in this definition.[16] Besides, the division of governmental power need not indicate a division or absence of sovereignty so long as supreme authority remains with the people.[17]

If we turn to the *Second Treatise* itself, moreover, we find strong evidence for treating Locke as a theorist of popular sovereignty. That he accepts both freedom and equality is obvious enough; he describes man's natural condition as "a *State of perfect Freedom*" and "A *State* also *of Equality*." The consensual origins of political authority follow from "Men being...by Nature, all free, equal and independent" (II§§4, 95). Locke makes clear that by natural equality he "cannot be supposed to understand all sorts of *Equality*"; age, birth, virtue, merit, excellence, benefits, gratitude, and alliances are among the sources of precedence among people. Still, he maintains that these inequalities are compatible with "that *equal Right* that every Man hath, *to his Natural Freedom*, without being subjected to the Will or Authority of any other Man" (II§54). Thus for Locke freedom and equality unequivocally locate legitimate political authority in consent. In the Preface to the *Two Treatises* Locke expresses hope that his arguments are "*sufficient to establish the Throne of our Great Restorer, Our present King* William, *to make good his Title, in the Consent of the People, which being the only one of all lawful Governments, he has more fully and clearly than any Prince in* Christendom...."[18] Such statements, coupled with his insistence on the "supreme" and "perpetual" power of the community, seem as plain as any expressions of what is often called indirect or constitutive sovereignty.[19] This reading is also commonplace; advocates of popular sovereignty have invoked Locke for centuries, and many of his distinguished interpreters *do* read him as a theorist of popular sovereignty.[20] Besides, what Locke intended is probably less important for our purposes than what he has come to mean.

There can be no doubt that Rousseau was a champion of popular sovereignty; his statement of the doctrine has subsequently been modified and restated but never outdone. "Since the American and French Revolutions...it has sooner or later come to be the prevalent doctrine" most everywhere.[21] In Rousseau's view, the state is "a moral person whose life consists in the union of its members."* Each individual, through the social contract, becomes a member of the sovereign (SC I.7.i); the sovereign "is formed entirely of the individuals who make it up" (SC I.7.v). Sovereignty is inalienable and indivisible; simply, it is either the will of the body of the people or it is not (SC II.1.ii; II.2.i). It "[owes] its being solely to the sanctity of the contract" (SC I.7.iii).

For our purposes the central question with respect to Rousseau's account of popular sovereignty concerns its foundations in freedom and equality. Rousseau's views on freedom are familiar and clear enough: "man is born free, and everywhere he is in chains" (SC I.1.i). But what about equality? Rousseau sees a rough equality among men in their natural condition. This equality consists mainly in their equal freedom, notwithstanding "differences in age, health, physical strength, and qualities of mind or soul."† Moral or political

---

* Jean-Jacques Rousseau, *The Social Contract and Other Later Political Writings*, ed. Victor Gourevitch, trans. Julia Conaway Bondanella (Cambridge, UK: Cambridge University Press, 1997), II.4.i, the *Social Contract* (hereafter SC).
† Jean-Jacques Rousseau, *Rousseau's Political Writings*, ed. Alan Ritter and Julia Conaway Bondanella, trans. Julia Conaway Bondanella (New York: W.W. Norton, 1988), 8–9.the *Discourse on the Origin and Foundations of Inequality Among Men* (hereafter DI), 8–9.

inequality, which "depends upon a kind of agreement and is established or at least authorized by the consent of men" grows imperceptibly out of natural inequality once society is founded: "from the moment any one man needed help from another, and as soon as they perceived that it was useful for one man to have provisions for two, *equality disappeared....*" (DI 40; emphasis added). In criticizing Grotius, Rousseau observes that inferring principles from political facts would lead us to conclude that freedom and equality belong only to a few individuals. He asks satirically "whether the human race belongs to a hundred men or so, or whether these hundred men or so belong to the human race?" (SC I.2.v), clearly suggesting that freedom and equality are *human* attributes. Popular sovereignty, established through the social contract, restores and strengthens men's original freedom and equality, grounding them in convention and right (SC I.9.viii).

The appeal and utility of universal principles of freedom and equality to a thinker like Locke, whose party was struggling with the Stuart monarchy over the origin and extent of governmental power and the limits of political obligation, is clear enough.[22] These principles have a leveling effect that undercuts natural hierarchy and subjection, providing a theoretical foundation for government by consent. This logic won the battle of sovereignty for the people; by the time Rousseau formulated his doctrine of popular sovereignty less than a century later, the doctrine had come full circle, extolling the ability of the social contract to establish freedom and equality in right and justifying the unfettered sovereignty of the people themselves. Having located the "popular" aspect of popular sovereignty in universal freedom and equality, it remains to inquire into its sovereignty.

Sovereignty, Popularized

According to Hirst and Thompson, modern democratic theory in effect begins with the transfer of sovereignty to the people.[23] Although democracy developed mostly after sovereign states emerged, they argue, it adapted easily to the framework of the state: popular sovereignty, the idea that the will of the people is supreme, follows relatively straightforwardly from the idea of sovereignty as the will of the prince. The rights and interests of citizens supplant the whims of princes as the subjects of the sovereign's concern. Hurrell, observing that in the modern international system states act as agents of the people, misleadingly suggests that in so doing they do not act as sovereigns.[24] This terminology misleads because in securing the rights and interests of the people the modern state reflects its justification in *popular* sovereignty.

As we have seen, the key theoretical innovation in justifying this shift from princely to popular sovereignty was the introduction of natural freedom and equality, principles which ground authority in consent. More gets transferred, however, than meets the eye. The ingenious argument based on freedom and equality leaves the architecture of sovereignty intact while transposing it from prince to people. Sovereignty describes the nature, location, and limits of political authority; in whom sovereign power rests makes surprisingly little difference with respect to the logic and requirements of the doctrine itself. Popular sovereignty differs from the original neither in the nature and extent of the political power it describes nor in the particular justification of authority on which it depends. This is precisely the point for the doctrine's proponents, whose writings and revolutions contested the royal monopoly on sovereign power within established states, not the *idea* of sovereignty. So the transfer from princely to popular sovereignty preserves the spatial and normative characteristics of the sovereign state, which provide the requisite legitimacy for governing;[25] the popular element gets grafted on to the preexisting account of rightful rule. Thus popular sovereignty remains an account of final and absolute political authority within a fixed, exclusive territory and of the consolidation and centralization of all functional authority within that territory.

While the transfer of sovereignty is logically straightforward—universal freedom and equality ground political authority in consent—it is hardly so in practice. The main difficulties concern how these universal principles come to apply only within a particular territory, only within the so-called "public" realm, and only (initially) to a very limited subset of that territory's population. Given the importance of universality to the argument for popular sovereignty, how is it that the social contract constitutes authority in this highly particularized way? How is it, in other words, that the universal principles of freedom and equality get reconfigured and reconceptualized to conform with the logic of sovereignty? How is that logic preserved in theories of popular sovereignty? The answers, I shall argue here, lie hidden in the state of nature.

The state of nature is a conjectural device, a hypothetical condition whose features model a theorist's assumptions; those assumptions, in turn, shape the social contract, which is a solution to the problem posed by the state of nature. Proponents and critics of such arguments agree that whatever one builds into the state of nature one gets out again in the specifics of the social contract.[26] Conversely, we can surmise that whatever one gets out of the state of nature must have been built into it. Sovereignty, on this view, should be present in the state of nature. It is not, however, obviously there: the classic accounts of the state of nature depict a prepolitical (and for Hobbes, presocial) condition populated by free and equal individuals. In Locke's state of nature all people "[share] all in one Community" (II§6). The state of nature is defined by the lack of common authority; there are no states, no borders; none, apparently, of the hallmarks of sovereignty.

Still, sovereignty *is* discernible in the state of nature if we know where to look for it. Recall the analogy between individuals in the state of nature and states in the anarchic realm of international relations. The explanatory power of this analogy is usually acknowledged to flow in only one direction: we learn about states in the international system by comparing them with individuals in the state of nature. Reading the analogy "in reverse," however, suggests that sovereignty in an anarchic system lies in the constituent units—in individuals—at least in accounts of popular sovereignty. A sovereign individual has all the attributes of a sovereign state. He (it is always he—more below) is independent, master of himself (subject to no external authority), and as a result he enjoys considerable autonomy. He possesses natural proprietary rights over himself, his capacities, and his real property (he is rightful ruler of his domain). In all of these attributes he is roughly equal with his sovereign peers, who confront one another in competitive, anarchic conditions.*

"Natural" sovereignty is difficult to recognize because we are accustomed to look for sovereignty in states; their obvious absence makes it easy to conclude that sovereignty is also absent. Even when we recognize the sovereignty of natural individuals its significance is easily missed; John Scott, for instance, has argued that Locke's natural individuals are sovereign but still later described Locke's state of nature as "sovereignless."[27] Of course, in the traditional sense he is right: states of nature being prepolitical, there is no governmental power of any kind, sovereign or otherwise. Again, that was precisely the point of this way of arguing, to eliminate claims for political right arising in natural and especially familial relations. The sovereignty of natural individuals, like their freedom and equality, only assumes political form in the states created through the social contract. But precisely the innovation in theories of popular sovereignty was to locate sovereignty in natural individuals. Understanding the political form of popular sovereignty, then, requires that we reconstruct its institution through the social contract. The first step in that reconstruction is to ask who the parties to the contract are.

Sovereigns All?

The argument from universal freedom and equality was extremely effective in eroding the patriarchal foundations of absolutism, but its very effectiveness posed a problem: what was to prevent it leading to democracy? If the language of universal freedom and equality eliminated all the natural foundations of rule, critics wondered, "how was such a language to be used, in the interests of the responsible and respectable, without placing an ideological weapon in the hands of 'the multitude' and of those who claimed to speak on

---

*The story is slightly different for Hobbes, but I cannot pursue these differences here. But it is hardly surprising on this account that just as Hobbes and Locke wind up with different accounts of sovereignty inside the state, they also wind up with different accounts of the international system. I shall return to this point briefly below; on the Hobbesian and Lockean conditions of anarchy, see Alexander Wendt, *Social Theory of International Relations* (Cambridge, UK: Cambridge University Press, 1999), chap. 6.

its behalf?"[28] The answer was to ensure the mastery of this respectable class, to exclude the multitude from rule. Inconveniently, however, the argument from natural freedom and equality requires universality, as we have seen. So the theorists had to devise a way of ensuring the subordination of free and equal individuals. They resolved this difficulty through contract; "the multitude" consents to its own subordination.

As both Locke and Rousseau make perfectly clear, the social contract is a contract among equals. Locke argues that *political* power is concerned with those individuals who are independent, subject or subordinate to no one; it is power constituted among equals (II§§4, 95).* Rousseau similarly contends that subordinate individuals must be excluded; the supreme power in a political community does not and cannot consist in an agreement between superior and inferior (SC I.4.viii).† While all individuals are free and equal "in respect of Jurisdiction or Dominion one over another" Locke carefully specifies that they are not equal in respect of age, birth, virtue, merit, excellence, benefits, gratitude, and alliances (II§54). Inferior reason, as in the case of children, is another source of distinction (II§55). Rousseau likewise makes clear that the moral or political equality people enjoy originally consists in their equal natural freedom; they are distinguished by all sorts of natural or physical inequalities including "age, health, physical strength, and qualities of mind or soul" (DI 8). These distinctions make possible a fairly simple argument: people are free and equal enough to be naturally independent, that is, free from the domination and jurisdiction of others, yet unequal enough that some will always find it necessary or convenient to subordinate themselves to others through consent. These natural differences motivate the inferior parties to accept and agree to contractual relations of subjection or subordination.

Contract was the preferred way to secure consent—or rather, to depict it as having been secured—among theorists of popular sovereignty ("contract theorists"). While ostensibly a device for securing or imagining consent, contract theory is primarily about a way of creating social relationships constituted by subordination...."[29] These relationships must be *created* precisely because the leveling effect of universal freedom and equality destroys their foundation in nature and custom. Contract theory recreates the natural subordination destroyed by universal freedom and equality as consensual political subordination. By disguising subordination in consent, the theorists hoped to reap the benefits of arguments from universal freedom and equality while avoiding their more democratic logic. This consensual disguise does

---

*My reading of Locke and Rousseau in the following passages is deeply indebted to Pateman, *The Sexual Contract*.

†Cf. Rousseau, *Rousseau's Political Writings*, the *Discourse on Political Economy* (hereafter DPE), 61.

create a theoretical inconvenience; namely, that certain individuals must always consent to subordination of certain kinds —specifically, marriage and employment or servitude. The inconvenience arises in explaining why women and servants always agree to such contracts.

Both Locke and Rousseau resolve this inconvenience by invoking all of those differences and distinctions said to exist among people in nature despite their moral and political equality. For Locke, man is "abler and stronger" than woman (II§82); woman is to be fully subject to a man unless her contract explicitly exempts her from such subjection (I§47). These distinctions have their foundation in nature (I§47), which presumably helps explain why Locke thinks it among the rights of a man to marry his daughter to whom he chooses.[30] Similarly, when the poor man makes a compact with the wealthy man for his subsistence, "the Subjection of the Needy Beggar began not from the Possession of the Lord, but the Consent of the poor Man, who preferr'd being his Subject to starving" (I§43).* This subjection—note the term—is based in consent; the freeman makes himself a servant to another and in so doing puts himself into the family of the master and subjects himself to the master's discipline. So when Locke turns to consider the foundation of the commonwealth, he contrasts it with the situation of the "*Master of a Family* with all these subordinate Relations of *Wife, Children, Servants* and *Slaves*" united under his domestic rule (I§86). Whatever the implications of this argument for Locke's attack on the patriarchal politics of Filmer, it clearly establishes the political subjection of women and servants or workers to their masters. Thus the subtle—and often overlooked—shift from the free and equal individuals populating the state of nature as Locke first describes it (II§4) and the "free, equal, and independent" individuals who "cannot be put out of this [natural] Estate, and subjected to the Political Power of another, without [their] own *Consent* (II§95). The crucial addition of *independence* as a requirement for accession to the social contract that constitutes civil society excludes all those who stand in subordinate consensual relations to others.

Similarly, Rousseau finds that "for several reasons derived from the nature of things, it is the father who should be in command" in the family (DPE, 59–60). This is to do partly with "the indispositions peculiar to the woman," which force her to inactivity on a regular basis (ibid.). Also, husbands need authority over their wives to avoid being cuckolded—a concern which crops up with surprising frequency in Rousseau's works.[†] *Emile* is a veritable

---

*This passage, following hard on Locke's insistence that "*Charity* gives every Man a Title to so much out of another's Plenty, as will keep him from extream want, where he has no means to subsist otherwise" and that he cannot subject him to vassalage because of his poverty, seriously challenges efforts to reconstruct Locke as a social democrat.

†DPE, 60; see also Jean-Jacques Rousseau, *Emile, or on Education* [Book] (Institute for Learning Technologies, 1762 [cited December 4, 2004]); available from http://www.ilt.columbia.edu/pedagogies/rousseau/.(hereafter E), ¶¶1160, 1260.

encyclopedia of stereotypical and prejudicial views about women, from their extreme fragility (which impedes kite flying) to their suitability for indoor work and their superior knowledge of bodily matters, but inferiority in morality and understanding (E¶¶488, 699, 1200 among others). As Rousseau makes clear, "woman is made to please and to be subjected..." (E ¶1256); she is "made for dependence" (E ¶1298). For these, among other reasons, it is good fathers, sons, and husbands who make good citizens (E ¶1271-2), while nature has fitted women to be mothers (E ¶1266ff., among others). While Rousseau sometimes seems more sympathetic than Locke to the plight of the poor (e.g., SC II.11.ii; DPE 81–3), servants nonetheless owe obedience to the father/husband, as do women and children—though as for Locke, this obedience lasts only as long as the agreement between them (DPE 59–60). Thus women and servants, as subordinates and inferiors, cannot make contracts with their masters and superiors (SC I.4.viii).

As Pateman puts it, classic contract arguments demand that women's personhood be affirmed and denied, that women be considered both persons and property, that they both possess and lack the capacity to enter contractual relations; the same holds for workers.[31] The marriage and employment contracts are not pacts among equals but among natural superiors and their natural inferiors or subordinates. Women and servants are free and equal enough to make contracts, but inferior enough always to make poor ones; they always contract into relations of subordination, into marriage or servitude (employment).* These contractual relationships create a political right that husbands and masters enjoy with respect to wives and servants. That marriage establishes the political right of husbands over wives is well known; Mill writes that the husband was "lord" over his wife, "literally regarded as her sovereign."[32] Something similar happens in the case of servants, who do not lose ownership of their labor or other capacities through employment; they lose their independence. Their subjection has typically been overlooked because of the fiction that labor power is something separable from the person whose property it is; in fact, the inseparability of worker and labor power means that the worker is subject to the owner of his labor power as specified in the terms of the contract.[33]

Natural inferiority is built into the state of nature; differences in the natural endowments and condition of servitude among free and equal persons compel some always to confirm their inferiority by contracting into subjection. These natural inferiors lose their independence, give up their political right, by consenting to contracts establishing their subordination to husbands and

---

*Women who did not make such contracts remained in a perpetual state of dependency upon fathers and brothers (though the law was full of anomalies and exceptions). Similarly, individuals without means who do not accept wage labor either become wards of the state through relief schemes or imprisonment.

masters. This subordination leaves only husbands and masters with their natural autonomy and independence, but it does so without strictly violating the universal logic of freedom and equality on which contract arguments rely. That this result is reached through what seem like rather dubious arguments to contemporary readers hardly matters (though critics were quick to note the fallacious quality of appeals to nature in such arguments).[34] The natural sovereignty of male, propertied individuals is just the flip side of this coin; only those individuals who are free, equal, and *independent*—who are not contractually subordinate or in subjection to others—can consent to the social compact and become citizens of the state and members of the sovereign. Only they are owners of real property and of exclusive rights in their own capacities. Only they become parties to the social contract, the explicit purpose of which is to protect the property of its signatories. Only they become citizens or "members of the sovereign" as Rousseau styles them. The others are brought into civil society through their masters; they are part of it, but not members of it.[35] Thus the original contract explains why popular sovereignty was less "popular" than its universalistic foundations might lead us to expect: only sovereign individuals can be parties to the social contract. In the state of nature, everyone is free and equal, but only some are sovereign.

This argument raises a puzzle: why did the contract theorists couch their arguments in universal terms, only to reintroduce natural differences that undermine that universality? The traditional Whiggish explanation attributes these exclusions to the theorists' unfortunate views about the nature or capacities of women and servants: but for some backward beliefs that blinded them to the full logic of their own ideas—beliefs understandable for men of their time—these theorists would have been modern democrats. There is some truth to the argument that the texts might be wiser than their authors; the core democratic principles of universal freedom and equality have an appeal far beyond the limited purposes to which these authors put them. Still, this explanation does not dispatch the question of why thinkers who obviously had no practical commitment to universality nonetheless used it in their theories, and it distorts their arguments. Rather than restricting "universality" to propertied men, the theorists actually ascribed freedom and equality to everyone, only to swindle them away from all but a select handful—the swindle itself being pulled off through dubious arguments about voluntary contracts based in the natural inferiority of certain "free and equal" persons.

The Whiggish account understates the theorists' awareness of the leveling power of the principles they unleashed and obscures the steps they took to check it. For me both facts are important. In making freedom and equality universal, the theorists of popular sovereignty forged a double-edged sword; with one bold stroke they smote kings and severed the link between nature and authority. But these principles proved so effective in erasing privilege and social hierarchy that to avoid a truly democratic backswing the theorists had to reassert the natural sovereignty of some individuals. In so doing they established the social contract as a sovereign contract.

The Social Contract as Sovereign Contract: Inside

In social contract theory, sovereignty is an artifice, something created by political agreement.* The social contract establishes political authority through the agreement of sovereign individuals. In this respect it is a sovereign contract, an agreement among natural sovereigns to establish political power by transferring their right to a contractually constituted sovereign whose authority their consent explicitly legitimizes. But in practice the state constituted by this contract must conform to the logic of sovereignty and the particulars of already existing sovereign states. By studying the details of this contract, we can see how freedom and equality get reconfigured to fit the limits of sovereignty.

Sovereignty inside the state assumes different forms depending upon the nature of the social contract—a contract designed to solve specific problems by different theorists. Locke's state of nature is plagued by "inconveniences" arising from the lack of an independent authority with recognized power to judge and enforce the law of nature. Each natural sovereign transfers just so much of his right to the commonwealth as is necessary to constitute a power sufficient to rectify these inconveniences and secure his property (II§§128–31, 135ff.). Rousseau has less interest in limiting the power of the sovereign; for him, the fundamental problem of politics is "to find a form of association that defends and protects the person and possessions of each associate with all of the common strength, and by means of which each person, joining forces with all, nevertheless obeys only himself and remains as free as before" (SC I.6.iv). The solution to this problem is a social pact through which "each of us puts his person and all his power in common under the supreme control of the general will, and, as a body, we receive each member as an indivisible part of the whole." Individuals in effect contract with themselves in forming the sovereign (SC I.6.ix). Their equality as members of the sovereign makes them free, subject only to laws of their own making.

The original contract reconciles freedom and equality with sovereignty by restricting their universality; consensual subordination leaves only sovereign individuals to become citizens through the social contract and exercise sovereign authority inside the state, collectively in the public sphere

---

*Thanks to Fred Whelan for helping me clear up the argument in this section.

and individually in the private. These two spheres are mutually constitutive.[36] In the public realm citizens address common concerns collectively, either directly or through representatives. One of these concerns is securing property, and among the property citizens possess is their property right in contracts, including those contracts establishing their sexual and economic mastery. One advantage of structuring subordination through contract is that it turns what had been natural relations of mastery and subjection into publicly enforceable contractual roles.

The regulation of marriage and labor contracts is paradigmatic: though it is technically true that the power of husbands and masters is not political, the distinction collapses because it is husbands and masters, wearing the public hats of citizens, who create and enforce the rules governing private relations of subjection.[37] At the same time, citizens remain sovereign in private; they enjoy a presumption of noninterference from public authority in their private affairs. So while contracts are publicly regulated, sovereign citizens enjoy the power and benefits of mastery and contractual property rights.

Thus, the rights of these [male] individuals to be free from intrusion by the state, or by the church, or from the prying of neighbors, were also these individuals' rights *not* to be interfered with as they controlled the other members of their private sphere—those who, whether by reason of age, or sex, or condition of servitude, were regarded as rightfully controlled by them and existing within *their* sphere of privacy.[38]

Men's ongoing sovereignty in the private sphere, in turn, assures that their public mastery as citizens remains unchallenged. Again, the international analogy helps us recognize these arrangements as characteristic of sovereignty. In the international system, respect for the sovereignty of other states creates a norm of noninterference in domestic affairs; among the prerogatives of sovereignty is the enjoyment of absolute and final authority at home. Similarly, sovereign individuals are unmolested in their private or "domestic" affairs. The analogy is in this case imperfect, however, because the creation of a public sphere at the state level allows collective regulation of the private sphere through contract; international public authority (contracting out) is excluded by hypothesis.

The social contract establishes the collective sovereignty of citizens in the public domain and protects their individual sovereignty in private. Sovereign citizens are free and equal in the public sphere, where each possesses an equal say in the affairs of state. In private, they are equal in their rights as citizens, benefiting from the noninterference of public authority in their private affairs and from the publicly guaranteed contractual mastery over members of their family, "their" domestic sphere. This distinctive configuration of rule characterizes popular sovereignty inside the state.

The Social Contract as Sovereign Contract: Boundaries

The exclusive character of freedom, equality, and citizenship, upheld by the division between public and private, describes the internal limits of popular sovereignty: its inside. But this is only part of the story: because sovereignty is a theory of rightful rule *within a particular territory*, that territory must be delineated. The boundaries of the sovereign state must be explained as well. In practice, this space was usually identical with the king's realm; the state had come to be understood as independent of both ruler and subjects, and its territorial dimensions were essentially fixed.[39] Yet this practical result was difficult to explain in theory. As Filmer objected in his critique of Hobbes's consensual argument for sovereignty, basing government on the consent of naturally free and equal individuals suggests that "if all the men in the world do not agree, no commonwealth can be established."[40] Filmer seems to have recognized that where consent is supposed to provide the only legitimate foundation for government there is no neat way to explain territorial political differentiation.

As Bernard Yack has argued, the definition of the state and its people is circular in most popular sovereignty arguments. The people is taken to be prepolitical, its consent constitutive of the state, yet who constitutes "the people" is usually inferred from the borders of the state they are said to create. The people is at once a prepolitical and postpolitical concept.[41] This problem is pronounced in Rousseau, who claims that "the act by which a people becomes a people"—"the true foundation of society" which "is necessarily prior" to the act creating government—"presupposes unanimity" (SC I.5.ii–iii).* Given Rousseau's explicit recognition of a plurality of states, unanimity assumes a prepolitical population, and thus a prepolitical polity, just as Yack describes. The problem for Locke is less dire only because he is less committal, referring to unanimous agreement among "any number of Men" while apparently leaving open who these men might be (II§101).

Once again, if we read the social contract as a sovereign contract, we can reconstruct how the territorial limits sovereignty requires get instituted in popular sovereignty. On the standard Lockean interpretation, parties to the social contract bring their property with them into civil society (II§§120, 123).[42] This stands to reason for Locke: securing property rights, which are precarious in the state of nature, is the primary rationale for creating political society in the first place (II§124). Rousseau makes this connection explicit; the state's territory is determined by the original act that forms society: "the

---

*Cf. Rousseau, *The Social Contract and Other Later Political Writings. The State of War* (hereafter SoW), 167, where Rousseau argues that once the first society has formed each person must decide whether to join or dissent from it.

adjoining properties of private individuals are united and become public territory, and…the right of sovereignty [extends] from the subjects to the land they occupy" (SC I.9.v). The sovereign state acquires its territory directly through the social contract, which establishes the boundaries of the political community.[43] By linking the state's territory to the property of its citizens, the social contract explains how in popular sovereignty theories the sovereign—the people—comes to have property in its territory. The sovereign citizens rule "their" state with the same proprietary right by which the sovereign rules "his" realm. This right to rule is recognized in natural law discussions of noninterference, in which a connection between property, territory, and sovereignty is "distinctly implied."[44]

The social contract explains the citizens' right to rule within a particular territory, their property; certain peculiar features of this contract explain how the state's territory becomes fixed and stable. According to Locke, men lose an important right in their property when they join civil society: it becomes permanently attached to the commonwealth.

> Every Man, when he, at first, incorporates himself into any Commonwealth, he, by his uniting himself thereunto, annexed also, and submits to the Community those Possessions, which he has, or shall acquire, that do not already belong to any other Government. For it would be a direct Contradiction, for any one, to enter into Society with others for the securing and regulating of Property: And yet to suppose his Land, whose Property is to be regulated by the Laws of the Society, should be exempt from the Jurisdiction of that Government, to which he himself the Proprietor of the Land, is a Subject (II§120).

When an individual joins a commonwealth, all of his land "joins" with him, except, tellingly, any lands already part of another state. This "annexation" is permanent: anyone who comes to enjoy any property under a government, whether by purchase, permission, ownership, inheritance, or other means, submits that property tacitly (by default) to the government's authority and jurisdiction (ibid.).

Strangely, unless and until an individual explicitly incorporates himself into civil society, "the Government has a direct Jurisdiction only over the Land, and reaches the Possessor of it…only as he dwells upon and enjoys that: *The Obligation* any one is under, by Virtue of such Enjoyment, *to submit to the Government, begins and ends with the Enjoyment*" of the property. If that enjoyment has not been formalized by a specific declaration of consent, a man may, "by Donation, Sale, or otherwise, quit the said Possession"; he is then at liberty to join another society or to form a new one with others *on the condition that he renounces title to his land*, which cannot be separated from the civil society (II§121). Heirs must accept their property on the terms under which their fathers had it; that is, they must acknowledge it as part of the commonwealth (II§73).*

Rousseau makes this direct link between territory and rule even more explicit. He notes that while ancient monarchs styled themselves leaders of men rather than masters of countries—kings of the Persians, the Scythians, and so on—today's rulers more cleverly call themselves kings of France, Spain, England. By holding the land, Rousseau argues, they are quite sure of holding its inhabitants. The transfer of land from individual to society and then back to the citizen places the landowners in greater dependency and makes their strength itself the guarantee of their fidelity (SC I.9.v). Sovereign power then applies to land as well as men, which is clear since "when the state is instituted, residency implies consent; to inhabit the territory is to submit to the sovereign authority" (SC IV.2.vi). Once society is constituted, moreover, the sovereign cannot submit to any outside authority or alienate any portion of its territory without nullifying the social contract (SC I.7.3). These arguments clarify that the social contract establishes rightful rule within a particular territory and only by extension over particular subjects whose loyalty is a function of oath or creed. They also exemplify the intellectual contortions required to align the hypothetically contractual state with existing sovereign states. Authority is linked to territory, ostensibly through consent, but in fact through convention.

After the French Revolution, sovereignty became increasingly associated with the people qua nation. As this association developed, the related territorial claims become more complicated, as do the accounts of who qualifies as one of "the people" in the first place. The rightful territory of "the nation" comes to include lands with special historical or cultural significance and areas with large populations of national members, even if these areas lie outside the existing boundaries of the national state.[45] While it has been common to regard nationalism, especially in its virulent forms, as antiliberal and antidemocratic, from the early 1990s liberal nationalists have argued that it can support liberal and democratic values.[46] Tamir goes further, arguing that liberal democratic theory relies on hidden nationalist values: for instance, in restricting the community of distributive justice to members and in explaining why there is no global contract.[47] I demur only in that I think sovereignty—though sometimes in its nationalist guise—is the core issue; nationalists are some of sovereignty's strongest contemporary advocates. While not all nationalist justifications of authority are democratic,

---

*Locke is careful to point out that "enjoyment" (in the broad sense) of an inheritance signals only tacit consent; fathers cannot, by passing along property, bind their heirs to the state. However, if the heir wishes to leave civil society, he leaves his property behind.

most do appeal to some notion of popular sovereignty; insofar as they *are* democratic, membership of the nation becomes another of the natural criteria required for citizenship.[48]

The Social Contract as Sovereign Contract: Outside

The social contract constitutes authority inside the state and fixes its territorial dimensions. It also constitutes, indirectly, the international system; that is, relations outside among states.[49] This international system is famously anarchic, as we saw in the previous chapter. We can now also see—the objectivist harrumphing of neorealists and the righteous indignation of their critics notwithstanding—that this anarchic system rests on deep moral foundations. Its constitution and laws flow from the normative assumption that rightful rule inheres in the state. Thus political authority created by consent introduces a moral imperative for anarchy: only an anarchic system prevents abrogation of the sovereign people's right to rule. As Walker argues, the realist tradition in international relations is unthinkable without the priority it assigns to the moral claims of political authority inside the state.[50]

The implications of anarchy's moral foundation are far-reaching. Wendt argues that the Westphalian system is not a Hobbesian war of all against all characterized by enmity but rather a "Lockean" anarchy characterized by rivalry; this distinction resides largely in whether a right to sovereignty is reciprocally recognized by states in the system.[51] Certainly neither Locke nor Rousseau accepts the Hobbesian version. Locke characterizes the people, united as one body, standing in relation to other societies so united as individuals within the state of nature (II§145). As we know, in Locke's state of nature individuals are natural owners of, and have rights to, their lives, liberty, and property. By analogy with such individuals, states would have a right to sovereignty; this is evident primarily in Locke's discussion of why conquest does not confer just title on the conqueror or establish his authority (II§§182–84). These passages not only affirm Locke's view of natural law in the state of nature but also clearly indicate respect for contractually constituted authority in other states.

Rousseau adamantly rejects the Hobbesian characterization of international relations (SoW 164ff.), though his own views remain opaque. He considers war properly as a term reserved for conflict among states (SC I.4.x; SoW 175). While acknowledging that peace among sovereigns is both possible and desirable,[52] Rousseau also maintains that sovereigns exist in a state of nature with respect to one another (DI 45) and that war among them is legitimate because they are public, moral persons (SoW 175ff). Together these views seem at least to indicate a reciprocal recognition of sovereignty among states, as we would expect from a theorist of popular sovereignty.

This international system of reciprocal recognition of sovereignty applies only among European states, however; as Charles Mills has argued, all of the classic contract theorists took rather different views of aboriginal peoples in America and of Asians and Africans.[53] Many of the same arguments that justified the contractual subjection of women and workers—deficient rationality, moral immaturity, or incapacity—were used to explain the "absence" of civil(ized) society in these lands. Locke, for example, frequently cites America as a contemporary example of men existing in a state of nature (e.g., II§§14, 45, 48, 49, 65, 92). More subtly, however, Locke implies that the absence of government or sovereignty in America flows from a lack of reason and moral character. The argument, briefly, is that rational and industrious men will acquire private property (II§34), the protection of which is the "great and *chief end*" for entering civil society (II§124). We can infer from the absence of government an absence of property and thus of reason and moral character as well.[54] For Rousseau, savagery—which is buried in the primordial European past or confined to bizarre cases of infants raised by wolves—exists widely in the world today, in Africa and America in particular (DI 12ff.).[55] Hottentots and Americans resemble animals in their possession of keen senses of sight, smell, and hearing (and correspondingly coarse senses of taste and touch); this is why Americans can track Spaniards in the wilderness "as well as the best dogs" (DI 15). For Rousseau, leaving the state of nature through agreement to the social contract is a necessary step in the moral transformation of human beings; it is this social compact that creates them as moral persons (SC I.8.i–iii). Thus existence in a state of savagery affirms the immorality, the arrested civilization, of the savages.[56]

There is a growing debate on the role of Enlightenment thinking in shaping and resisting empire and colonialism, a debate I cannot join here.[57] The point I want to emphasize is that the denial of sovereignty to colonized or expropriated peoples is perfectly consistent with other arguments limiting universal freedom and equality used by popular sovereignty theorists—though no less objectionable for this consistency. Like women or servants, savages might be morally free and equal, but their evident deficiencies meant that their mastery by Europeans was, for them, appropriate, providing vicarious enjoyment of the benefits of sovereignty.* This denial of sovereignty, and the moral capacity for sovereignty, helps to explain the jealous guardianship of sovereignty by formerly colonized states, who often see globalization as neocolonialism precisely because it resembles another Western attempt to deny their hard-won sovereignty.

---

*As Mills notes, the racial contract takes a form different from the original and social contracts. "Whites" agree on the moral and political inferiority of "nonwhites" and further agree to misunderstand the world in a way supportive of this agreement (13). The racial contract is thus an agreement among "Whites" rather than between whites and nonwhites.

Sovereign Democracy

The social contract is a sovereign contract. It (re)creates sovereignty: a supreme political authority within a territorially exclusive state. The social contract constitutes sovereign authority in the citizenry or demos through a transfer of right from sovereign individuals; it defines the rightful extent of that authority through the consolidation and incorporation of their private property into the exclusive territory of the state; and, it establishes a normative order among sovereign states and among "subject" peoples. Modern democracy develops within the empirical framework of the sovereign state and the conceptual framework of popular sovereignty. Theorizing about democratization traces back to arguments for rule by the people, arguments based in universal freedom and equality. These arguments provide logically necessary and politically expedient grounds for leveling natural hierarchies and anchoring political authority in consent.

But popular sovereignty remains a theory of sovereignty, though its very success as an idiom for modern democracy renders the conceptual framework of sovereignty invisible to most theorists working within it. It is, as we noted at the outset of this chapter, taken for granted. This sovereign framework becomes evident, once we look for it, in the strange limits modern democratic theory places on its universal principles. Freedom and equality are limited inside by the demarcation of public and private spheres and the restriction of citizenship; they are limited outside by the exclusivity of states. These limits generate profound tensions that have remained largely invisible because modern political theory depicts its limits as universal. Citizenship is the quintessential example: "universal" suffrage refers to suffrage for everyone within a state. But as Walker observes, *all* universals in political theory are similarly particularistic: they are claims about or on behalf of the citizens of some particular state. Political theory maintains a studied silence about international relations to preserve this fiction of universality.[58] By constituting the world outside the state as anarchic and unsuitable for politics, political theory hides the extreme particularism of its "universal" claims. (Conversely, realism, the consummate theory of sovereignty outside the state, keeps quiet about politics to preserve its own fictions about relations among states.)

Something analogous happens inside the state, where freedom and equality are professedly universal yet remain limited to citizens in their public capacities, in the public sphere. Political theory long observed silence about this internal sphere of "domestic" politics as well. Over time, however, these internal tensions were exposed. Popular sovereignty was democratized internally through challenges to and struggles over the meaning and limits of universality; externally, until quite recently, the silence and the limits have been maintained.

Still, despite several centuries of democratization, many familiar features of modern democracy are artifacts of sovereignty; they reflect its core assumptions and can only be fully apprehended and justified with these assumptions in mind. Briefly consider three examples: the public/private distinction, accountability, and collective autonomy through representative government. In modern democracy political (democratic) authority is limited to the public sphere, leaving certain important spheres of life—such as family, the economy—outside democratic control. While these spheres are regulated by the public authority, the presumption remains that democratic principles do not apply to governance and authority within these spheres. Nothing about freedom and equality or rule by consent explains this distinction; as we have seen, however, the private rights of sovereign citizens require the bifurcation.

Accountability is the norm that rulers must be responsive and ultimately responsible to those they rule and from whom they derive their authority. But without prior assumptions about who the citizenry—the people—comprises, this notion loses all coherence. Many decisions impact people who are not citizens or who live outside the jurisdictions where the decisions are taken; those who experience this impact are in a real sense "ruled" by the decision makers, yet in modern democratic theory those decision makers are not accountable to such persons. Freedom and equality alone do not explain this arrangement; sovereignty, rightful rule within a particular territory, does. Attempts to extend accountability outside the state, beyond the citizenry, founder not on technical grounds but on normative ones; popular sovereignty imparts to democratic legitimacy a requirement that citizens, and only citizens, rule within their territory.

Or consider the closely related idea of collective autonomy through representative government, a key feature of modern democracy. That there should be some fixed territory in which all the (qualified) inhabitants rightfully decide political questions through their representatives to the exclusion of other interested and affected parties cannot be explained solely with reference to freedom and equality or to government by consent. Sovereignty supplies the territorial distinction as well as its normative justification.* I am not suggesting that there is anything wrong or undemocratic about accountability or representation in the abstract (restriction of democracy to the public sphere is more problematic). My point is simply that without further assumptions to do with sovereignty these notions are underspecified and unworkable. Modern democracy looks the way it does and works the way

---

*Some critics will insist that nationalism supplies an alternative justification; as I have already indicated, I agree, though with the caveat that nationalism itself piggybacks on notions of popular sovereignty.

it does because it has incorporated sovereignty's territorial and conceptual limits. The connection between them is more than merely incidental and not easily severed.*

Modern democracy's entanglement with sovereignty and the sovereign state is deep and long standing. Democratic legitimacy is predicated upon limits difficult to explain or justify solely through democratic principles; supreme rule by the people within a particular territory and within a limited public domain are the hallmarks of sovereignty. The central argument of this chapter has been that popular sovereignty transforms an argument that begins with free and equal individuals in a prepolitical state of nature into a justification for territorial political rule shared among the members of an exclusive demos or citizenry. The sovereign contract reconciles the universal principles needed to effect the transfer of sovereignty with the limits sovereignty requires. These limits, masquerading as universals in modern political theory, restrict and redefine freedom and equality within the sovereign democratic state. The restrictions have been challenged with some success inside the state, but the external limits of sovereign democracy have been mostly ignored.

Popular sovereignty has been indispensable to modern democracy—it has made freedom and equality possible within the modern state. But it also endows democracy with all of sovereignty's characteristics, limiting universal freedom and equality by reconfiguring them to fit sovereignty's spatial and normative requirements. Modern democracy is sovereign democracy; this, I shall argue in the next chapter, is the crucial fact in understanding globalization's effects on democracy.

---

*I shall return to these important points in later chapters.

CHAPTER 4

Globalization and the Paradox of Sovereign Democracy

We began by analyzing contemporary debates about how globalization affects democracy. Conceptual confusions bedevil these debates, confusions stemming from treating states and democracy as if they fit together unproblematically. The conventional wisdom that states are the natural and appropriate containers of democracy combines a spatial claim regarding the configuration of rule with a normative claim concerning its propriety; both of these interdependent assumptions derive from sovereignty, and both inform modern democracy, shaping its meaning and its institutional form. More specifically, sovereignty justifies supreme political authority within a particular territory; its normative persuasiveness as an account of rightful rule hinges on its empirical plausibility as a description of the global political system. Supreme rightful authority inside the state requires territorial exclusivity in an anarchic international system of notionally equal sovereign states. Modern arguments for democratization take the state's sovereignty and the Westphalian system of sovereign states for granted. By introducing principles of universal freedom and equality, theorists of popular sovereignty successfully grounded political authority in consent; instead of challenging sovereignty, however, these arguments transfer it to the people. Freedom and equality get reconciled with sovereignty through the social contract, which reestablishes the sovereign state on new, consensual foundations. Thus the transfer of sovereignty to the people also transmits the normative and empirical limits of sovereignty into modern democracy. Popular sovereignty becomes the idiom of democratic theory; modern democracy is sovereign democracy.

Now, having specified the link between modern democracy and the sovereign state, we can consider why globalization affects democracy. In this chapter I shall argue that globalization is transforming the modern configuration of rule, radically remaking contemporary governance in ways that undermine sovereignty and sovereign democracy by undercutting the spatial and normative assumptions on which they depend. Globalization dissipates sovereignty, eroding its coherence as a normative account of politics. Moreover, globalization reveals a paradox: as universalization proceeds, sovereign democracy simultaneously requires and rules out supranational governance. This paradox stems from the strange universalism of modern democracy: as the global configuration of rule evolves, a tension develops between the universal principles of freedom and equality and their limited realization within the sovereign state. This tension, long submerged beneath the anarchic assumptions of Westphalia, makes modern democracy incoherent. Globalization does not cause this paradox, it heightens and highlights it by transforming politics and established notions of political authority. This paradox is most evident outside the state, where globalization transforms sovereign democracy's external limits. Yet a similar, and instructive, paradox occurs inside the state as democratization challenges the limits sovereignty imposes on freedom and equality. I conclude by drawing some provocative parallels between the external and internal processes of universalization in the sovereign state and exploring their implications for contemporary democracy.

I begin with a brief overview of sovereignty emphasizing the interdependence of its spatial and normative aspects and stressing its difference from control and independence. Next, I show how globalization erodes sovereignty by transforming the configuration of contemporary governance arrangements and by displacing politics in the lives and perceptions of modern citizens. While defenders of traditional sovereignty insist that current events represent little change, transformationalists insist that sovereignty is being remade by globalization. I show that each of these views is deficient—the first because it misapprehends the nature and significance of the changes underway and the latter because it clings to the nomenclature of sovereignty and confuses the new world order with an older one. Defending an alternative understanding of contemporary developments, I argue that ongoing changes in the configuration of rule must be understood in their own terms, not as a rehash of the Middle Ages or a refabrication of sovereignty itself. Globalization dissipates sovereignty by destroying its plausibility and usefulness as an account of politics—and in so doing reveals the paradoxical nature of modern democracy. This paradox highlights the tensions between sovereignty on the one hand and freedom and equality on the other, both outside and within the state. I conclude by suggesting that we would do better to conceive globalization as a challenge to democracy—to the universality of freedom and equality—than as a threat to it.

The Decline of What?

Sovereignty, as we saw in chapter 2, is a vexed and vexing concept, one embroiled in heated controversies over its meaning and its future. At the outset of a chapter arguing that globalization dissipates sovereignty and that sovereign democracy is in decline, it seems appropriate, in light of this imbroglio, to recapitulate those dimensions of sovereignty I have been stressing thus far. I shall do so by means of emphasizing three distinctions often lost in the contemporary literature. The first is between sovereignty as a spatial and normative discourse and legal sovereignty. "When international lawyers say that a state is sovereign, all that they really mean is that it is independent, that is, that it is not a dependency of some other state."[1] When I argue that globalization dissipates sovereignty, I do not mean to imply that it is eroding the legal independence of states. Rather, my concern is with sovereignty's spatial and normative requirements: fixed, exclusive territory, supreme political authority within it, and the justification of that authority as rightful or legitimate because of its territorial basis. This broader definition entails independence, but the two are hardly equivalent; we can easily imagine legally independent entities that are not sovereign in this sense.

The second distinction is between sovereignty and control. Many contemporary analysts talk about sovereignty or authority when they are actually referring to de facto control. But control is an empirical variable; it deals with material, technical, and coercive capacities exercised by a wide range of actors and agents across a wide spectrum of functional domains. Sovereignty is a normative concept; it explains and justifies control or rule. Control can be analyzed independently of its rightfulness or propriety; not all control is justified, and not all legitimate control is justified in the same way. Sovereignty is rightful rule within a particular territory; while sovereignty implies rule or control, to have control is not to be sovereign and to be sovereign is not to exercise absolute control. Sovereign states vary in the degree of control they exercise, while sharing a common justification for their exercise of it.

Finally, we must make a distinction between sovereignty and the state itself. The two ideas are so closely associated that states' ongoing existence and centrality in world politics are frequently taken as evidence that sovereignty remains the organizing principle of international relations. While sovereignty assumes the state, states do not, conceptually, require sovereignty. "State" is the name of the political community in which sovereign authority is justified through its territorial connection, but the modern state has developed a legal and institutional identity compatible in principle with various configurations of authority. Put differently, legally independent states need not claim or possess the supreme territorial authority sovereignty entails.

Globalization and Sovereignty (I)

In the first chapter I defined globalization as universalization, the trend in social activity and interaction in the broadest sense, including economic, political, and cultural activity, toward the supranational. I emphasized its tendency to challenge all kinds of familiar borders and boundaries; to cite again Rosenau's apt depiction, "any technological, psychological, social, economic, or political developments that foster the expansion of interests and practices beyond established boundaries are both sources and expressions of" globalization.[2] How do these developments affect sovereignty? At least two effects are directly relevant here.

First, in challenging familiar borders and boundaries globalization also challenges the presumption that supreme political authority rests with (and within) the state. Economic globalization is a textbook example: market forces associated with globalization tend to break down borders and resist control by state-based political systems.[3] Economic globalization creates "new spaces" of economy and politics outside any state's authority and control. These spaces extend beyond, cut across, and overlay existing political spaces (states), transforming the political cartography of Westphalia. That state actions—in easing capital controls, for instance—helped fuel economic globalization in the first place might complicate the simplistic view of states as victims of economic globalization, but it has little bearing on broader claims about the empirical trend being discussed here.[4] Transnational corporations (TNCs), investors, and speculators all exercise a great deal of control and influence within these spaces[5]; they manifest both internally, in the form of TNCs evading some forms of domestic regulation and taxation, and externally, in the form of so-called market discipline and restricted policy autonomy.

While economic changes are perhaps the paradigmatic instances of globalization in this respect, they are hardly unique. Increased and increasingly easy flows of people, ideas, and information across borders significantly undermine the state's presumed status as the site of politics. This is a change that bears directly on sovereignty's distinctive (if factually questionable) claim that the state is a natural and appropriate container of politics and arena of political activity. States often resist these flows—by trying to (re)establish control over borders, airwaves, cyberspace—but technology and human ingenuity often seem determined to thwart them. So there is an empirical dimension to this change, to be sure, but also a perceptual one: growing awareness of interconnections and interdependence is a hallmark of globalization. We see this awareness reflected in claims about the shrinking planet, the global village, and so on.

Globalization's second important effect on sovereignty is closely related to the first. As the number and density of supranational activities and interactions increase, so does the need for mechanisms through which they can be regulated and through which problems arising from them can be effectively addressed. Put simply, globalization generates the need for governance. In response, states create supranational governance regimes: broadly, international governance organizations (IGOs), treaty organizations, and other international forums and institutions that fulfill control or steering functions at the supranational level.[6] International financial institutions (IFIs) like the IMF and World Bank are perhaps the most familiar (notorious?) examples, but the variety is staggering, encompassing familiar organizations like the UN, WTO, NATO, and the European Union; regional trade organizations like those associated with NAFTA; and, all sorts of functionally specific organizations like the International Whaling Commission or the International Labor Organization. These regimes can be understood as responses to globalization and as instances of globalization in their own right. They are increasingly common: in 1909 there were 37 IGOs, but by 1996 the number was 260; the number of international treaties in effect among governments rose from 6,351 at the end of the World War II to 14,061 a mere thirty years later.[7] In addition to these formal regimes, less formal bodies like the Group of 8 (G8) industrialized nations or the Asia-Pacific Economic Cooperation Forum (APEC) play important coordination roles and are taking on growing policy roles as well.

Together, supranational governance arrangements reveal "an image of extremely intense and overlapping networks of global, regional, and multilateral governance."[8] It is notable that states, especially rich democratic states, have been the key actors creating and supporting such regimes. Cerny argues that in a highly interdependent world, states "are increasingly drawn into the construction of interstate institutions or 'regimes' in pursuit of their national interests."[9]* Recall that these interests include protecting and promoting the rights and interests of citizens, at least in democratic states. Other critics argue that while states do in some cases delegate control to supranational governance organizations, power is sometimes assumed or accumulated by the organizations themselves.[10] Still, there is widespread agreement that these regimes represent a "new geography of power" crucial to the management

---

*On this basis he concludes that globalization is a process of "political structuration"; see Phillip G. Cerny, "Paradoxes of the Competition State: The Dynamics of Political Globalization," *Government and Opposition* 32, no. 2 (1997): 253.

of "new" spaces created by globalization.[11] Again, we see that an empirical change is linked to a perceptual one: trends in global governance affect how people conceive governance and authority, as reflected in talk about new world order or complaints about bureaucrats in Brussels and Geneva.

Whatever their origin, supranational governance regimes represent a significant challenge to sovereignty. They represent new sites and sources of authority, militating against the sovereign notion that supreme rightful rule resides within territorially exclusive states. So globalization challenges sovereignty's empirical and normative assumptions. Empirically, the trend of social activity toward the supranational challenges the presumption of the state as a site of politics and political authority; normatively, the reallocation of authority concomitant with that trend strains sovereignty's distinctive territorial justification of rule. But assessments of this challenge and its implications for sovereignty differ widely. Traditionalists maintain that contemporary developments are greatly exaggerated and pose no threat to sovereignty, while transformationalists insist that globalization is remaking the world order and sovereignty with it. Both views are wrong, but both instructively so. We can best understand how globalization is affecting sovereignty by learning from their mistakes.

Good Old-Fashioned Sovereignty?

When traditionalists survey the "new geography of power," the landscape looks more or less the same as it always has.* Traditionalists view claims about globalization's transformative significance as grossly exaggerated; Waltz calls globalization "a fad."[12] On the traditionalist view, entering into treaties and other cooperative arrangements, far from diminishing or abrogating sovereignty, expresses an important attribute of it. These arrangements enhance states' effectiveness in realizing and protecting their interests (though admittedly at the cost of policy autonomy) and are therefore wholly consistent with sovereignty.†

Traditionalists stress the rationality of states' decisions to participate in supranational governance regimes. States agree to such arrangements in the first place because they calculate that doing so will enhance their control or effectiveness in certain policy domains or lead to more optimal outcomes. Integration is a rational way for sovereign states to avoid the often unacceptable costs of isolation and to maximize their influence over policies and

---

*This is hardly surprising; recall Waltz's comments about the striking sameness of the international system throughout the ages.
†This view is reflected in the *Wimbledon* Case, in which the Permanent Court of International Justice declined to see any treaties by which states undertake or refrain from undertaking particular actions as abandonments of sovereignty. Instead, the Court held that the right to enter international engagements is an attribute of sovereignty; Malanczuk, *Akehurst's International Law*, 18.

decisions that will affect them regardless of their explicit participation. Such arrangements are nothing new, traditionalists emphasize, and they do not diminish states' sovereignty.[13] It is not my intention to survey the traditionalist literature; rather, I want to reconstruct the logic underlying this view so that we can assess one of its key claims: that supranational governance regimes pose no threat to sovereignty.[14]

We saw in chapter 2 that sovereignty explains and justifies a change in the configuration of rule in early modern Europe. The increasing de facto role of territorial states was difficult to comprehend through the older, more encompassing narratives of political community and authority that had provided a conceptual anchor for the chaotic hierarchies of medieval political life. Sovereignty represents a new political subjectivity, one that starts from the assumption of an already-defined political space, an inside. This empirical fact becomes a theoretical postulate, one which makes politics outside or above this space impossible. In a world comprised of sovereign states, authority inside is predicated upon and requires anarchy outside; states are conceived as analogous to individuals in the state of nature. There is no common authority among them and each has the right (and duty) to defend and preserve itself and its interests. While they differ on whether this international state of nature should be understood in Hobbesian, Lockean, or Kantian terms, realists, constructivists, and idealists agree that states, unlike natural individuals, cannot contract out of anarchy.[15]

This point seems clear enough in respect of Hobbes and Locke but might seem dubious in respect of Kant, who famously argues that a (domestic) constitution capable of administering justice universally [sic], and facilitating realization of human beings' moral capacities, requires an external constitution guaranteeing the security and rights of states.[16] So states are ultimately compelled to form a common constitution: "not a cosmopolitan commonwealth under a single ruler, but a lawful *federation* under a commonly accepted *international right*."[17] Indeed, Kant makes clear that the contract inside the state fulfills the sovereignty of the people, and that this external contract can in no respect violate, circumscribe, or supersede this sovereignty; it is required solely for the internal justice, security, and stability of independent civil societies. So the Second Preliminary Article of Kant's scheme for Perpetual Peace guarantees the independence of existing states,[18] and the Second Definitive Article emphasizes that the right of nations is based on a federation of free states. This federation is in some ways analogous with the state of nature, but it cannot lead to an international state, because

> State involves a relationship between a superior (the legislator) and an inferior (the people obeying the laws), whereas a number of nations forming one state would constitute a single nation. *And this would*

contradict our initial assumption, as we are here considering the right of nations in relation to one another insofar as they are a group of separate states which are not to be welded together as a unit.[19]

So Kant sees pacific federation as crucial to human moral development but as ancillary to popular sovereignty achieved through civil society in the independent state. Like other contract or popular sovereignty theorists, Kant thinks that supranational authority is a moral and political contradiction.

For popular sovereignty theorists, contracting out of anarchy would violate the postulate about the inside space of politics; it would abrogate the domestic social contract that constitutes sovereign authority inside and must therefore be considered logically and temporally prior to any *international* relations (as emphasized in Kant's initial assumption). Crucially, this is not an empirical claim: states are of course capable of making agreements that abrogate sovereignty. The point is that, as Kant puts it, independent states "are not to be welded together." In a world structured by sovereignty, permanent anarchy is an empirical and normative requirement of supreme territorial political authority. This requirement, which proscribes contracting out, implies limits on the kind of supranational governance regimes consistent with sovereignty: such arrangements must be temporary, voluntary, and limited. Permanent, nonvoluntary, or open-ended transfers of authority to supranational institutions or entities would violate sovereignty's requirements of supreme political authority within a particular territory. (Treaties specifying the terms of peace or specifying agreements resolving specific disputes or issues do not fall afoul of this requirement; even if they are meant to be final, they are not permanent in the sense of creating an ongoing, autonomous system of governance.)

Traditionalists are right to insist that not all cooperative arrangements and international agreements violate sovereignty. They are also right to insist that there is nothing new in cross-border flows and economic interdependence or in the arrangements states make to deal with them—after all, the Westphalian system has always been a good deal messier than the notion of sovereignty would suggest. Military interventions and financial and economic interference have been regular features of the system. Authority in numerous domains has been transferred to, contested, or simply seized by a variety of outside agents. Many such arrangements have been conceived as permanent, and many have lasted for significant periods of time. Alliances, security pacts, even functional governance regimes, are familiar features of the Westphalian landscape: the first IGO, the International Telegraph Union, established in 1865, hardly threatened sovereignty or tamed international anarchy. Besides, exceptions and modifications to exclusive territoriality have been necessary almost from the start: diplomatic immunity and rights of embassy are pragmatic accommodations that bend the rule to preserve its viability.[20] As Kobrin so concisely puts it, "absolute territorial sovereignty has always been easier to imagine than to construct."[21]

The traditionalists' key claims are less incorrect than they are beside the point. Whether globalization dissipates sovereignty cannot be answered by dismissing the novelty of certain of its empirical features; documenting previous exceptions to or compromises of an ideal that was anyway primarily prescriptive has little relevance to an assessment of globalization's cumulative effects on the international system. We are concerned with whether globalization results in a qualitative change in the configuration of rule in the international system and with how that change impacts sovereignty's normative and empirical presumptions. I believe that contemporary changes are qualitatively different and do undermine sovereignty's conceptual foundations. There exists today something akin to a permanent, nonvoluntary, and open-ended system of governance at the supranational level.[22] Consider permanence: many organizations, such as the WTO and numerous IFIs, exist not to resolve particular issues or problems but to manage trade and the global economy on an ongoing basis. The international criminal court—if it survives American hostility—aspires to be a *permanent* tribunal for trying war crimes and crimes against humanity. The UN, through the security council and through some of its subsidiary committees and organizations, has established ongoing mechanisms for international governance, as have regional suprastate organizations like the European Union. NATO, which has outlived its original purpose, prefers an uncomfortable limbo and a fraught search for a new justification to disbanding. The list might go on and on. The point is not that any one agency or regime pretends or is likely to achieve permanence; the League of Nations probably had similar pretensions. The point is rather that the number and density of "permanent" supranational regimes has increased to an extent that signals an important shift in the configuration of political authority globally.

Further, many of these new governance arrangements are nonvoluntary in two important respects. First, even though states retain a choice in whether to join or withdraw from IGOs, treaties, and other arrangements, participation in networks of governance is increasingly *necessary* for states. Consider again economic regimes: for states hoping to deliver economic growth and stability, membership of the WTO, for instance, has become vital. Compliance with IMF mandates is crucial for maintaining investor confidence and avoiding economic ruin; many states' "agreements" with the IMF are little more than bitter pills they find themselves obliged to swallow to ward off capital flight and currency collapse related less to economic fundamentals than to willingness to take one's medicine.[23] In short, the costs of opting out of international economic regimes are extremely high; the alternative to integration is increasing isolation, political inefficacy, and economic inefficiency; notably, this is true even for states that choose the dubious path of autarkic growth.[24] This Hobson's choice illustrates that states' juridical freedom in matters of economic and political integration frequently counts less than their material circumstances.

Second, many contemporary governance regimes are highly coercive. Conditions attached by the IMF to its various loans and other economic development programs are frequently cited as examples of such coercion; the governmental and public-sector reforms demanded by the Fund are notoriously far-reaching (and critics would add, wrongheaded). Again, while states have the option of rejecting the Fund's assistance, to do so would in many instances invite economic and political chaos. The coercive nature of these requirements primarily affects developing countries, but similar constraints are being formalized in the developed world as well. The stabilization and growth pact associated with the single European currency, for instance, limits spending and constrains policy for member states.* In the political domain, the membership requirements set by the EU for prospective members are also broadly intrusive.† Participation in such arrangements is not mandatory, but remaining outside them can be extremely costly. The point, once again, is not that nonvoluntary and coercive arrangements are new or unprecedented; it is that they have become so commonplace, and the costs of avoiding them so high, that they represent a significant change in the configuration of rule. As Joe Rogaly, a columnist for the *Financial Times* so aptly put it, "Britain *could* regain all the powers divested to various international bodies by withdrawing from them—if it was prepared to pay the price of becoming the Western world's first totally sovereign stone-age island."[25]

Finally, consider the open-ended mandates of many of these same governance regimes. Growing numbers of IGOs exercise not just traditional monitoring and enforcement power but also decision-*making* power. States are increasingly delegating or simply ceding their control in a range of policy domains to supranational organizations, agreeing to be bound by outcomes they cannot control or veto (short of withdrawal). This is a qualitative difference from treaty organizations or other specific agreements dealing with a proscribed set of issues. State cession of binding authority to external agencies—the dispute resolution mechanisms of the WTO and many features of European Union policymaking are textbook examples—violates the stricture that supreme authority be located within the state. Again, the

---

*Whether some of Europe's major economic players—Germany, for instance—can continue to violate the pact with impunity remains to be seen.
†Which is not to say "bad," as I noted in chapter 1.

question is not whether historical precedents for such arrangements can be found but whether their cumulative effect today amounts to an alteration in the Westphalian system of governance. I maintain that, considered together, recent developments in global governance *do* constitute a significant change in the modern configuration of rule. Supranational governance arrangements are not only increasingly common but also increasingly permanent, less voluntary, and more expansive in their scope and autonomy; they have gone from exceptions to the Westphalian rule to constituting a new, hybrid form of rule. Traditionalist conceptions of sovereignty cannot make sense of these changes.

Sovereignty Transformed?

Another group of scholars, recognizing the limits of the traditional approach, argues that contemporary developments should be seen not as the end of sovereignty but as part of its necessary transformation. These "transformationalists" agree that "a new 'sovereignty regime' is displacing traditional conceptions of statehood as an absolute, indivisible, territorially exclusive and zero-sum form of public power."[26] They argue that changes underway in the international system demand that the concept of sovereignty be stripped of its associations with territory and exclusivity and reconceptualized in a way that captures the complexity of contemporary political interactions and interdependencies.

Many of these scholars see the Middle Ages as model and metaphor for the changes associated with globalization; for them, medieval Europe represents an archetype of nonexclusive territorial rule.[27] These theorists see the territorial complexity of authority in medieval Europe as a historical referent for the spatial transformation of contemporary politics. In a sense, they try to see the new world order more clearly through the optic of what we might call the Old World order. The provocative imagery of a new medievalism is an effective descriptive device,[28] but growing numbers of observers take the possibility of a return to something like medieval politics quite seriously as a way to tackle the "triple challenge" of coming to terms with globalization, fragmentation, and the persistence of the nation-state.[29]

Many transformationalists hold that recent trends associated with globalization are leading us back toward a medieval future: a complex, overlapping system of political authority and allegiance resulting from a decline in the salience of national borders. They argue that sovereignty, state power, and territoriality stand in a more complex relationship today than during the era following the modern state's emergence. "This is not to argue that territorial boundaries retain no political, military, or symbolic significance but rather to acknowledge that, conceived as the primary spatial markers of modern life, they have become increasingly problematic."[30] The example of the Middle Ages, Mann argues, shows that "there is no necessary reason why all [the modern state's] functions should be located within the same political agency…for most of history, they were not."[31] States increasingly *share* the functions of governance with a range of nonstate actors situated at various levels of global politics, giving up final control or authority in certain areas to enhance their regulative and administrative capacity. Agencies like the IMF, the WTO, or the European Union should be understood, according to this logic, as evidence of states' willingness to cede authority to entities better positioned to carry out certain governance functions.

Sovereignty is being "unbundled" on this view, variously pooled and parceled out to a range of governance agencies across numerous functional domains.[32] Functional unbundling does not entail or imply the disappearance of states; in point of fact, states remain the primary agents of enforcement for many decisions and regulations originating at the supranational level, and in those areas where they retain authority their capacities might well increase.[33] The unbundling hypothesis helps us reconcile states' continuing strength and vitality with the reorganization of authority driven by globalization. The point is neither that states are dying nor that they remain essentially unchanged, but that their role and functions are in the midst of wholesale reconstruction.

The neomedievalists accurately describe many of the changes reshaping the global configuration of rule, but characterizing this transformation in terms of sovereignty confuses more than it clarifies. Transformationalists reduce sovereignty to control, ignoring the spatial and normative connections constitutive of the Westphalian system. Held, in a typically transformationalist locution, argues that "any conception of sovereignty which interprets it as an illimitable and indivisible form of public power—entrenched securely in in-dividual nation-states—is undermined" by globalization.[34] Held's larger point is well-taken, but his suggestion that other conceptions of sovereignty would fare better misses sovereignty's distinctiveness and significance. Sovereignty *is* precisely an illimitable and indivisible form of political authority operating within the fixed, exclusive political space of the state. It is not an infinitely malleable concept, nor is it merely a synonym for control or authority; it is an argument about the rightfulness of rule within a particular territory, a justification of political authority within a particular political space. The transformationalists' sensitivity to increasingly complex and overlapping structures of governance is a welcome counterpoint to traditionalists' strange insistence that nothing much has changed. Still, talk of unbundled sovereignty or functional sovereignty or deterritorialized or multilayered sovereignty, strictly speaking, is nonsense.

Globalization and Sovereignty (II)

Today we are in the midst of something similar to the theoretical crisis that accompanied the medieval–modern transition: old ways of describing the world are increasingly inadequate for making sense of contemporary events. Just as the early modern theorists struggled to justify a world of sovereign states that no longer matched up with theories of Empire and Christendom, it is becoming difficult today to explain and justify recent developments linked to globalization through sovereignty.

Globalization generates a demand for supranational rule, attenuating the link between territory and authority characteristic of the Westphalian order. Traditionalists try to account for this change through good old-fashioned sovereignty, but they overlook or underestimate the extent to which the emerging configuration of rule violates the requirements of sovereignty through its permanence and its nonvoluntary, open-ended character. Transformationalists, on the other hand, recognize the changing realities of governance under globalization, usefully describing these changes as a functional unbundling of control. But in redefining sovereignty to fit the world they observe, transformationalists ignore sovereignty's history and its normative significance. Both mistakes make it impossible to assess globalization's impact on sovereignty and, by extension, on sovereign democracy.

The full significance of contemporary functional unbundling can only be appreciated in this context, in light of the functional bundling of authority that preceded it. To see this, consider again the medieval–modern transition. Medieval authority had been based around a cosmological conception based in organic conceptions of a pan-European Christian community. This shared worldview provided an underlying unity that held the otherwise fragmented system together and justified its complex, overlapping layers of authority. Neomedievalism obscures this unity and its distinctive justifications, emphasizing only the superficially similar patterns of overlapping, functional rule in the contemporary system. Profound social changes associated with the onset of modernity significantly transformed this system of rule. Sovereignty provided plausible answers to the central problems of authority associated with these changes, with the emergence of the modern state: territoriality, functional consolidation, and the revaluation of political subjectivity. Sovereignty explained and justified these new features of political life. Today another new configuration of rule is emerging, one in which authority is increasingly multilayered, supranational, and functionally organized.

In describing the emerging configuration of rule in terms of sovereignty, then, neomedievalists miss that globalization *dissipates* sovereignty. For sovereignty is not a natural or unchanging feature of the political world, nor is it the object of some eternal quest or the solution to any riddle of history.[35] It is a political argument, a set of answers to problems concerning the form and location of rule, the meaning and significance of political community, and the nature of the political world. As globalization remakes the geography of rule, as the problems of political authority change, this set of answers is becoming increasingly irrelevant; the old answers supplied by sovereignty no longer persuade. Empirical changes wrought by globalization make it implausible to conceive of authority as a function of territory, either descriptively or normatively. Crucially, this is true regardless of whether globalization is old or new, regardless of whether it is more or less advanced than it was a century ago, regardless of whether states are dying or evolving, waxing or waning, driving change or succumbing to it. Sovereignty might always have been a fiction, but today it is an increasingly less useful one for making sense of politics.

The Paradox of Sovereign Democracy

Sovereign democracy, like sovereignty itself, is an account of the rightfulness of a particular configuration of rule. Also, like sovereignty, it takes that configuration of rule for granted. As social activity and interactions push up against and run over the older spatial and conceptual boundaries of the state—as globalization proceeds—emergent configurations of rule dissipate sovereignty, undermining its distinctive territorial justification of rule. In doing so, globalization also undermines sovereign democracy.

To see this, consider again Mann's comment regarding the functional unbundling of control: "there is no necessary reason why all [the modern state's] functions should be located within the same political agency." There might be no *necessary* reason for these functions to be bundled together, but there is a *democratic* one. Mann includes among the sovereign state's functions that it provides a site or container for democracy.[36] But as we have seen, the relationship between sovereignty and democracy, though contingent, is not merely empirical. Modern democracy assumes and requires sovereignty; popular sovereignty depends on the bundling of all functional authority within the state to make rule by the people possible. When control or rule gets unbundled it is no longer susceptible to the popular will, to the sovereign's authority. Globalization destroys the fit between democracy and the broader configuration of authority; supranational governance regimes violate sovereign democracy's territorial conception of political authority and undermine the presumed "symmetrical and congruent relationship between political decision-makers and the recipients of political decisions" that popular sovereignty requires.[37] The modern notion of a sovereign people supreme within a particular territory becomes fragmented and unworkable. As Görg and Hirsch argue, "the reciprocal founding relations of democratic self-government and freedoms—in the radical tradition of the sovereignty of the people ... forbid every form of outside interference in the affairs of the state."[38] Popular sovereignty is no longer theoretically viable in conditions of interdependence.[39]

This problem is much more severe than typical depictions of disjunctures and deficits make it appear. Disjunctures, remember, represent gaps between global politics and state-based democratic authority. The problem is not simply that issues and institutions do not match up, however; it is that they cannot in principle match up because democratic legitimacy depends upon the contingent empirical proposition that the state is the site or container of politics. Globalization creates a disjuncture between an account of political authority predicated on the assumption that states contain politics and a universalizing trend in social activity and interactions belying that assumption. Similarly, democratic deficits cannot be resolved through procedural reform or institutional innovation because sovereign democracy's account of legitimacy is inextricably linked to territory. Sovereign democracy entails a specific answer to the question "representative of and accountable to whom?" Even if supranational governance were made representative and accountable they would remain illegitimate because of their location outside the rightful political community. Put differently, globalization creates a deficit between a theory of democracy that locates rightful rule within state-based institutions and a political practice in which rule is increasingly independent of these institutions.

It seems, then, that sovereign democracy rules out supranational governance. Yet, paradoxically, sovereign democracy also seems to require it. Popular sovereignty transfers authority from the prince to the people; in so doing it creates the rights and interests of the citizens as the state's paramount concern. The state is the vehicle through which citizens protect and promote their rights and interests, both domestically and in the international arena. Globalization multiplies the threats originating or manifesting outside the state's exclusive territory: to invading armies, maritime marauders, and stone-hearted creditors it adds speculative capital flows, deadly pathogens (natural and manufactured), ozone depletion, global terrorism, trafficking in narcotics and human beings, transnational social and religious movements, and much more besides. Most of these phenomena are not new; what makes them significant is their sheer number, their significance in the daily lives of growing numbers of people, and their impact on the rights and interests of citizens. Given this impact, supranational governance seems like a rational democratic response to globalization. By unbundling and pooling control along functional lines, states can exert at least some influence and control in areas where changing patterns of social activity and interactions make their territorial jurisdiction a poor instrument of rule. As participants in such regimes, states give a voice to their citizens, however limited and indirect it might be. Sovereign democracy thus also seems to require state participation in supranational governance arrangements.

This paradox originates in the modern democracy's strange account of universality. Sovereignty posits the universality of the state: there is only anarchy outside, making politics outside impossible. Modern democracy reconciles the universal principles of freedom and equality on which it is predicated with these territorial limits through the social contract; it accepts this particularistic account of universality through its silence about international relations. So long as sovereignty provided a plausible account of the real world of politics, there was no difficulty; that is the point of saying that the social contract *reconciled* freedom and equality with sovereignty's limits. Now, globalization exposes a latent tension between the universal precepts that ground authority in consent and their limited realization in and through the modern state. Once territorial authority no longer satisfactorily guarantees the rights and interests of citizens, once political universality can no longer plausibly be construed as excluding most of the world's population, this tension emerges into a full-blown paradox. Sovereign democracy both requires and rules out supranational governance because it is simultaneously universal and particularistic. Globalization does not cause this tension; it reveals it by exacerbating the contradictions that have always been present within sovereign democracy but which have until recently remained invisible beneath sovereignty's peculiar account of universality. As globalization reshapes the configuration of modern rule this account loses its capacity to persuade.

Universalization Inside Out

Universalization exposes a long-standing tension within sovereign democracy, a tension between democracy's universal principles and their limited realization through sovereignty. The resulting paradox makes sovereign democracy incoherent, contradictory. This is most obvious outside, where universalization takes the form of globalization, but there are intriguing and suggestive parallels inside the state as well.

We saw in chapter 3 that the social contract created a polity comprising two conceptual domains: a public, political sphere where free and equal citizens share sovereignty, and a private sphere where relations of mastery and subordination remain sacrosanct. Sovereign individuals were independent, masters of themselves, in both domains. In the public sphere this mastery was achieved through popular rule or collective autonomy among political equals; in the private sphere it was secured through the publicly enforced contractual subjection of natural inferiors, whose subordination disqualified them from politics. But those persons denied citizenship through this logic of sovereignty did not acquiesce in their exclusion. They saw immediately that the boundaries of categories like man and citizen could be challenged using the language of universality itself.[40] Seizing on the logic of universality, they fought for and eventually won citizenship.*

We can reconceive this familiar story of democratization within the modern state as a process of universalization (think "universal suffrage") that challenged the limits of sovereign democracy. Just like globalization outside, universalization inside reveals tensions and contradictions within sovereign democracy. Two such contradictions are relevant to our discussion here. The first concerns the social contract's protection of citizens' sovereignty by making them equals in public and guaranteeing their rights and property in private. Initially this guarantee included the contractual mastery of husbands over wives and masters over servants. The public/private distinction facilitated this protection by simultaneously limiting the public power's "interference" in private affairs and using that power to protect and enforce citizens' rights in private. The universalization of citizenship creates a paradox when "natural inferiors" become citizens or members of the sovereign: they achieve formal equality in the public sphere, but their newfound political freedom and equality also require the state to guarantee their rights in the private sphere, where structures of subjection remain firmly entrenched in homes and workplaces. The paradox is that ensuring the rights of these new citizens requires curtailing the long-standing privileges of other citizens through an active reorganization of the private sphere—exactly the type of interference that the restriction of public power is meant to forestall. Sovereign democracy cannot reconcile its obligation to the equal rights of all with its promise of noninterference in the private affairs of citizens once citizenship becomes universal.

The second contradiction concerns the idea of collective autonomy at the core of sovereign democracy. Held argues that

> the idea of democracy derives its power and significance...from the idea of self-determination; that is, from the notion that members of a political community—citizens—should be able to choose freely the conditions of their own association and that their choices should constitute the ultimate legitimation of the form and direction of their polity.... If democracy means "rule by the people," the determination of public decision-making by equally free members of the political community, then the basis of its justification lies in the promotion and enhancement of autonomy, both for individuals as citizens and for the collectivity.[41]

---

*I shall develop this account of democratization extensively in part II.

This collective autonomy is a function or attribute of citizens' sovereignty—a point Held's formulation ignores. Popular sovereignty stipulates that all citizens are members of the sovereign; the only way to preserve their freedom and equality is for them to govern themselves collectively. Popular sovereignty demands collective autonomy, not the other way round. The paradox here is that democratization, by "universalizing" citizenship, dilutes each citizen's share of sovereignty to the vanishing point. The division of sovereign power among eight thousand or so citizens in a face-to-face community gives each less than spectacular but still real and effective autonomy.[42] But among eighty thousand? Eight million? India, the world's most populous democracy, now has over a billion citizens. Casting that single vote among scores or hundreds of millions hardly seems like a meaningful exercise of autonomy or sovereignty; it is far from obvious that in casting it one has governed oneself in any meaningful way.[43]

Some theorists might maintain that what collective autonomy really requires is a political process in which individuals have the best chance of living under rules of their own making. What really matters is that the process of participation is fairly structured in a way that gives each individual a real equality of opportunity in influencing outcomes.[44] But as Dunn rightly observes, such "minimal unfairness" is hardly much to get excited about; it seems quite unlikely that it could inspire revolutions, topple dictators, or even motivate people to wait for hours in withering heat or driving rain to cast their ballots.[45] Besides, the minimal unfairness view does not really address the extreme diminution of sovereignty entailed by expanding citizenship. Dunn concludes that the practical difficulties with popular rule are insurmountable, restating this conclusion as a point of theoretical skepticism: "the promise to give each of any set of human beings full control over their [sic] own lives is barely conceptually coherent."[46]

My point in this section is to highlight that universalization inside the state, in the form of democratization, erodes sovereignty, changing democracy's meaning and its practical form. The logic of universal freedom and equality ultimately overwhelms the arguments designed to check its universal implications, proving the early critics of such arguments right.

Conclusion

Universalization affects sovereign democracy by exposing deep tensions between its universal principles and their limited realization in and through the sovereign state. Outside, universalization takes the form of globalization; inside, of democratization. In both cases, universalization reveals sovereignty's limits on freedom and equality. These parallels suggest that democratization inside the state might be a useful guide to thinking about the challenges of globalization and the prospects for democratization outside. I am not proposing some facile thesis of identity or compatibility between globalization and democratization; many of the emerging patterns of social activity and interaction linked to globalization create new forms of subjection and exclusion that are patently malign and uncontestably antidemocratic. While universalization inside has been closely tied to democratization and has had a beneficial effect on the realization of freedom and equality, universalization outside is driven by a variety of processes with uncertain implications for democracy. Still, both globalization and democratization push up against borders and boundaries long accepted as natural and legitimate. Both represent challenges to the ordering principle of sovereignty that structures modern politics and political thinking. Both, as we saw here in the cases of expanding citizenship and supranational political integration, render sovereign democracy incoherent and contradictory.

The parallels between universalization inside and outside suggest that we should not conceive globalization solely as a threat to democracy. Insofar as we take freedom and equality as constitutive of democracy and as the driving force of democratization, globalization helps us to see that sovereignty represents the primary impediment to democracy inside and beyond the state. For freedom and equality to remain meaningful and appealing principles, democracy must be stripped of its theoretical and institutional associations with sovereignty, which have limited its universal promise inside and beyond the state. This is a radical proposition. It entails giving up on the ideas of citizenship and popular rule as we know them. It requires abandoning long-held assumptions about the democratic legitimacy of states and exclusive citizenship. It implies rethinking the purpose of and justification for territorial representative institutions. Perhaps most significantly, it demands that we find ways to secure and promote the rights and interests of all without regard for the borders and boundaries that structure modern democracy. These are the requirements of freedom and equality in the age of globalization.

CHAPTER 5

The Limits of Modern Democracy

I argued in the first chapter that communitarian and cosmopolitan democratic responses to globalization differed less in their views about globalization than in how they conceived the link between state and democracy. Communitarians conceive this link as necessary and appropriate, understanding democracy as something that is ethically and politically about states and their citizens. Cosmopolitans, by contrast, see the link between states and democracy as contingent, treating the relationship as empirical but not normatively required. Another way of stating this disagreement is that communitarians and cosmopolitans disagree about the conditions in which democracy can be realized in the age of globalization: communitarians are committed to the view that democracy can only be realized within the state, while cosmopolitans maintain that democracy must be realized globally. The most puzzling question arising from this debate is not whether democracy requires exclusive citizenship in a bounded political community or whether it demands a global political framework, but rather how to account for its seeming to do both.

The account of sovereign democracy developed in the intervening chapters explains this paradox by revealing how globalization increasingly brings democracy's universal and particularist elements, long reconciled within the sovereign state, into tension. It turns out that both communitarians and cosmopolitans are both right and wrong about modern democracy: there is a normatively compulsory connection between democratic legitimacy and the exclusive citizenry of a bounded political community, yet the plausibility and persuasiveness of this account of legitimacy depend upon a specific and contingent configuration of rule in the global political system, one which globalization has transformed. The paradox stems from the *interdependence* of democracy's normative and empirical dimensions: democracy's link with the state is at once normatively compulsory and empirically contingent.

My aim in this final chapter of part I is to consider the limits of modern or sovereign democracy in the age of globalization. I shall argue that both communitarians and cosmopolitans offer unworkable democratic responses to globalization. In defending sovereign democracy's territorial exclusivity and bounded citizenship, communitarians rightly emphasize democracy's normative ties with the state, but in ignoring how globalization transforms the political conditions that give these ties meaning and coherence, they wind up advocating an anachronistic model of democracy. The anachronism lies not in any failure or problem with democracy's values but rather with the changing conditions in which they must be realized. Cosmopolitans, in emphasizing the contingency of democracy's empirical ties with the state, rightly envision extending democracy's political reach to grapple with issues thrown up by globalization and interdependence. However, in ignoring how existing modes of democratic legitimacy presume a specific spatial configuration of rule, they wind up advocating a model of democracy devoid of compelling moral foundations. The problem lies not with the institutions, mechanisms, or procedures of modern democracy themselves but rather with their detachment from the ethical and political context in which they make sense. Put differently, communitarians and cosmopolitans, in different ways, retain sovereign democracy's unique justificatory framework; once globalization shatters the Westphalian configuration of rule, this framework also shatters. There is no way to put Humpty together again.

I begin by considering communitarian defenses of state-based democracy. Focusing on liberal nationalist and neorepublican accounts of popular sovereignty, I argue that these accounts ignore how changes in the global configuration of rule make the normative account of state-based democracy they share anachronistic. Communitarian democratic proposals can neither deal adequately with interdependence nor offer a compelling account of democracy "at home." Next I consider cosmopolitan approaches, focusing on proposals for global civil society (GCS) and for a global democratic constitutional framework, the two most thoroughly developed alternatives to state-based democracy. In both cases I show that the justificatory accounts animating these global schemes become incoherent when detached from the state context. While the values and social empowerment promoted by GCS are laudable and often effective, and while cosmopolitan democracy's global institutional ambitions are admirable and apposite to changing political conditions, both err in replicating inherently sovereign models of democracy at the global level. I conclude by arguing that sovereign democracy's conceptual limits render it unworkable in the age of globalization; we must abandon sovereign democracy and reconstruct democratic theory from its core principles.

The Limits of Community

In an insightful pair of recent essays on democracy and community, Charles Taylor stresses that "the revolutions which ushered in regimes of popular sovereignty" established the people for the first time "as an entity which could decide and act together, to whom one could attribute a will."[1] Despite appearances—popular sovereignty seems to require nothing more than "majority will, more or less restrained by the respect of liberty and rights"—the people qua willing entity cannot survive without strong bonds of community.[2] For individuals to accept being outvoted requires something more than a theory of democracy that purportedly makes them free because they rule themselves; a mere agglomeration of individuals will not accept the shared burdens and obligations of citizenship or develop adequate levels of reciprocal trust. Without a strong sense of common identity, democracy or popular sovereignty cannot survive because citizens cannot have confidence that their rights will be respected and their views taken fairly into account.[3]

Liberal nationalists and neorepublicans alike share Taylor's view that a strong sense of identity and belonging underpins popular sovereignty and that modern democracy cannot do without such communal solidarity. For communitarians this need for solidarity demonstrates why democracy requires a bounded political community and exclusive citizenry: democracy is only possible when underlying commonalities unite the people. Responding directly to Held's notion of a "community of fate," Will Kymlicka argues that it is not the flows associated with globalization but rather the reactions of particular groups to those flows that define communities.[4] Communities are "morally self-originating" entities in this sense, a fact which for the communitarian has a huge bearing on their legitimacy: community is morally necessary because it creates and defines itself as moral community.[5] This definition takes different forms: neorepublicans stress the constitutive function of deliberation, which promotes reciprocal recognition of all members of the community as free and equal citizens. Some critics worry, however, that deliberation promotes an ideal of a "concrete, substantively integrated ethical community" with exclusionary tendencies.[6] Liberal nationalism, by contrast, emphasizes the political dimensions of membership, making it potentially more inclusive and more plausible than deliberation on the scale required by contemporary democracies.[7] Critics worry, however, about the illiberal tendencies of nationalism and their negative impact on democracy.[8]

Important differences and critical reservations notwithstanding, both neorepublican and liberal nationalist justifications of democracy take communal solidarity as a necessary element in the political legitimacy of collective decision making. As Taylor stresses, the modern democratic state relies on such cohesion in claiming to be the bulwark of freedom and locus of political expression for its citizens: "whether or not these claims are actually founded, the state must be so imagined by its citizens if it is to be legitimate."[9] Put differently, the *idea* of the community of fate, however defined, legitimates sovereign democracy. Within this justificatory framework, reciprocity, shared trust, and mutual understanding bind citizens in political and ethical relations without which democracy cannot function. Such cohesion becomes necessary when "the people" emerges as a collective agency with a will and the ability to decide. The link between state and democracy is necessary because it provides the ethical/political unity on which democratic self-rule—popular sovereignty—is predicated.

Some cosmopolitan critics object to communitarian views because of their ethical particularism. Communitarian democrats are right to insist, against these critics, that ethical particularism is consistent with certain universal commitments—to democracy and human rights, for example.[10] Moreover, the bounded political community can be "a universal source of particularist values."[11] Both views are consistent with popular sovereignty, which in its Rousseauan, Kantian, and Hegelian variants is a precondition for moral development, and both views are universalist insofar as self-determination through civil society can be consistently desired for and practically extended to all. The universality of freedom and equality can be reconciled with the particularism of the state so long as everyone lives in a state through which all members can realize their moral capacities. It will not do, then, to criticize communitarian responses to globalization merely for their particularism, which is wholly compatible with one version of democratic universalism (the version logically entailed by sovereign democracy). The problem with communitarian defenses of state-based democracy in the age of globalization lies in the implausibility of their underlying empirical assumptions and the concomitant attenuation of democratic norms and legitimacy.

We have seen that globalization is transforming the global configuration of rule, relocating control in supranational governance regimes of various kinds; as a result, many key decisions are no longer taken by the people. At the same time, growing interdependence means that many decisions the people do make have a significant impact on the lives of outsiders who are excluded from the political process. In light of these facts, popular sovereignty cannot remain a compelling account of political legitimacy for two reasons. First, it loses its persuasiveness as a vehicle for expressing the freedom and equality of citizens as those citizens recognize that they are increasingly governed from outside. An independent state with exclusive citizenship no longer sufficiently guarantees self-determination. Second, since communitarian democrats accommodate democracy's universality through recognizing a multitude of self-governing, independent states, popular sovereignty of the citizens of any one state leads to a performative contradiction: by exercising their own freedom and equality citizens can dominate people in other states. Democratic citizens are implicated in outsiders' lack of freedom, revealing the limits of universal democratic citizenship realized through a multitude of sovereign states.* Thus popular sovereignty no longer offers a compelling and coherent account of freedom and equality in the age of globalization and no longer provides an effective guarantee of the rights and interests of citizens.

Let me emphasize that the problem with communitarian accounts is not that they are undesirable or unappealing in the abstract. The problem is rather that popular sovereignty is ethically and politically unworkable once the state is no longer the locus of (most) social activity. Communitarians might object that democracy simply *is* about the state—about the relationships, obligations, and understandings that bind citizens together in a collective political enterprise. There is no arguing that this is true of what modern democracy *has been*. My argument is that, due to globalization, democracy *can no longer be* about the state, at least not without contradicting its core commitments to freedom and equality for all. Just as proponents of the organic cosmology of medieval Christendom undoubtedly held to their ethical and political commitments as they had always understood them, many democrats will continue to defend the link between state and democracy as necessary for and definitive of democracy. They are not so much wrong as, from the perspective adopted here, on the wrong side of history.

The Limits of Cosmopolitanism

Communitarian democrats conceive the link between states and democracy as necessary and offer a principled defense of it. Unfortunately, they miss that no defense of this normative ideal can survive globalization's impact on the empirical configuration of rule that made this link necessary and appropriate in the first place. Cosmopolitan democrats appreciate that globalization radically transforms the empirical context of democratic politics and so attempt to extend the democratic ideal globally. In this section I shall argue that cosmopolitans miss that democratic ideals cannot survive transposition out of the context in which they were originally worked out; no empirical reworking can rescue the normative ideal from incoherence outside the sovereign state. I shall focus here on GCS arguments and on Held's cosmopolitan

---

*Pacific federation on the Kantian model cannot resolve this problem because Kant's model, as I argued in the previous chapter, presumes the sovereignty of citizens within each state. Kantian schemes work only for very limited degrees of interdependence.

democratic constitutionalism, showing that both founder in trying to realize sovereign democracy's normative ideal outside the state.*

In the case of GCS, the problem consists in the uncritical application to global politics of a state-based conceptual framework of democracy. I show this by establishing that the purported democratic effects of democratic civil society depend upon assumptions regarding the interdependence of state and civil society that do not and cannot hold at the global level. In the case of Held's cosmopolitan constitutionalism, the problem consists in his attempt to reground popular sovereignty by replacing territorial political communities with fluid empirical ones comprising all those affected by an issue or decision. This attempt, I argue, ignores that the justification for and legitimacy of collective decision making cannot be detached from its normative foundation in sovereignty's territorial conception of rightful rule.

Global Civil Society[12]

Growing numbers of democratic theorists and activists, observing the proliferation of supranational NGOs and transnational social movements, and impressed by their increasing role and influence in supranational affairs, talk about GCS as a model or framework for global democracy. GCS comprises a "medley of boundary-eclipsing actors—social movements, interest groups, indigenous peoples, cultural groups, and global citizens" which constructs network and political practices that are reshaping global politics.[13] Much of this activity transpires in "new" political spaces constructed by "the conscious association of actors, in physically separated locations, who link themselves together in networks for particular political and social purposes."[14]

GCS theory conceives of supranational social and political activity primarily in neo-Tocquevillean terms: trust building among citizens of a global public; development of transnational social capital and the articulation of a global democratic will; counterbalancing of global governance agencies and competing social interests; and so on.† This neo-Tocquevillean perspective clearly shapes characterizations of GCS activity: the constituent groups of GCS are described as voluntary and often issue- or identity-related; they seek social or political influence and generate bonds and social capital across state borders; and they serve as channels for information, creating opportunities for transnational learning and dialogue that facilitate the recognition of common experiences of global problems and the emergence of transnational identities.[15]

---

*I do not engage reformist cosmopolitan models separately, primarily because they comprise such a disparate collection of proposals. Most of the criticisms offered of global civil society and constitutional models apply to reformist schemes as well.

†Some global civil society theorists invoke what I have elsewhere called an "antiauthoritarian" model of civil society, a model patterned on movements of resistance and rehabilitation in Eastern Europe and Latin America. I shall not focus on this model here, but it is susceptible of the same criticisms I shall make of neo-Tocquevillean models; see Goodhart, "Civil Society."

Proponents argue that such networks and associations are well suited to checking the "statelike" system of global governance made up of institution-alized regulatory arrangements (regimes) and less formalized norms, rules, and procedures.[16] According to Smith, global groups and networks represent "the most promising source of enhanced democratic participation in the emerging global polity."[17] In her view, participation in such organizations "helps enfranchise individuals and groups that are formally excluded from participation in international institutions. It strengthens the global public sphere by mobilizing this disenfranchised public into discussions of global issues, thereby democratizing the global political process." Participation thus serves a representative function that widens discussion of the global public good and expands both the agenda and the range of policy options considered.

Transnational networks usually target specific global issues or institu-tions.[18] Their influence derives from their efficacy in shaping the inter-national agenda, in negotiating within various international forums, in strengthening and supporting local organizations and networks, and in using their moral authority to pressure officials and raise consciousness.[19] Such networks frequently draw on already-established norms of democracy and human rights to construct frames for collective action and opposition to oppressive regimes.[20] GCS can claim some success in influencing states and international regimes: the expanding role of NGOs and other organizations in global summits and conferences, and even in some formal governance regimes, further encourages the hope that they might play an important role in democratization.[21]

Proponents see this constellation of activity as a nascent global democracy "legitimated by the growing competence of societal actors relative to the inability of states to confront problems that increasingly escape the grasp of territorially delimited actors."[22] Dryzek, for example, concludes that GCS provides democratic legitimacy to the emerging system of global governance; networks promoting transnational deliberation (and thus shaping transna-tional discourse) are "the most appropriate available institutional expression of a dispersed capacity to engage in deliberation" that promotes democratic legitimacy.[23] GCS is thus able to reconnect politics with the moral purpose and values associated with democracy. Falk and others refer to this process as one of "globalization from below," in which grass- and cyber-roots activists (will) remake the international order through civilizing activities based in a commitment to progressive political norms.[24]

Despite these potentialities, GCS provides a deeply flawed model for global democracy. Before demonstrating its shortcomings, however, I want to clarify two important points. First, my argument "against" GCS is in no way an argument "against" or dismissive of supranational network and as-sociational activity in itself. As the foregoing account suggests, there is a vast range of politically significant supranational network and associational activity that has constrained and influenced global governance in positive and important ways.[25] Many of the actors engaged in transnational political activity are unquestionably motivated by a commitment to democracy and human rights and vigorously promote these norms through their activities. Moreover, it is nearly impossible to imagine a more democratic global order without also imagining a significant role for GCS in achieving and sustaining it. But my argument here is not about whether this supranational political activity is a good thing or has positive effects on global governance; it is rather about whether GCS provides an adequate and appropriate model for global democracy; that is, about the wisdom of conceiving global democracy in terms of GCS. The second clarification is that my critique does not concern the role of transnational networks and associations in fostering *domestic* political change. Democratic transitions in Eastern Europe and Latin America in particular were catalyzed by links forged between domestic opposition groups, international NGOs, and other transnational associations.[26] The distinction between these two types of activity has become blurred, but I want to insist on it here: my critique pertains to the suitability of GCS as a model for global democracy, not to the efficacy of transnational actors in promoting domestic democratization.

GCS is a flawed model for global democracy because the purported democratic functions and effects of domestic civil society models rely on statist assumptions about politics; these assumptions do not hold for supranational politics.* These assumptions become easier to identify when we consider that the neo-Tocquevillean model on which these democratic claims are based is not a complete account of democracy. Rather, it explains how a well-functioning civil society supports and facilitates democracy. Three assumptions about the relationship between civil society and the state emerge in this account of civil society's ancillary role in democratic societies. The first assumption is that civil society and the state are coterminous; they share the same territory, jurisdiction, and membership. The autonomous sphere of associational life occupies a distinct conceptual space, but the state delimits that space in practice. The political authorities and institutions with jurisdiction in civil society are those of the state, creating a fit between civil society activity and political authority. Finally, the members of civil society are simply the citizens of the state. We can speak sensibly, for instance, about American or Canadian civil society as distinct entities.

---

*I call these "purported" democratic effects because each of the claims surveyed above rests on empirical foundations that might well be challenged. As Ian Shapiro argues, the increasingly popular view that democracy needs civil society is "perhaps more often asserted than argued for or even persuasively explained…" Ian Shapiro, *Democratic Justice* (New Haven, CT: Yale University Press, 1999), 100.

Another key assumption of neo-Tocquevillean models, which builds on the first, is that a "democratic symmetry" exists between civil society and the state. This symmetry legitimates civil society's role as a site for discursive will formation that guides or determines state policy. Given that civil society is independent of the political sphere by definition, its steering function can only be democratic if there is an identity between civil society's members and the state's citizenry. What matters is not merely that public opinion gets formulated according to deliberative norms but also which public does the formulating. This democratic symmetry reconciles the formation of public opinion and the generation of political demands with the necessary use of state power to enact or enable policy.

A third central assumption underpinning neo-Tocquevillean civil society's democratic effects is that civil society and the state are mutually supportive and constitutive.[27] The state's laws structure civil society, defining its members' rights and its civic spaces. The state's institutions uphold the laws, regulating activities within civil society and guaranteeing rights;[28] they are responsive to the demands of civil society, providing points of access and influence. The state's norms shape civil society and the groups populating it; as Walzer puts it, "only a democratic state can create a democratic civil society, and only a democratic civil society can sustain a democratic state."[29] There is an obvious but instructive circularity here: the democratic functions and effects of civil society can only work where participation, representation, and deliberation are valued and institutionalized politically; only in these circumstances does civil society strengthen and support political democracy. These circumstances obtain only within democratic states.

None of these assumptions, all of which are directly implicated in civil society's democratic effects, holds for GCS. Clearly there is no global polity, no political unit whose borders, jurisdiction, and membership correspond with those of GCS. International governance organizations (IGOs) do perform many "statelike" roles, but these roles are typically organized func-tionally, often overlapping with one another and with state roles. The "new" political spaces constructed around these institutions differ from states in important ways, perhaps most significantly in that they lie on top of exist-ing political spaces. As a result, GCS is highly differentiated politically: it is only as open or as tolerant as the underlying political spaces in which its activities manifest, making it very unevenly democratic. In addition, there is no unique jurisdictional correspondence between IGOs and a particular citizenry, and thus no way to determine "membership" according to familiar democratic models.

This indeterminacy is most problematic in light of the second assumption regarding democratic symmetry. Once membership is no longer given by the boundaries of the state, the requirements of democratic symmetry become ambiguous: should all persons be considered members of GCS at all times, or should the functional jurisdictions of IGOs set political boundaries? Is membership based on residence within such boundaries or by some version of the "all-affected" principle favored by many deliberative democrats? This ambiguity directly diminishes the representative and deliberative legitimacy of public will formation in GCS. Public will formation through deliberation *counts* as democratic because the rightfulness of the citizens who do the deliberating can be taken for granted. But the self-originating character of the democratic polity discussed by communitarians is a moral quality predicated on the fixed boundaries of the political community; once this presumption is relaxed, the ambiguity immediately appears. Moreover, without global political institutions to translate the public will into law and policy, it is not clear what the political meaning of global deliberations is or should be; nor is it clear what should happen if the "global democratic will" conflicts with the particular will of a democratic state. Theorists who place a huge burden on the steering role of transnational democratic deliberation underestimate the difficulties in theorizing a democratic will or discourse outside the normative and political limits of the state. Given these difficulties, it becomes unclear what exactly the democratic functions of global opinion, discourse, and deliberation might be.

The lack of a global state means that there is no political framework to constitute and support GCS. Democratic civil society requires the rule of law as well as explicit guarantees of citizens' rights; it requires norms of openness, freedom, equality, and participation; and, it requires institutions that are open to influence and scrutiny by the public. This is what Walzer meant by saying that "only a *democratic* state can create a democratic civil society" (emphasis mine). In considering GCS as a model of global democracy, however, we must also consider whether only a democratic *state* can create a democratic civil society. Global governance is not characterized by the rule of law; at the global level there is no extensive legal system and few institutions to enforce those important laws that do exist. The rights possessed by members of GCS are their rights as citizens of particular states, and they vary tremendously. While governance regimes perform many statelike functions, they typically do not guarantee anyone's rights (which is not to say they do not affect anyone's rights). Moreover, while IGOs are responsible for much global governance, the absence of a global government means that a variety of other actors—from NGOs and transnational social movements to transnational corporations, organized crime, terrorist networks, private militias, and sex traffickers—also exercises significant governance functions in the supranational domain. Many do not promote democracy locally, where they operate, or globally. States can, at least where they have the capacity, constrain the governance roles of such actors domestically, but their ability to do so supranationally is highly limited. As Pasha and Blaney note, civil society itself often calls forth an expansion of the state apparatus as an agent of social reform.[30] One of the key achievements of the postwar democratic welfare state was subordinating the capitalist economy to public—democratic—authority. Where key governance institutions are not unified or even coordinated, democratic purposes become difficult to achieve and maintain.

Democratic civil society is not democracy; GCS cannot support democracy in the way that neo-Tocquevillean civil society does because the latter's democratic functions cannot work outside a democratic state. Identifying the interdependence of state and civil society in the neo-Tocquevillean model in no way constitutes a criticism; it simply makes explicit the assumptions upon which the model's democratic claims depend. Associational life might manifest many of its salutary effects quite apart from the state—in large associations, in nongovernmental institutions, and in local communities of various kinds—but we cannot understand these effects to be democratic without understanding the interdependence of civil society and the democratic state.[31] As one critic has observed,

> the notion of civil society itself makes little sense apart from the notion of the state against which it was originally articulated as a form of politics contained within its boundaries, a form of domesticity, sometimes public and sometimes private, that depends first and foremost on the capacity of states to carve out the spatial domains necessary for any kind of politics worthy of the name to be constituted.[32]

Democratic politics on the neo-Tocquevillean model requires the democratic political space of the sovereign state; it is sovereign democracy. This perspective makes clear that GCS provides an inadequate and inappropriate model of global democracy.

Held's Cosmopolitan Democratic Constitutionalism

Like GCS theories, David Held's proposals for cosmopolitan democracy begin from an appreciation of the state's democratic limits in the emerging global order. Held recognizes that the state's important democratic functions are constrained by their embeddedness in the framework of sovereignty and concludes that cosmopolitan democracy requires an alternative framework of empowerment based in a global democratic constitutional confederation. His account is valuable not only for its obvious insights and ingenuity; because Held is keenly aware of democratic theory's embeddedness in the sovereign state, his proposal's shortcomings are also instructive. Moreover, Held's views are broadly representative of cosmopolitan democratic approaches.

Held's reconstruction of democratic theory stems from his awareness that self-determination raises serious questions about "the relation between the state and democracy."* He is skeptical of both state and popular sovereignty; the former gives too much power to the state while disregarding the community's right, while the latter makes precisely the opposite error (146). Held looks to what he calls the "principle of autonomy" for an alternative to these unacceptable positions. This principle states that

> persons should enjoy equal rights and, accordingly, equal obligation in the specification of the political framework which generates and limits the opportunities available to them; that is, they should be free and equal in the determination of the conditions of their own lives, so long as they do not deploy this framework to negate the rights of others (147).

Building on this principle, Held develops an account of democracy as autonomy that balances the demands of state sovereignty and popular sovereignty through constitutionalism while stressing that the people must determine the conditions of their own association. He articulates a set of "empowerment rights" or "entitlement capacities" derived from the principle of autonomy; these rights are to be anchored in a cosmopolitan democratic legal framework. They are not citizenship rights, Held argues: citizenship implies a national framework of empowerment and a structure for common political action limited to the framework of the nation-state (222–23). This framework is too restrictive because the interconnections typical of globalization dictate that "autonomy can prevail in a political community if, and only if, it is unimpeded by threats arising from the action (or non-action) of other political communities, or from the networks of interaction which cut across community boundaries" (226).

In other words, the pursuit of individual and collective projects requires a common structure of action or common democratic framework fostering respect for the legitimate boundaries of one's own and others' autonomy. "In a highly interconnected world, 'others' include not just those found in the immediate community," Held writes, "but all those whose fates are interlocked in networks of economic, political, and environmental interaction." This condition is not met if "the quality of life of others is shaped and determined in near or far-off lands without their participation, agreement or consent" (231). The obligation to ensure everyone's participation, agreement, and consent in an era of heightened global interdependence means that a community of all democratic communities must be among the highest priorities of democrats. It would entail the enjoyment by all individuals of

---

*David Held, *Democracy and the Global Order: From the Modern State to Cosmopolitan Governance* (Stanford, CA: Stanford University Press, 1995); hereafter I shall use in-text page citations in referring to this work.

multiple citizenships in each of the diverse communities that significantly affect their lives (233).

For Held these requirements dictate a reconceptualization of sovereignty. The cosmopolitan democratic law replaces what Held calls the "'artificial person' at the center of the idea of the modern state" as the legitimate subject of sovereignty.

> In this conception, sovereign authority or sovereignty would derive its legitimacy from this law.... While such a system requires an overarching set of institutions to nurture the entrenchment and application of basic law, it could be composed of a diverse range of decision-making centers which are autonomous, that is, which act within their own sphere of competence subject only to meeting the requirements of democratic law (234).

These decision centers could be states or other types of association. "Thus, sovereignty can be stripped away from the idea of fixed borders and territories and thought of as, in principle, malleable time-space clusters. Sovereignty is an attribute of the basic democratic law, but it could be entrenched and drawn upon in diverse self-regulating associations, from states to cities and corporations" (234).

Within this overarching framework, associations will be self-governing at diverse levels. Held explains that

> the issues and policy questions which rightly belong to local, workplace or city levels are those which involve people in the direct determination of the conditions of their own association—the network of public questions and problems, from policing to playgrounds, which primarily affect them. The issues which rightly belong to national levels of governance are those in which people in delimited territories are significantly affected by collective problems and policy questions which stretch to, but no further than, their frontiers. By contrast, the issues which rightly belong to regional levels of governance are those which require transnational mediation because of the interconnectedness of national decisions and outcomes, and because nations in these circumstances often find themselves unable to achieve their objectives without transborder collaboration. Accordingly, decision-making and implementation belong to the regional level if, and only if, the common interest in self-determination can only be achieved effectively through regional governance. By extension, the issues which rightly belong to the global level are those involving levels of interconnectedness and interdependence which are unresolvable by local, national, or regional authorities acting alone (235).

Sovereignty will be reapportioned to various authorities according to calculations of extensiveness, intensity, and comparative efficiency (236–37). *Extensiveness* gauges the range of groups and people significantly affected by an issue or decision; *intensity* assesses how significantly they are affected, and thus what level seems most appropriate for determining the matter; *comparative efficiency* evaluates (presumably at a later stage) whether the desired objective can be attained through action at a lower level (235–36).

Creation of this framework entails that territorial boundaries of systems of accountability be reconfigured to bring issues that escape the control of the state under better democratic control; that the role and place of regional and global regulatory and functional agencies must be transformed so that they can provide a sharp focal point in public affairs; and finally, that political institutions within key groups, agencies, associations, and organizations must be made compatible with the democratic process (267–68). In other words, the basic framework of liberal democracy must be extended horizontally into domains like the market and the economy and vertically to stretch from the local to the global. As Held puts it, "the possibility of democracy today must...be linked to an expanding framework of democratic institutions and procedures," a common framework of political action through which autonomy can be realized (267). Held derives the requirements of the democratic process and the content of the democratic law from the principle of autonomy. He recognizes that extending the framework of autonomy to the global level requires an account of its "most feasible and appropriate political anchor," and he locates this anchor in a reconceived notion of sovereignty that forms the basis of the democratic law. Sovereignty gets reconfigured more loosely as the subject of legitimacy at the center of a cosmopolitan conception of democracy (234). This "subject" is stripped from its territorial moorings and redefined as "malleable time-space clusters."

This account confuses more than it clarifies. To begin with, it is circular: the new conception of sovereignty provides legitimacy for cosmopolitan democratic law, and the cosmopolitan democratic law justifies reconceptualizing sovereignty. But sovereignty is both an attribute of the cosmopolitan democratic law and its source of legitimacy; the law is authorized by sovereignty, which is authorized by the law. The political anchor for Held's framework never touches bottom amid these tides of definition and redefinition. Perhaps aware that this formulation leaves his new conception of sovereignty adrift, Held offers a second anchor, tying rightful decision making to an empirical and procedural account of legitimacy as well. Two related difficulties raised by this attempt to reground sovereignty empirically stand out. The first has to do with making actual determinations about who decides. In Held's autonomy-based account, individuals must enjoy citizenship in all of the various associations that shape or influence their lives. The point of these multiple and overlapping memberships is precisely to extend the meaningful framework of autonomy or empowerment beyond the limits of the state. As Held acknowledges, given the intensiveness and extensiveness of interdependence, these boundaries are likely to be fluid and difficult to ascertain. In a footnote, he acknowledges that

> the principle that decisions about public affairs should rest with those significantly affected by them, or their representatives, will, of course, not always lead to clear demarcations among the appropriate levels of decision-making, even with the aid of the proposed filter principles and tests. Disputes about the appropriate jurisdiction of particular communities will in all likelihood be complex and intensive... (237).

He proposes issue-boundary forums or courts to address these complexities.

Held's criteria describe how we might determine the level at which a given decision, from local to global, is to be made by divining the impact of a particular issue or decision on individuals and then ascribing authority to those individuals who are significantly affected. Numerous difficulties plague this procedure. How do we determine impact: is it an economic, sociological, or psychological question? Is the determination subjective, left to individuals' feelings of impact or affinity, or objective, made by experts or politicians (chosen by whom)? How do we deal with intensity of preferences and interests? Will significance be uniform at each level? Held's own account of globalization emphasizes cross-cutting flows and complex interdependence, suggesting that people at any given level will be affected differently by different issues or decisions. Besides, who will be affected and how are usually among the points at issue in political decisions, so how can these points be decided in advance?[33]

Let me offer two examples to illustrate the difficulties just described.* First, with respect to levels, consider the decision whether to locate a toxic waste storage site in a particular locality. Suppose, perhaps implausibly, the community decides it might prosper by importing hazardous materials for storage, generating jobs and other revenues. Should each resident have one vote, or should the immediate neighbors of the site get extra say because they are intensely affected? Let us assume the community democratically decides in favor of this option, whatever that means. Now the surrounding localities, which will not share directly in the economic benefits but will still bear an elevated risk—the toxic stuff will pass through these areas in transit to the storage facilities—demand their say. If enough people in enough neighboring localities are allowed to vote, they might scupper the plan. But suppose the wider regional community might also reap benefits through taxation and

---

*In presenting these examples I take no substantive positions on the issues raised.

might bear much less direct risk—they are not located along major highways used for transit and would enjoy the general benefits of economic stimulus. At the national or global levels, industry groups (and, indirectly and probably unwittingly, consumers) might be desperate for a safe place to store such stuff, while greens would adamantly oppose transporting toxic waste in the first place. How should their views figure into the process? All are, to varying (and difficult to quantify) degrees, affected. Who decides?

In the second example, imagine that Subsidia, a rich democracy, is considering a new economic assistance program for its declining garment industry. This policy would preserve jobs in several localities throughout Subsidia but would also increase the taxes of all Subsidians and raise the prices they pay for garments. At the same time, Subsidia's policy would cause job losses in Textilia, an emerging democracy whose garment industry operates at lower cost. Subsidia's policy will make Textilia's garments uncompetitive in the vast Subsidian market; moreover, it will spur surplus production likely to be dumped on the world market, further reducing demand for Textilia's goods and putting even more workers there out of jobs. Suppose the decision about this policy is taken by Subsidians: how does one weigh garment workers' intense preference for jobs against the much more diffuse but aggregately much greater economic interest of taxpayers and clothing buyers? (How should the latter weigh their individual pocketbook concerns against their social interest in decent jobs for their compatriots?) What about the Textilians and Textilian democracy? Now suppose Subsidians and Textilians are given a joint choice. Subsidia has a larger population and its garment workers decry labor and environmental conditions and low wages in Textilia. The subsidies are implemented; have Textilians had a fair say? Has the global democratic framework increased their autonomy? Suppose the world made the choice, as it touched larger trade-related issues, and populous low-wage countries like Textilia prevailed. (Should the decision be taken by country or by individuals?) Would the dreaded "race to the bottom" destroy the comparatively quite generous welfare state citizens of Subsidia and other rich democracies expect? Should "others" be allowed to "make that choice for them"? Why should democracy for rich Subsidians entitle them to condemn Textilians to greater poverty for the sake of generous vacations and prescription drug coverage?

These examples illustrate that empirical measures of extensiveness, intensity, and comparative efficiency are hopelessly inadequate for resolving such questions. This is not just some analytic quibble: my concern is not that Held or other cosmopolitans define terms like *impact* and *significance* inadequately, nor is it the (obviously unfair) gripe that they provide no simple remedy for these difficult problems. My concern is broader and theoretical: there is *no plausible way* to extend an account of democratic legitimacy based in collective autonomy beyond the specific empirical context in which it makes sense.* In what I have called sovereign democracy, the rightfulness of decisions flows from their being taken by an antecedently recognized authority, that artificial person Held identifies as being at the heart of the modern state. Sovereignty offered a general solution to questions about authority within a particular territory; popular sovereignty merely extended this justification to collective authority and autonomy in the form of rule by the citizens. But crucially, in both its state and popular forms, the artificial person has a territorial personality. Once sovereignty is stripped of its territorial associations, its personality dissolves, along with the account of autonomy it demanded and licensed.

Held tries to finesse this issue by transposing the normative question of popular will into an empirical problem,† replacing the territorial political communities with empirically based ones. Apparently he hopes to locate the rightfulness of decisions in their being taken by the appropriate community, understood as all those significantly affected. This is why cosmopolitan citizens hold multiple citizenships: they must be members of all those communities where their rights and interests are at stake. These communities become the foundation of legitimacy in Held's scheme. But this means that determination of the proper boundaries and membership of each community—if that word even makes sense when boundaries and membership change with each issue—is essential to the legitimacy of its decisions.

I doubt, given the problems we have seen, that determinations of sufficient precision to support this burden of legitimacy can in principle be made. In giving up the territorial conception of sovereignty Held gives up the very essence of rightful rule in modern democracy. This is why his new conception of sovereignty cannot provide legitimacy for the cosmopolitan democratic law. Without the territorial definition of a rightful community on which it was based, sovereignty becomes a mere synonym for control that carries no independent account of the origins or justification of its own legitimacy. This is a strange oversight for Held, who was among the first to see that globalization destabilizes the democratic idea of a community of fate.[34]

This leads directly into the second problem with his account: the cosmopolitan framework is designed to provide structures through which autonomy can be realized in an interdependent world, but this commitment

---

*As the first example suggests, this account is not always helpful even within the context of established democracies.

†Note that the propriety of the empirical tests constitutes an indirect normative claim in its own right. Cf. Thomas W. Pogge, "Cosmopolitanism and Sovereignty," *Ethics* 103, no. 1 (1992): 64, who collapses the empirical and normative claims: individuals have a "*right* to an international order under which those significantly and legitimately affected by a political decision have a roughly equal opportunity to influence the making of this decision—directly or through elected delegates or representatives" (emphasis mine).

to autonomy itself becomes unsustainable without an anchor in sovereignty. We have already seen that the justification of democracy based in individual autonomy or self-government is reduced to incoherence by the size of the modern state; obviously this justification will fare no better at the global level. What about collective autonomy? Once its justification in individual autonomy collapses, collective autonomy can only be justified with reference to an ongoing political community, one recognized as rightful by its members. Once political communities get replaced by constantly changing agglomerations of far-flung strangers who are by some measure equally significantly impacted by some threat or decision, it becomes hard to discern the subject whose rights and interests require a framework of collective autonomy in the first place; collective autonomy becomes a moral requirement with no clear referent. It cannot be required by the sovereignty of clusters whose legitimacy is itself justified by the requirement of collective autonomy; as we saw withGCS, such bootstrapping arguments do not persuade. Moreover, the unavailability of independent democratic criteria for defining the polity and demos renders suspect the very notion that collective autonomy is a *democratic* imperative. Absent a strong sense of shared, legitimate community, even wholly transparent, accountable democratic institutions do not convey legitimacy upon political authority.

There is ample evidence to support this view. Consider just one example: Canada and the United Kingdom are two rich, stable, well-established democracies. Yet in both countries the larger community is thought to be invalid by some within it: for instance, many Québécois and certain indigenous groups in Canada, many Scots, Welsh, and residents of Northern Ireland in Britain. These democracies are straining because the larger polities that contain the various communities, even though they are among the most democratic in the world, are not recognized as legitimate by all of their members; the boundaries of the political community cannot be taken for granted. That we might expect new supranational democratic institutions on the same model to command more legitimacy, even though they refer neither to historical or ethnonational communities, seems far-fetched. Moreover, empirically based communities would be unlikely to gain much independent legitimacy over time because of their constantly changing constituencies. My point is not that representative political institutions cannot be justified; it is rather that they cannot be justified through collective autonomy once the rightfulness of the collectivity can no longer be taken for granted.

Again, my critique of Held is not that he fails to resolve difficult practical questions about global democratic decision making. It is instead that he and other cosmopolitan democrats continue to conceive global democracy as collective autonomy and self-determination—as sovereign democracy—when their own arguments demonstrate that globalization undermines sovereignty.

These questions are so difficult because they are posed in a framework that makes them irresolvable.

Conclusion: the Limits of Modern Democracy

Communitarian and cosmopolitan democratic approaches together demonstrate the limits of modern or sovereign democracy in the age of globalization. Its normative ideal can only be realized within the sovereign state, but sovereignty has been undermined by globalization. Ironically, communitarians and cosmopolitans make the same mistake: both fail to appreciate and reckon with the interdependence of sovereign democracy's normative and empirical dimensions. Sovereign democracy is, in a word, untenable in both its traditional and cosmopolitan variants; it only makes sense in the Westphalian order, an order which no longer exists.

Communitarians defend sovereign democracy's normative ideal, which I have argued is indefensible on *empirical* grounds. There is a danger in holding on to this ideal despite its empirical implausibility: it sanctifies democratic forms that evolved within the sovereign state, creating the illusion that sovereign democracy *is* democracy, that democracy would look more or less the same regardless of whether it had developed within the sovereign state or in some other context, and that any theory of democracy must look more or less like those with which we are familiar. This sanctified view confuses the institutions through which democracy is realized at the state level with democracy itself, transforming traditional democratic institutions into ends rather than—as they should be regarded—means of translating democratic principles into practice.[35]

Cosmopolitans try to reconfigure the empirical framework of sovereign democracy's ideal, which I have argued is unworkable on *normative* grounds. Again, there is a danger in naïvely assuming that there is no theoretical difficulty in decoupling democracy from the framework of the sovereign state. We must not assume that extricating a concept from the context in which it was theorized and institutionalized leaves the *meaning* of the theory or the institutions intact. With respect to the theory, I have tried to establish (throughout part I) how deeply our understanding of what democracy is and how it works is tied up with its realization in the Westphalian state. The very idea of an autonomous polity with a unified collective will is in many respects just an artifact of sovereignty colored by the romantic patina of classical Athens. Now we must seriously reconsider even our most basic intuitions about what democracy might mean apart from that context. With respect to the institutions, I have shown that familiar democratic processes and mechanisms, from voting and deliberating to participating in associational life, must be understood (at least partly) as artifactual in this way:

elections, parliaments, participation, and representation make sense largely because we take for granted the boundaries and propriety of the polities in which they are embedded.

A related confusion arises when we treat the scale and reach of democratic institutions as unrelated to democracy's meaning and purpose. The territorial limits of modern democratic institutions are not mere contingencies; they are directly related to democracy's foundational normative assumptions concerning the demos and its sovereignty. Democratic institutions are located where they are in part thanks to historical contingencies, but this history itself informed the theorization of modern democracy.[36] The idea of a people whose will is supreme within a particular territory and whose consent legitimizes government *follows from* the idea that states are natural and appropriate containers of politics; that is, from sovereignty. Democracy's territorial institutions reflect this assumption; they are legitimate not because they are representative but because they represent an already constituted people in an already-constituted political community. Thus it is impossible to change the scale or reach of democratic institutions without changing the meaning of democracy itself: about this communitarians are unquestionably correct.

There is an irony in cosmopolitan responses to globalization. The state-based models of democracy on which many cosmopolitan proposals are patterned are frequently seen, or were prior to the furor over globalization, as inadequate models of democracy at the state level. Elections and parliaments are corrupted by money and the power it buys; government is said to be distant, out of touch, dominated by corporate interests; bureaucracy is said to be stifling and oppressive; civil society is stratified by extreme inequalities, and the demands of associational life privilege the wealthy and well-educated; the economy remains largely outside democratic control. The irony is that cosmopolitan defenders of what amounts to global pluralism and global liberal democracy advocate democratic models widely regarded as narrow, conservative, and insufficiently egalitarian and representative at the state level as radical solutions to the challenge of democracy at the global level. Thus cosmopolitan responses to globalization entail the risk that we might get what we wish for: a global democratic regime modeled on domestic arrangements with which we are anyway dissatisfied.

We need a theory of global democracy, not just the application of existing democratic theory to the global context. We need it because our current democratic theory is inadequate and increasingly inappropriate for the age of globalization. In developing this new theory we must avoid the easy but problematic assumption that global politics is fundamentally similar to domestic politics—an assumption reflected in both GCS and cosmopolitan constitutional theories. This assumption encourages us to treat the challenge of globalization as a challenge of application, of figuring out how to fit familiar models and institutions to new problems. An alternative approach would begin with democracy's core principles and try to work out their requirements and methods for their realization that avoid the empirical and conceptual entanglements of sovereignty. This is the approach I adopt in part II.

PART **II**
Democracy as Human Rights

CHAPTER 6

The Emancipatory Tradition
of Democratic Theory

In the second part of this book I undertake a critical reconstruction of democratic theory informed by my analysis of sovereign democracy. This theory, which I call democracy as human rights (DHR), reinterprets democracy's core principles of universal freedom and equality for the age of globalization. DHR defines democracy as a political commitment to universal emancipation through securing the equal enjoyment of fundamental human rights for everyone. I shall articulate and defend this conception in the following chapters; here, I want to set the stage for that argument by outlining the broader democratic tradition to which DHR belongs. That tradition, I shall argue, conceives emancipation as the goal or aim of democratization and invokes human rights as the language of democratic empowerment.* The insights and limitations of this tradition provide the key historical resources upon which the subsequent reconstruction of democracy draws.[1]

Anything like a proper historical survey is impossible here. Instead, I shall pursue three more modest goals. First, I shall sketch the central concepts of this tradition and discuss several of its key thinkers; second, I shall argue that the understanding of democratization these thinkers share can be usefully redescribed as the dismantling of the obstacles that sovereignty poses for democracy; finally, I shall suggest that the emancipatory democratic tradition, despite its historical concern with democracy and democratization

---

Empowerment is a problematic term; where it means that some person or persons gives power to others—as when some international financial institution "empowers" a local population—it is not very democratic. Throughout this chapter I have in mind empowerment's more limited meaning of "enablement" (a neologism for which I do not want responsibility). My position is that the thinkers in this tradition all share the view that human rights are politically enabling toward emancipation, and I shall use "empowerment" strictly in this sense.

inside the state, offers an attractive way of thinking about democracy and democratization globally.

I want to be clear that what follows is not intended as a proof of DHR or even as a historical argument for it; DHR will have to persuade on its own merits. Nor is my intention to suggest that the emancipatory tradition I shall highlight here is somehow a unique or correct interpretation of democracy: it is one of many currents in democratic theory, with many points of confluence and divergence from other streams, points I shall emphasize in the following account. My main purpose here is to establish that, however strange or unfamiliar it might seem, there is good historical and theoretical warrant for thinking about democracy as emancipation and for conceiving human rights as a crucial part of the democratic vocabulary.

The Language of Democratic Empowerment

Democracy and human rights share deep historical ties, especially in the Anglo-American liberal tradition, but not only there. Some theorists have questioned the relevance of early theories of rights to modern political arguments,[2] but broadly speaking, their influence can hardly be doubted. At least since the American and French revolutions, freedom and equality have been closely associated both with democracy and with human rights; the roots of this connection extend back as far as the English Civil War.[3] Soboul has argued that while the Levellers and Locke, and through them the American revolutionaries, based their theories on natural human rights, it was for the French in 1789 to insist upon the universality and equality of rights, making the French *Déclaration des Droits de l'Homme et du Citoyen* genuinely democratic.[4]

In its specifics this analysis is faulty: as we have seen, Locke and other theorists of popular sovereignty do begin from universal freedom and political equality, though other natural inequalities nonetheless yield an exclusive conception of citizenship. Besides, the exclusion of women and belated, half-hearted recognition of the rights of black men belie Soboul's too enthusiastic claims about the "truly democratic" quality of the *Déclaration*.[5] Yet it is hard to quarrel with the more general point that the French revolution established an ideal to be realized, a "direction of intention" that shaped the evolution of democracy.[6] As Hunt describes, many women at the time recognized that "human rights had an implacable logic," even if it had not yet worked itself out fully.[7]

Indeed, "from the time that modern argument about democratization began in the seventeenth century, it has embodied a promise couched in the universal language of citizenship, consent, rights, equality, and freedom."[8] One way of conceiving arguments about democratization in this vocabulary—and

I stress that it is only one way—is in terms of *emancipation*. What I mean by emancipation is an egalitarian state of nondomination and noninterference achieved through rights, including the crucial right to suffrage; democratization consists in achieving emancipation for more people by arguing for their inclusion in the enjoyment of rights and by pushing to extend rights to encompass a wider set of social relations and institutions, including economic and "private" ones. From the seventeenth until the nineteenth century, radical democratic thinkers argued for more thoroughgoing democratization in the egalitarian language of human rights.

This emancipatory view of democratization combines theoretical elements often associated with the liberal and republican traditions; it insists on traditional liberal ideas like protection of rights and noninterference, but talks about emancipation using republican terms like *virtue, independence*, and *nondomination*. There is a significant contemporary debate about the dividing lines between liberalism and republicanism, with both sides claiming key figures (including several I discuss here) as their own. I shall not join this debate here; rather, I want to draw attention to a group of thinkers, "emancipatory democrats," notable for their concern with both types of infringement upon freedom and equality. Calling them democrats recognizes that, as Ian Shapiro argues, "democracy is as much about opposition to the arbitrary exercise of power as it is about collective self-government," even though this oppositional aspect of democracy is not frequently mentioned in the academic literature.[9] Self-government can play an instrumental role in securing emancipation; it is enabling as well as protective. Calling these thinkers democrats also helps to highlight their *egalitarian* understanding of emancipation. Michael Walzer argues that democratic egalitarianism is at heart a negative idea, one originating in abolitionist practices.[10] As he puts it, "the experience of subordination—of personal subordination, above all—lies behind the vision of equality.... The aim of political egalitarianism is a society free from domination."[11]

Assimilating these thinkers into either the liberal or republican tradition obscures what from the democratic perspective stands out as significant about their thought: emancipatory democracy is oppositional and enabling; it is egalitarian; it envisions emancipation through human rights. We could call this radical liberalism—the view that Locke provides all the necessary theoretical resources for achieving democracy: rights, freedom, equality, and independence.[12] These concepts are all important in emancipatory democracy, yet liberalism's emphasis on property rights and privacy and its general inattention to domination mean that it captures only part of what the emancipatory theorists mean by freedom and independence. Also recall that Locke sees independence primarily as a category denoting a particular status of nonsubjection, of individual sovereignty. Given the emancipatory theorists' hostility to domination, we might try to understand them as republicans. Doing so creates an anachronism, however, because as contemporary defenders and critics of republicanism agree, the classical republican conception of freedom could not be universalized. It rested on intertwined notions of virtue, virility, and wealth that made citizenship for women or servants inconceivable.[13] It was also skeptical of rights, instead stressing a notion of public virtue that potentially licenses quite a bit of state interference in the name of the common good. Moreover, classical republican thinkers always regarded independence as a marker of citizenship rather than a political objective.[14]

I want to insist, then, on the distinctiveness of this particular current of thought in which emancipation for all is conceived and guaranteed through equal rights. Doing so underlines what is distinctively democratic about these thinkers even as it highlights important points of confluence with other theoretical traditions. From the perspective adopted here, contemporary reconstructions of two competing traditions in seventeenth- and eighteenth-century political thought seem to oversimplify a more fluid and complex reality.[15]

Emancipatory Democracy

The theorists I shall focus on here share an egalitarian commitment to emancipation through natural or human rights. From the mid-seventeenth century, when arguments for popular sovereignty were first articulated in terms of freedom and equality, emancipatory democrats pushed for greater inclusion in citizenship and for greater independence in social and economic life. In what follows I do not mean to suggest that all of these thinkers share the same view or hold these commitments to the same extent; my aim is to single out important similarities in their views and highlight their democratic implications.

The Seventeenth Century: The Levellers

The Levellers were traditionally viewed "as harbingers of the democratic revolutions of later centuries" until C. B. Macpherson read into their views a theory of possessive individualism according to which he classified them as "radical whigs."[16] For a time Macpherson's view was grudgingly accepted,[17] though now the pendulum seems to have swung back in the other direction. Sharp, in his introduction to the "Cambridge Canon" edition of their writings, acknowledges that most critics see the Levellers as democrats of some kind, though just what kind remains contentious.[18] I want to emphasize three related aspects of Leveller thought in identifying them as emancipatory democrats: their belief in natural rights, freedom, and equality; their opposition to all forms of bondage or subjection, including economic dependence; and, their commitment to a wider (though not universal) suffrage.

Hampsher-Monk argues that over time the Levellers' arguments relied increasingly on claims grounded in reciprocal natural rights.[19] In the postscript to "The Freeman's Freedom Vindicated," for instance, John Lilburne argues that all men and women, as descendants of Adam and Eve, are "by nature all equal and alike in power, dignity, authority, and majesty—none of them having (by nature) any authority, dominion or magisterial power, one over or above another."[20] They believed "in the existential equality of authority among human beings, their natural right to sustain and defend themselves and their natural duty to defend and succour others."[21] The Levellers understood economic domination on a par with political domination; in whatever form, such domination destroys freedom and independence.[22] Amid endless rhetoric of bondage, slavery, tyranny, and oppression we find numerous references to subjection originating in poverty and economic dependence. Lilburne, who was something of an "egalitarian agitator,"[23] consistently saw domination and oppression both in the arbitrary exercise of law and authority and in the conditions of economic dependence constraining many commoners.[24] In the "Petition," the "Manifestation," and in the "Agreement of the Free People.…" Lilburne and his collaborators reiterated and refined proposals for economic reforms designed to ameliorate poverty, including ending trade monopolies, eliminating debtors' prisons, opening the commons, undertaking limited redistribution, and other measures.[25]

What makes the Levellers' thought distinctively emancipatory, in the sense in which I am using that term, is their conviction that guaranteeing men's natural rights, including crucially the right to the franchise, is the surest and only way to ensure their independence. In "An Arrow Against All Tyrants" Overton asserts that all individuals possess by nature a propriety which is not to be usurped or invaded by any.[26] This propriety consists in right and freedom, as well as in subsistence.[27] Quite consistently throughout the debates at Putney, Rainsborough (the Leveller spokesman) reiterates the position that poverty should not be grounds for domination and that only the franchise can prevent such domination.

> Even the poorest he that is in England has a life to live as the greatest he; and therefore truly … I think it's clear that every man that is to live under a government ought first by his own consent to put himself under that government, and I do think that the poorest man in England is not at all bound in a strict sense [to any government he has not consented to].[28]

After Ireton objects that manhood suffrage will mean the end of property, Rainsborough retorts: "I am a poor man, therefore I must be *oppressed*?"[29]

Later, citing the remarks of Colonel Rich to the effect that the ratio of rich (enfranchised) men to poor was one to five, Rainsborough laments that "the one part shall make hewers of wood and drawers of water of the other five, and so the greatest part of the nation be enslaved."[30]

So even as they vehemently denied any plan to confiscate estates or otherwise "level" property,[31] the Levellers insisted on economic reform and on manhood suffrage to end the slavery of poverty and the domination of the poor by the rich. They understood guarantees of natural rights—in particular the right to vote—as the best way to ensure the natural independence and "propriety" with which nature endows everyone. It is important to stress that the Levellers were not—like Winstanley's Diggers or "True Levellers"—advocates of communism; they believed in the right to estate, but understood this right as part of a larger constellation of freedoms that together guarantee independence. It is this complex, egalitarian conception of independence and its connection with human rights that distinguish Leveller thinking as democratic.

The Eighteenth Century: Paine and Wollstonecraft

Paine is a complex and controversial figure: he is remembered for his impassioned pleas for American independence, for his debate with Burke, for his life as an international revolutionary, and for his notorious (supposed) atheism. He is often dismissed primarily as a pamphleteer, a thinker lacking in insight and originality, yet his legacy is also contested by liberals and republicans alike. In short, Paine's life and thought remain enigmatic.

Nonetheless, Paine is clearly committed to emancipation as a political ideal and to human rights as the means for achieving it. Paine's devotion to human rights is well-known: his *Rights of Man* defends not only the principle of rights but also the revolution the French had made by invoking it. His proposed Declaration of Rights, written in collaboration with Condorcet as part of the approved but never implemented Constitution of 1793, makes his position eminently clear. These rights are not limited narrowly to the classic liberal trinity of life, liberty, and property; rather, natural rights also include "…equality, security…social protection, and resistance to oppression."[32] These important additions reflect Paine's awareness that natural rights are not merely individualistic liberties on the Hobbesian model; he conceives rights as an inheritance promising a better life. Paine frequently contrasts "the wretched condition of man under the monarchical and hereditary systems of Government" with the new political order possible through revolutions in the principle and construction of government. The "wretched condition" includes a person "being dragged from his home by one power, or driven by another, and impoverished by taxes more than by enemies.…"[33] Obviously Paine has in mind not just civil and political liberties but something like emancipation as I have described it here; arbitrary authority, subjection, and poverty are equally mentioned as among the defects in government that a rights revolution will rectify.

Largely on the basis of certain of his early writings in defense of commerce, Paine is sometimes labeled a liberal or bourgeois theorist.[34] He is certainly a friend of commerce and an opponent of taxes, but in his more complex understanding of the egalitarian social function of rights he balances this prohibition with public need: "no one can be deprived of the least portion of his property without his consent, *unless evidently required by public necessity*" and then only "for the general welfare, and to meet public needs."[35] Paine is no leveler: he believes in the power of commerce and money to elevate the condition of individuals and of humanity in general, but insists that the negative impact of commerce be attended to as well. "I care not how affluent some may be," he writes, "provided that none be miserable in consequence of it."[36] Paine is also frequently described as a republican thinker, but this view obscures the radical democratic thrust of his views.[37] While he certainly emphasizes virtue, favors commerce, and opposes corruption, tyranny, and arbitrary government, Paine also develops an emancipatory account of rights as crucial to ameliorating subjection; the interdependence of political rights protects citizens against arbitrary rule and social guarantees protect them from economic dependence.

This theme is clear throughout his later writings, where Paine links the inheritance of rights with the achievement of universal civilization, a condition he contrasts with the situation in many "advanced" countries where the multitudes remain impoverished. "Poverty . . . is a thing created by that which is called civilized life," he argues;[38] "when, in countries that are called civilized, we see age going to the workhouse and youth to the gallows, something must be wrong in the system of government." Despite superficial appearances, "there lies hidden from the eye of common observation, a mass of wretchedness that has scarcely any other chance, than to expire in poverty or infamy." The role of civil government, Paine argues, is to "[make] that provision for the instruction of youth, and the support of age, as to exclude, as much as possible, profligacy from the one, and despair from the other."[39] It is in response to such depredations that Paine lays out a scheme for poor relief in the *Rights of Man* that he later reformulates and expands in *Agrarian Justice*. This social support, Paine emphasizes repeatedly, "is not of the nature of a charity, but of a *right*."[40] Thus "public succours are a sacred debt of society" and instruction is owed to all members of society equally.[41]

Crucially for my case, Paine understands rights as an egalitarian means for realizing emancipation, and holds that "equality consists in enjoyment by every one of the same rights."[42] In his view the social unrest that spawned several plots against the revolutionary government in France originated in the Republic's failure to recognize that "every individual in the world is born therein with legitimate claims on a certain kind of property, or its equivalent," that property or right being a guaranteed social minimum. This right has been ignored, and social dissatisfaction aggravated, because of the "constitutional defect" that places a property restriction on suffrage.[43] Paine comprehends the interdependence of all rights and the crucial role political rights play in securing emancipation, a realization expressed in his proposal for a right to "legal means of resisting oppression."[44]

I have emphasized how for the Levellers and for Paine emancipation, by which they meant something like social, economic, and political independence, was realized through rights. I have not mentioned some shortcomings in their theories: for instance, that the Levellers apparently did not believe that "universal" suffrage encompassed women. Such exclusions are puzzling: could Rainsborough repeatedly question how the franchise came to be possessed by only *some* freeborn Englishmen without also wondering how it could be denied to freeborn Englishwomen? Other writers of the revolutionary period, among them Condorcet and Olympe de Gouges, did recognize that the logic of human rights extended to *all* people, women as well as men, but the clearest and most forceful advocate of women's human rights in the eighteenth century was Wollstonecraft.

For Wollstonecraft, rights are clearly linked to a state of emancipation constitutive of political modernity; moreover, she shows that unless rights are shared equally by both sexes both will remain vulnerable to moral corruption. In her view, virtue can only flourish among equals; domination of any kind "blasts" all the prospects for social, economic, and political reform needed to complete the revolution Wollstonecraft applauded.[45] Her "republican" emphasis on virtue and emancipation is reconciled with her "liberal" insistence on rights through an egalitarian democratic intuition on the universality of both.[46] Thus in Wollstonecraft's thought we see an explicit egalitarian and universalist recognition that denying rights to one class of persons undermines the rights and virtue of all people.

In the dedicatory letter of the *Vindication of the Rights of Woman*, Wollstonecraft writes to Talleyrand-Périgord that in his recent pamphlet he had glimpsed the truth on which her vindication of women's rights rested:

> [you wrote] "that to see one half of the human race excluded by the other from all participation of government, was a political phaenomenon [sic] that, according to abstract principles, it was impossible to explain." If so, on what does your constitution rest? If the abstract rights of man will bear discussion and explanation, those of woman, by a parity of reasoning, will not shrink from the same test.[47]

In countering Burke's arguments against the rights of man, she urges that "it is necessary emphatically to repeat, that there are rights which men inherit at their birth, as rational creatures, who were raised above the brute creation by their improvable faculties; and that, in receiving these, not from their forefathers but, from God, prescription can never undermine natural rights."[48] Wollstonecraft's hostility to prescription animates both of her *Vindications*: she repeatedly denounces submission to traditional authority as debasing, arguing that virtue is incompatible with servility and dependence. Virtue is only possible, in her view, when rational beings exercise reason for themselves; it thus requires independence, the medium in which reason flourishes.[49] Women, like the poor and the idle rich, cannot be expected to develop virtue or become good democratic citizens unless, through independence, their reason is cultivated.[50]

Wollstonecraft blames inequality between men and women for much of the moral corruption in society; women's dependence makes them dull, incapable of being good mothers or good citizens. Without reason, which flourishes in independence, virtue withers; without rights, social duties become null.[51] Interestingly, Wollstonecraft links the vices of poverty to dependence in precisely the same way; in the first *Vindication* she is adamant that protection of property inhibits the virtue of the poor. Those suffering in poverty, she argues, have "a *right* to more comfort than they at present enjoy."[52] Her proposals for land and inheritance reform for women and the poor exemplify her belief that any kind of dependence, social, economic, or political, has a corrupting and corrosive effect on society. In this vein, she insists that greater equality is the key to moral improvement in society.[53] For women this equality entails a secure civil existence, whether they are married or single. Once woman's independence is guaranteed by anchoring her rights in law, once she is "allowed to be free in a physical, moral, and civil sense," her character will be transformed.[54] Wollstonecraft is thus profoundly convinced that "as sound politics diffuse liberty, mankind, including woman, will become more wise and virtuous." Woman will "grow more perfect when emancipated."[55] This emancipation includes economic independence as well as independence from slavish subjection to men and husbands.[56] Wollstonecraft sees thoroughgoing democratization—a "revolution" in female social, economic, and political roles—as crucial to women's emancipation and full human dignity.[57]

These views are confirmed in Wollstonecraft's reflections on the French Revolution, where she argued that "the *Déclaration*…with its basic guarantee of equal rights, was both an expression of popular will and a simplified set of political truths." In codifying this list of rights in law, the French were creating the tools for democratizing their revolution and "[producing] a virtuous citizenry capable of fully democratic self-government."[58] Thus rights, once recognized and fully implemented, would guarantee for all citizens the emancipation necessary for realizing individual and social virtue. While focusing on her language of virtue and independence tempts us to link Wollstonecraft with the republican tradition, focusing on her language of rights tempts us equally to associate her with liberalism. Yet her thoroughgoing egalitarian commitments make such simple associations impossible. Like the other thinkers we have surveyed, Wollstonecraft synthesizes aspects of what contemporary scholars call liberalism and republicanism into an emancipatory ideal of democracy.

The Nineteenth Century: Stanton, Douglass, the Chartists—and Marx

Elizabeth Cady Stanton is usually read as a feminist and suffragist; too often, her importance as a theorist of democratization and proponent of human rights and emancipation gets overlooked. I shall emphasize three aspects of her thought here: her understanding of the struggle for women's emancipation as one aspect of a broader struggle for universal freedom and equality; her stress on women's economic independence; and, her recognition of suffrage as a necessary tool for achieving emancipation. Without political power, Stanton realized, the oppressed would always remain oppressed; only votes would allow them to transform their social and political subjection into full equality as citizens.

Stanton's belief in equality between men and women and her unrelenting opposition to women's subjection are plainly articulated in her famous *Declaration of Sentiments* delivered at Seneca Falls in 1848. Brilliantly mimicking Jefferson's *Declaration of Independence*, Stanton simultaneously exposes the sexist nature of that document and stresses that its fundamental logic applies to women as well as to men: "We hold these truths to be self-evident: that all men and women are created equal; that they are endowed by their Creator with certain inalienable rights" including life, liberty, and the pursuit of happiness. Continuing the allusion in turning toward a consideration of women's subjection, she argues that human history is a record of "repeated injuries and usurpations on the part of man toward woman, having in direct object the establishment of an absolute tyranny over her." Only the equal recognition of women's rights could put an end to this tyranny.[59]

Stanton's profound understanding of the tyrannical nature of oppression, and her unequivocal faith in the emancipatory power of rights, aligned her not just with fellow feminists but also with key figures in the antislavery movement. Her activity in both causes undoubtedly shaped her conviction that women and slaves shared much in common; both suffered the degradations of bondage as members of subject classes.[60] This is why she saw emancipation for women and slaves as logically and politically inseparable. Both were "chained to the great Gibraltar-truth of human freedom and equality."[61] She notes in a speech supporting twin referenda in Kansas that would have extended the suffrage to blacks and to women, that such an extension required no special arguments; rather, it was justified according to the same principles that justified the extension of suffrage to all white men in the United States, that is, to the basic truth of universal human rights for all citizens.[62]

Stanton always championed social and economic independence as crucial to emancipation. She saw self-support for women as the only way to end their dependence on men and achieve equality in the public and private spheres.[63] In her later years Stanton advocated what she called "self-sovereignty" on the basis of the existential singularity of every human life, a condition which demanded women's "complete emancipation from all forms of bondage, of custom, dependence, [and] superstition."[64] But whatever the ultimate justification for emancipation, Stanton never wavered in her conviction that suffrage was the indispensable right for its achievement. Through votes women could effect changes in the laws that impacted all aspects of their lives.[65] She argued that "as long as man makes, interprets, and executes the laws for himself, he holds the power under any system"; recognition of women's political equality and their vote would "revolutionize" social relations, including marriage, and ensure women's full enjoyment of their rights.[66] Thus for Stanton, political emancipation is both required by and achieved through human rights, and it initiates more comprehensive social democratization.

It is useful to consider Stanton's thought alongside that of her friend and contemporary Frederick Douglass. Among the most eloquent and forceful spokesmen for emancipation of the slaves, Douglass was also an early champion of women's rights, seconding Stanton's motion for endorsing the *Declaration of Sentiments* at Seneca Falls. Douglass always accepted the sufficiency of the American promise of emancipation through rights and forcefully advocated extending this promise to everyone. In his many speeches he was successful in highlighting the hypocrisy of restricting rights to certain classes of persons. His powerful address on "The Meaning of July Fourth for the Negro" argues that the *Declaration of Independence* had already put the case for abolition as clearly as was possible. After noting that blacks work as doctors, ministers, engineers, account clerks, metal workers, in virtually all the professions, he says there can be no question that they are "men" and asks:

> Would you have me argue that man is entitled to liberty? that he is the rightful owner of his own body? You have already declared it. Must I argue the wrongfulness of slavery? Is that a question for Republicans? Is it to be settled by the rules of logic and argumentation, as a matter beset with great difficulty, involving a doubtful application of the

principle of justice, hard to be understood? How should I look to-day, in the presence of Americans, dividing, and subdividing a discourse, to show that men have a natural right to freedom? speaking of it relatively and positively, negatively and affirmatively. To do so, would be to make myself ridiculous, and to offer an insult to your understanding. There is not a man beneath the canopy of heaven that does not know that slavery is wrong for him.[67]

As this argument demonstrates, Douglass recognizes that the belief in one's own freedom logically entails recognition of the freedom of others as well.

After years of collaboration and friendship, Douglass and Stanton found themselves bitterly divided over the issue of "precedence" for manhood suffrage for emancipated blacks. The issue arose in connection with the proposed Fifteenth Amendment to the United States Constitution, which would (and eventually did) grant suffrage to recently freed black (male) slaves but not to women. At a meeting of the American Equal Rights Association, this issue split the assembly, with Stanton repeating some famously racist arguments in maintaining that if precedence had to be granted to anyone it should be women. Douglass countered by asserting the manifest urgency of votes for southern blacks, who lived under the constant threat of intimidation and even death at the hands of Klansmen and others, ignoring that many women lived under similar threats from husbands and fathers.* Aside from providing a salutary reminder against sanitizing or sanctifying our intellectual heroes, this debate highlights that the indivisibility of rights is crucial to their emancipatory function.† Lucy Stone seemed to recognize this in her remarks to the assembly:

> Mrs. Stanton will, of course, advocate the precedence for her sex, and Mr. Douglass will strive for the first position for his, and both are perhaps right. If it be true that the government derives its authority from the consent of the governed, we are safe in trusting that principle to the uttermost. If one has a right to say that you can not read and therefore can not vote, then it may be said that you are a woman and therefore can not vote. We are lost if we turn away from the middle principle and argue for one class.[68]

Dividing people into different classes with respect to the rights they enjoy subjects them to domination through the biases, prejudices, and classifications others inflict upon them.[69]

---

*Division over this issue ultimately split the Association, with Stanton and Susan B. Anthony leaving to form the National Woman Suffrage Association.
†I am grateful to Brooke Ackerly for making this aspect of the argument clear to me.

The emancipatory tradition of thinking about democratization often manifested in collective social movements in the nineteenth century, movements like the abolition and suffrage causes to which Stanton and Douglass were devoted. The British Chartists, with their appreciation of the interconnection between rights and emancipation, provide another example. The Chartists understood rights as a vital defense against the arbitrary power of the ruling classes and an instrument "to emancipate the working-class from wages-slavery."[70] As the radical Chartist leader Brontere O'Brien put it:

> universal suffrage is…a grand test of Radicalism.…Knaves will tell you that it is because you have no property that you are unrepresented. I tell you, on the contrary, that it is because you are unrepresented that you have no property.…Thus your poverty is the result not the cause of your being unrepresented.[71]

Such statements make eminently clear rights' role in achieving social and economic independence.

As well as establishing individuals' natural equality, the language of natural rights used by the Chartists "derived much of its polemical force from its critique of absolute or arbitrary restrictions imposed by one person on another person's freedom."[72] Democratic working class, agrarian, and populist movements in America voiced a similar critique in broadly similar terms, and theorists like J. S. Mill—for instance, in his essay on "The Subjection of Women"—understood social, economic, and political independence as a crucial guarantor of rights. When read in light of Mill's understanding of democracy's protective function, the interconnections among rights, democracy, and emancipation are plain. We might multiply examples of emancipatory democratic thinking at length; the point I want to emphasize here is that both in the works of leading theorists and in the struggles of social movements the connection between democracy, human rights, and emancipation was a powerful progressive theme.

The story does not end there, however; both the idea of human rights and the link between human rights and genuine emancipation came under severe challenge in the nineteenth century. Liberals in the Benthamite mold dismissed any notion of rights that went beyond strict positivism as metaphysical nonsense. Even more damaging for emancipatory politics, however, was Marx's critique of human rights in the famous "Essay on 'The Jewish Question.'" Marx differentiated political from what he called "human" emancipation, associating rights with the former and denigrating them for alienating man from citizen.[73] In Marx's view rights "legitimized the inequalities that were universal in modern societies"[74] by disguising them beneath the language of abstract political right. In particular Marx saw the right to private property as a major obstacle to genuine emancipation for workers; it not only reduced people to individualistic and egoistic beings but ensured that social control in the form of liberal-democratic politics would always remain subordinate to the power of capital. Thus for generations of Marxists natural or human rights were dismissed as bourgeois ideology.

It is not Marx's insistence on the social and economic aspects of human emancipation that marks his break with other radical democratic thinkers; he is distinguished rather by his rejection of human rights as a means to achieving this end. This is not the place to debate the merits and limitations of Marx's view; the crucial point is that thanks to this critique "the radical democratic tradition was ... deprived of its integral connections with working-class movements."[75] For much of the succeeding century democratic theory was bifurcated, with a more radical strand emphasizing social and economic empowerment through collective action while largely dismissing "bourgeois" political rights and a mainstream liberal variant emphasizing civil and political rights—their ties to social and economic rights ignored and their emancipatory logic suppressed—in defense of the status quo. Yet despite this acrimonious theoretical divorce, "progressive social change in the liberal democratic capitalist societies has followed the logic of collective opposition to oppression suggested by Marxian theory, while adopting the liberal language of rights and the goal of democratic empowerment."[76] In recent years, feminists, neorepublicans, critical theorists, left Rawlsians, progressive socialists, and other democrats have begun to reconsider the interdependence of rights, equality, and emancipation—the work of thinkers like Carole Pateman and Iris Marion Young provides some of the best examples. The central emancipatory insight remains attractive to contemporary proponents of democratization as well; as Nobel Prize winner Aung San Suu Kyi puts it,

> The basic requirement of a genuine democracy is that the people should be sufficiently empowered to be able to participate significantly in the governance of their country. The thirty articles of the Universal Declaration of Human Rights are aimed at such empowerment. Without these rights democratic institutions will be but empty shells incapable of reflecting the aspirations of the people and unable to withstand the encroachment of authoritarianism.[77]

Human Rights, Sovereignty, and Universality

In the emancipatory democratic tradition, emancipation is achieved *through* human rights. In this section I shall consider *why* human rights prove so effective as a language of democratic empowerment. Recall from part I that sovereignty imposes limits on freedom and equality, the principles on which popular sovereignty is based. The resulting tension between the universality of these principles and their limited realization was immediately exploited by opponents of the restrictive conception of citizenship entailed by popular sovereignty.*

The arguments used to exclude women and working people from the demos and from politics never convinced everyone; seventeenth- and eighteenth-century debates clearly show that who counted as a "man" when it came to claiming the rights of men was bitterly contested.[78] Arguments like those made by the Levellers at Putney, by Wollstonecraft, Paine, Stanton, Douglass, and others seized on the gap between the universality of the fundamental principles underlying popular rule and their limited realization in practice. They demonstrate how advocates of democratization have from the beginning used the language of universal rights to attack domination, oppression, and political exclusion and to extend rights, freedom, and equality to more and more people. Rights are a tool for breaking down barriers to democratic emancipation, and the thinkers surveyed here—in different ways and with different limitations—all employ the language of universal rights in arguing for a more thoroughgoing democratization of social relations and institutions. As Hoffman states, "it is the division between egalitarian form and unequal reality that provides every emancipatory movement with its case for change."[79]

We can usefully think about internal democratization as the struggle to eliminate the limits and boundaries that sovereignty imposes on freedom and equality inside the state. This set of internal restrictions has come under attack from the beginning, as democratizers set out to widen access to citizenship, redefine rights, and redraw the boundaries between public and private. The same logic that unseated kings and leveled medieval hierarchies gets turned toward dismantling limits on democracy itself. The argument from human rights proves effective against these limits because it appeals to the universal principles on which popular sovereignty arguments ultimately rest; arguments couched in the universal language of rights are difficult to deny or refute within the modern democratic idiom because that idiom is defined in part by the premise of freedom and equality for all. So we can usefully understand democratization within the state as an attack on sovereignty, or at least, on the limits that sovereignty places on freedom and equality.

Redescribing democratization in these terms allows us to see an important and revealing parallel. The universal logic that drives democratization and tears down sovereignty inside the state has a direct analogue outside the state,

---

*I am using citizenship here as a shorthand; much more was at issue; cf. Jean L. Cohen, "Changing Paradigms of Citizenship and the Exclusiveness of the Demos," *International Sociology* 14, no. 3 (1999).

where human rights also challenge the logic of sovereignty and the sovereign states system. As Bull puts it,

> carried to its logical extreme, the doctrine of human rights and duties under international law is subversive of the whole principle that mankind should be organized as a society of sovereign states. For, if the rights of each man can be asserted on the world political stage over and against the claims of his state, and his duties proclaimed irrespective of his position as a servant or a citizen of that state, then the position of the state as a body sovereign over its citizens, and entitled to command their obedience, has been subject to challenge, and the structure of the society of sovereign states has been placed in jeopardy.[80]

More recently, Rosenau has taken a similar position, arguing that "the emergence of human rights as a central issue of post-international politics testifies eloquently to the erosion of national sovereignty as an organizing principle."[81]

As these statements demonstrate, the logic of human rights runs counter to the logic of sovereignty outside as well as inside the state.* Again, this has to do with the universality of human rights claims. Sovereignty constructs political universality as a characteristic of states, while the universality of human rights is global and concerns all human persons as political subjects. Appeals to human rights inside the state further democratization because they establish greater freedom and equality for all—they push toward "universal" citizenship. Arguments for global human rights have not usually been conceived as arguments for democratization, however, in large part thanks to the widespread belief that politics, and thus democracy, is impossible outside the state.

Conclusion: Globalization and Emancipatory Democracy

In surveying the emancipatory tradition of democratic theory I have stressed that for some theorists and activists human rights have provided a language of democratic empowerment. Almost from the time arguments for natural

---

*Reus-Smit has recently challenged the conventional wisdom that sovereignty and human rights represent two mutually contradictory discourses, arguing that "the tensions that exist between sovereignty and human rights stem not from their separateness, from their status and parallel and antagonistic regimes…but from the inherently contradictory nature of the modern discourse of legitimate statehood, a discourse that seeks to justify territorial particularism on the grounds of ethical universalism"; Christian Reus-Smit, "Human Rights and the Social Construction of Sovereignty," *Review of International Studies* 27 (2001): 520. This is an important argument with which I am largely sympathetic. But there is a crucial difference between showing that sovereignty and human rights are caught up in a single, "inherently contradictory" *discourse* and showing that there is no tension between the two *concepts*. What, after all, makes the discourse contradictory if not the irreconcilable tension between sovereignty's territoriality and the universalism of human rights?

rights, freedom, and equality began, critics have appealed to the universal logic of human rights as a way of realizing freedom and equality for everyone. An egalitarian understanding of rights enables a more complete democratization of social relations and institutions—it enables emancipation. These arguments prove effective, I have shown, precisely because they appeal to norms of universal freedom and equality that theories constructed within the idiom of popular sovereignty cannot ignore. Outside the state, appeals to human rights also appeal to universal norms against sovereignty.

In concluding I want to push this analogy a little more. Human rights arguments enable democracy inside the state through appeals to universal freedom and equality; why shouldn't we understand global human rights arguments as potentially democratic in the same way? Traditionally we have thought of democracy as sovereign democracy, as requiring the state for its realization. Such a theory, as we saw earlier, is compatible with a universal commitment to human rights realized for everyone within sovereign states. I have shown, however, that neither the normative nor the empirical foundations of sovereign democracy can survive globalization; both communitarian and cosmopolitan arguments are flawed by their association with sovereignty. Initially sovereignty restricted the universal logic of democracy inside and outside the state: inside, by limiting citizenship; outside, by limiting self-determination to a handful of states. Democratization inside extends suffrage and citizenship to more and more people through appeals to universal human rights; similar appeals to human rights outside extend self-determination and sovereign statehood to more and more peoples.[82] The democratizing logic of human rights is nearly identical in both cases: their universality justifies extending freedom and equality to all, whether individuals or states. If this logic could be extended further, to do away with the very idea of sovereignty as a political condition for democracy among citizens or states, it would provide an attractive model for freedom and equality in the age of globalization.

By way of conclusion, I shall simply emphasize that I am not suggesting that this global conception is entailed by the arguments of the theorists discussed here. Nor, for that matter, would these theorists necessarily have embraced the egalitarian form of democratic emancipation as I have described it. I have only claimed that modern democracy has always included arguments couched in the emancipatory language of human rights; that arguments in this tradition are powerful and compelling because they appeal, against the logic of sovereignty, to universal freedom and equality; and, that the logic of human rights invites a similar critique of the sovereign states system. The global vision of democratic emancipation through human rights that I shall articulate and defend in the remainder of the book draws on this logic and tradition in *reinterpreting* democracy.

CHAPTER 7

Democracy as Human Rights

In this chapter I articulate and defend an approach to democracy that I call democracy as human rights (DHR). This approach reinterprets the core principles of freedom and equality on which modern arguments for democratization have long relied. Drawing on the insights of the emancipatory democratic tradition, DHR specifies the normative and institutional requirements of freedom and equality in the age of globalization; it promotes universal emancipation through securing human rights for all. I shall proceed by defining DHR and elaborating upon each element of its definition. Once its basic premises have been fully explained, I show how DHR implies a concern with governance that facilitates democracy's horizontal and vertical extension; that is, how it expands democracy's scope to encompass many domains of social relations and its reach from local through global systems of interaction. I consider several possible objections to this account of democracy and conclude with some brief reflections on the project of democratic reinterpretation.

The Normative Framework

DHR defines democracy as *the political commitment to universal emancipation through securing the equal enjoyment of fundamental human rights for everyone*. Let us consider each element of this definition in turn.

Democracy as a Political Commitment

What does it mean to describe democracy as a political commitment? It means that democracy is a choice, a creed people embrace based on reasons and passions. To be a democrat is to endorse democracy's core principles and their political implications. One might have a number of reasons for accepting democracy: it might be seen as the most fair system, the most just system, and so on. Emphasizing that democracy is a commitment does not suggest that it is irrational or inexplicable or indefensible—it is none of those things. Rather, this emphasis reflects a conviction that democracy cannot be deduced or demonstrated, it cannot be proven or disproved. Instead of seeking indubitable philosophical foundations for democracy we should defend and justify it by persuading people of its value.*

This position does not condemn us to a hopeless relativism regarding politics; on the contrary, democracy's strength lies in the moral and practical appeal of its principles, in the simple promise of freedom and equality for all. For those subject to prescriptive authority, the leveling effect of these two principles makes democracy quite attractive; antihierarchical and antiestablishment political activists, from Church reformers, Levellers, and feminists to gay men, lesbians, and opponents of the neoliberal economic order have all found democracy a potent weapon. But this emancipatory promise protects everyone more broadly, offering protection from unwarranted interference and domination that might limit individuals and communities in planning and pursuing their goals and values. Social cooperation requires the equal freedom of individuals so that cooperation does not become a form of domination of some over others. Put differently, freedom and equality for everyone dictate reciprocity.[1] My treating you as a free and equal being is the sole condition upon which I can expect you to treat me likewise. By treating you as less than free and equal, I acknowledge that I think valid reasons exist for denying the freedom and equality of others, even when they do not accept my reasons. Thus any justification I might give for treating you as other than a free, equal person would force me to accept your treating me in a similar manner. Only by treating everyone as free and equal can we all hope to get along.[2] In the following sections I outline a definition of democracy that builds on these ideas; I hope this fuller account demonstrates the broad appeal of DHR. My point here is simply to indicate how the political commitment to democracy can be supported without relying on dubious metaphysical foundations while still avoiding relativism. Implicit in my argument is the democratic conviction that no alternative ideology offers such an appealing or enduringly popular promise.

Framing and defending DHR as a political commitment suits its global aspirations; given the diversity of our world and the weighty burdens of judgment it seems highly unlikely that any metaphysical or deductive argument

---

*Put differently, the idea is less Rawls's "political not metaphysical," which concerns the *grounding* of principles, than Rorty's "ironism," standing for something despite our awareness of its irreducible contingency; see Richard Rorty, *Contingency, Irony, and Solidarity* (Cambridge, UK: Cambridge University Press, 1989); cf. John Rawls, *Political Liberalism* (New York: Columbia University Press, 1993).

for democracy will persuade everyone, making efforts to perfect rigorous philosophical defenses rather beside the point. Instead we should focus on arguments for democracy that showcase its broad appeal and increase its command of the widest possible acceptance. Of course, many critics argue that the doctrine of universal human rights, which in modified form provides the substance of DHR, reflects a particularly Western cultural experience or worldview, one mired in exactly the kind of foundationalist morass I am trying to circumvent. I have elsewhere addressed the cultural origins and universality of human rights and shall have more to say about this problem later in this chapter.[3] For now, let me emphasize that the definition of human rights offered here is not a deduction from metaphysical principles like autonomy, self-determination, natural law, the categorical imperative, or any others. It is a formal definition, one concerned with what human rights do and why we might find it appealing. Whether this account attracts support depends upon the substance and promise of the vision, not on the adequacy of its metaphysical premises or derivation.

Universal Emancipation

Emancipation   According to our definition, democracy is the political commitment to *universal emancipation*. Emancipation has long been associated with release from bondage or legal subjection, especially slavery. The term describes both a state of nonsubjection and the act of freeing or being released from subjection. Originally it denoted a struggle against legal and other constraints, including naked oppression; in the twentieth century it has also referred to struggles to achieve a new vision of society. This usage links emancipation with left or progressive politics and with efforts to remake the social, economic, and political order.[4] These two aspects of struggle and reform are closely related: creating a more just society is deeply tied up with eliminating structures of oppression and exclusion; that is, with emancipation from them.

Emancipation is often associated today with the republican ideal of nondomination. Republican thinkers maintain "that to live in a condition of dependence is in itself a source and a form of constraint,"[5] where by dependence they mean something like subjection to the will of another or to the right or power of arbitrary interference held by another.[6] Moreover, republicans seem to hold that any form of interference that might restrict freedom will also count as a form of domination, thus obviating the traditional liberal emphasis on noninterference or negative liberties.[7] But as Wall points out, a rule-following representative government might impose significant restrictions on its citizens in the name of the citizens' good—he mentions strict requirements concerning diet and exercise as examples. Even if these restrictions are legal, predictable, nonarbitrary, and publicly contestable, that is, not an instance of domination as republicans conceive it, they constitute a level of interference many would be unwilling to accept as consistent with freedom.[8] In talking about emancipation I follow the tradition surveyed in chapter 6. It proscribes both domination and unwarranted interference (as in the example above) as intrusions on human freedom; neither alone sufficiently describes the condition of nonsubjection essential to democracy.*

As this discussion suggests, and as my explication of fundamental rights below will make clear, DHR is not merely negative liberty or liberal rights repackaged, nor is it simply a rehash of republicanism. It requires a range of rights that, when institutionalized, eliminate subjection and guarantee emancipation. Importantly, these rights must include those guaranteeing social and economic independence.

Universality   Universality figures into DHR in two ways. The first is that democracy represents a "universal" value. Amartya Sen argues that we cannot judge the universality of a value by whether it commands the assent of everyone; if we did, universal values would be an empty category. "Rather, the claim of a universal value is that people anywhere may have reason to see it as valuable."[9] Democracy qualifies as a universal value in this sense, I contend, because of its historical and conceptual ties to emancipation. The promise of freedom and equality has motivated social struggles against subjection, with much success, for centuries. In developing DHR, I highlight this connection in hopes of making democracy's value clear and compelling. Calling democracy a universal value, then, does not imply that it is actually accepted by all, nor does it imply that people "must" find it acceptable, reasonable, nonrejectable, the subject of an overlapping consensus, or otherwise "valid" in any sense. The universality of democracy as a value does not concern its grounding; DHR is not a moral theory, in the usual sense of moral philosophy. Its morality lies in its account of "public ethical life."[10]

The second way universality relates to DHR concerns its scope. Democracy is meant to apply to everyone; it aspires to genuine inclusion.[11] This type of universality is more controversial and problematic. One problem concerns the political salience of difference. Frequently, difference serves as a pretext for justifying domination and subjection—consider the often-advanced arguments concerning the inferior or defective rationality of women, laborers, and people of color, which are used to justify their exclusion and subjection. Along with race, class, and gender, borders and boundaries provide another pretext for domination: whether internationally, in the normative foundations of political realism, or locally, in practices like zoning and district-based

*Hereafter I shall use the term *subjection* to refer to a condition of being dominated by or experiencing unwarranted interference from another or others.

school funding schemes.[12] Conceptual boundaries demarcating public and private spheres provide another familiar example.

Claims of universality often deny or ignore difference, implicating universality itself in the structures of subjection just described. Thanks to Marxists, feminists, and critical race theorists, we have a good idea of how universality works in this respect; unfortunately, I cannot begin to do justice to their rich and complex work here. The basic story, however, goes like this: theorists create categories—Man, Citizen, Reason, Equality—that are said to be universal and to include everyone while in fact they are open to and reflect only the interests and experiences of the powerful few. All those who do not qualify as rational men or equal citizens because of (usually "natural") differences are excluded, but their exclusion is hidden by the language of universality. Thus, universality masks particularity, constructing it as deviance from a purportedly general norm; this deviance then rationalizes exclusion and subjection precisely because it departs from the "universal." As these structures of exclusion come under attack, the inclusion of previously excluded individuals or classes of persons in the universal categories further accentuates the particularism that permeates the categories.

These failures of universalism have led many critics to abandon the idea altogether. Given the fact of irreducible pluralism, their argument goes, it is impossible to formulate any general precepts or categories that will be genuinely universal. This skepticism often sounds the retreat to a position enshrining incommensurable particularity as an epistemological principle.[13] The obvious difficulty with such a principle from a democratic perspective is that it offers no foundation for solidarity, no critical program or potential. It rules out the possibility of just those general or generalizable principles that might sustain democratic politics. Thankfully retreat is not the only available response to irreducible difference (in fact, it is a category mistake to conclude from biased definitions and deployments of concepts like Man and Citizen that universality is impossible or fraudulent). As Young argues, universality "in the sense of the participation and inclusion of everyone in moral and social life does not imply universality in the sense of the adoption of a general point of view that leaves behind particular affiliations, feelings, commitments, and desires."[14]

An alternative response to the ineliminability of difference would be to incorporate it into our understanding of what universality actually entails. In other words, instead of abandoning universality democrats must reconceptualize it. An epistemology grounded in difference commits democracy to an ongoing critique of how specific differences affect emancipation. Thus it focuses on actual instances of subjection; our understanding of what constitutes emancipation and what is necessary to achieve it cannot be based solely on abstract principles or deductive reasoning but must include the diverse experiences of real people.* Further, this epistemology will recognize that difference itself is a dynamic concept, "that specific differences may change from time to time and from place to place."[15] Difference is at once permanent and changing, always present but not always salient in the same ways.[16] This contingency of difference implies that a democratic conception of universality must also be contingent; what emancipation for everyone actually requires will vary with time and place as social conditions continually evolve. We can conceive democracy's task in such circumstances as the constant reassessment of when and where it is appropriate for difference to matter, and in what ways.

In DHR, the secure enjoyment of all fundamental human rights defines emancipation (I shall say more about this below). The contingent universality implied by a democratic epistemology of difference means that DHR's definitions of human rights will necessarily be provisional. Because DHR understands rights in terms of what they do, defining them will always be messy; the substance of rights must evolve along with changes in social conditions and in how difference matters. This is not to say that general statements and formulations of human rights are unimportant; on the contrary, the normative consensus they represent and the political and critical leverage they provide are invaluable. The point is rather that we must abandon the search for neat, general, and timeless definitions of rights. Human rights do real work in the real world, where theoretical elegance matters less than efficacy; our primary theoretical and practical concern is with guaranteeing emancipation. We value rights for what they do, for their political function, not for what they are.[17] We should always think of statements about rights as drafts, works in progress that will never be completed because the world in which they apply is always unfinished as well.

These epistemological observations indicate that participation is a methodological requirement of DHR. The critique of difference and universality that DHR demands can only occur through an open and ongoing process in which experiences of difference can be voiced and their implications assessed and debated. Critical theorists and deliberative democrats have exhaustively explored the conditions for open and inclusive dialogue, and I shall not reinvent that wheel here.[18] I shall simply note that DHR requires participation in three specific functions: the definition of rights, the creation of institutions designed to secure their enjoyment, and the critical evaluation of the rights and the institutions. This participatory aspect of DHR resonates with democratic theory's traditional emphasis on participation and with recent

---

*Booth suggests that "a universalist approach to human rights rests on the universality of human wrongs; the latter are universal social facts"; Booth, "Three Tyrannies," 63.

observations that any account of universal human rights must be provisional and contestable as well as participatory.[19] These requirements of DHR will become clearer as we consider the meaning and function of human rights in the theory.

Fundamental Human Rights

Fundamental human rights form the substantive core of DHR, which understands democracy as a political commitment to universal emancipation *through securing the equal enjoyment of fundamental human rights* for everyone. What are fundamental human rights, and what does it mean to secure them?

Fundamental Rights   In DHR rights are "fundamental" in two ways. First, they are fundamental in the sense of being *necessary to the goal of achieving emancipation.* Fundamental rights are the set of rights that together, when realized, constitute emancipation. When people are deprived of any of these rights, they are potentially subject to the arbitrary will or unwarranted inteference of another person, of the state, of a corporation, or of some other actor(s). Fundamental human rights, then, are all those rights necessary for protecting against potential subjection. *Potential* is an important modifier here: the threat of domination or the availability of means for interfering with people's rights themselves establish a state of subjection that democracy must not tolerate. On this view emancipation is defined by the secure enjoyment of all the fundamental human rights. This definition links democracy's commitment to freedom and equality for all with the specific guarantee of fundamental human rights, which become central to democracy's meaning. This definition also clarifies the relationship between emancipation and democratization in DHR.*

The second sense in which rights are fundamental in DHR concerns the relationship among them. I conceive the relationship among fundamental rights as one of indivisibility and interdependence: enjoyment of each of these rights is a necessary condition for the enjoyment of all other rights. Unless each fundamental right is secure, none is.[20] Unless all the fundamental rights are secure, emancipation is not assured. Shue's explication of the interdependence of basic rights can hardly be improved upon and is worth quoting at length. In this passage he demonstrates that a right to security is "basic."

---

*I do not mean to imply a division between some human rights that are fundamental and others that are not. In my view the term *human rights* should be restricted to those rights fundamental in the sense I am describing. Contemporary usage does not observe this restriction, however, describing as human rights some that are not fundamental in my sense; I therefore use the qualifier throughout.

No one can fully enjoy any right that is supposedly protected by society if someone can credibly threaten him or her with murder, rape, beating, etc., when he or she tries to enjoy the alleged right. Such threats to physical security are among the most serious and—in much of the world—the most widespread hindrances to the enjoyment of any right. If any right is to be exercised except at great risk, physical security must be protected. In the absence of physical security people are unable to use any other rights that society may be said to be protecting without being liable to encounter many of the worst dangers they would encounter if society were not protecting the rights.

A right to full physical security belongs, then, among the basic rights—not because the enjoyment of it would be more satisfying to someone who was also enjoying a full range of other rights, but because its absence would leave available extremely effective means for others, including the government, to interfere with or prevent the actual exercise of any other rights that were supposedly protected. Regardless of whether the enjoyment of physical security is also desirable for its own sake, it is desirable as part of the enjoyment of every other right.... Being physically secure is a necessary condition for the exercise of any other rights, and guaranteeing physical security must be part of guaranteeing anything else as a right.[21]

As Shue's argument makes clear, when a fundamental right is not secure, effective means remain available for others to interfere with or prevent one's exercise of one's other fundamental rights. (Failure to secure a right can also directly prevent the exercise of other rights, as with the right not to be killed.)

Importantly, the genuine universality of human rights is also crucial to their being secure. If any group or class of persons is denied rights, no one's rights are secure because similar arguments could be used to deny rights to other individuals in other groups or classes. So, for instance, racial profiling not only denies the rights of members of the group or class of persons singled out for heightened suspicion; it undermines everyone's rights by establishing the principle that in some cases, for some reasons, it is acceptable to curtail or violate some people's rights. The issue concerns social tolerance for limiting fundamental rights in the name of homeland security, defending public morals, or other such "emergencies," or for withholding rights from certain ethnic, gender, religious, or other minority groups. Where such tolerance exists, no one's rights are secure.*

The meaning of fundamental rights in DHR comprises both of these senses: substantively they are rights necessary to guarantee individuals against

---

*I am grateful to Brooke Ackerly for clarifying this point for me.

domination and oppression; epistemologically, they are universal and "basic" in Shue's sense, indivisible and interdependent. Some critics observe that Shue's definition is circular: unless at least one fundamental right is given, it is not clear how the definition gets off the ground; Shue attempts to sidestep this problem by beginning with what he calls an uncontroversial right, the right to security. But the dogged objector could counter that there simply are no uncontroversial rights. Even if we accept this objection, however, there is no difficulty for DHR: while interdependence and indivisibility are important features of rights, they are substantively anchored in democratic emancipation.

The fundamental human rights can be grouped into four clusters or closely related bundles of rights.* Rights relating to *liberty and security* concern the physical safety and integrity of individuals, their freedom of activity, choice, and movement, and their right to noninterference in matters of personal or intimate concern. Rights concerning *fairness* entitle people to equal and fair treatment under the law and in politics and society. These rights include guarantees concerning legal and criminal procedure (due process, an adequate defense, etc.) and equal access to public benefits and services. Rights essential to an *adequate standard of living* concern the satisfaction of basic needs and the conditions in which one works and lives. These rights include such things as food, shelter, affordable access to health care, a living wage, a decent education, choice in family and relationship status, and rights to enjoy and participate in one's culture. Finally, *civil and political rights* encompass rights and guarantees concerning one's social and political activities. These include freedom of assembly, conscience, and expression, a right to choose one's own lifestyle, and rights of access to and participation in government. Clearly a good deal of overlap exists among each of these clusters of rights. Nothing in the theory rides on the classification of any particular right or on the names assigned to the categories, however; grouping the rights into clusters simply makes it easier to talk about them in general terms.

We can briefly and usefully limn the argument for treating each of the clusters as fundamental; doing so clarifies what fundamental rights mean and illustrates how subjection is possible when fundamental rights are not secured. Rights to liberty and security are largely covered by Shue's example. Physical intimidation or force can be used effectively to thwart the enjoyment of other basic rights; similarly, without protection against unwarranted detention, individuals could be prevented from attending work, schools, places of worship, and political functions—obvious violations of other rights.

---

*The term is borrowed from Held, who uses it to denote bundles of rights associated with his seven sites of power in modern societies. The clusters I identify cut across Held's classification; see David Held, *Democracy and the Global Order: From the Modern State to Cosmopolitan Governance* (Stanford, CA: Stanford University Press, 1995).

Without the equality of protection guaranteed by rights to fairness, classes of persons can be arbitrarily singled out for mistreatment or denied the legal means through which to protect their other rights. If it is well known, for example, that the authorities will tolerate sexual harassment or the physical abuse of women, no woman can be said to enjoy any of her rights whose exercise might be checked by such violence. If the authorities commonly turn a blind eye to crimes against or harassment of members of particular racial or immigrant groups, members of those groups are similarly prevented from enjoying their other rights. So-called racial profiling puts the enjoyment of many rights—assembly, movement, fairness—under the cloud of arbitrary and potentially unwarranted interference; moreover, the implied threat of interference is a kind of social and psychological domination in itself. Lack of equal access to public services, or of guarantees against the arbitrary withdrawal or denial of such services, creates effective means for individuals or authorities to deprive individuals of their rights or to coerce them in other ways. A biased, corrupt, or capricious judicial system makes the enforcement of rights impossible.

Without guarantees of adequate income, nutrition, access to health care, and other core social rights, the exercise of many other rights becomes effectively impossible; children who have no food to eat cannot learn. Additionally, the threat of being without food, like other potential physical harms, can be used as a means of intimidation or coercion by criminal gangs, local officials, or whoever controls distributional channels. A threat to one's livelihood or health through loss of employment, whether made to squash labor activism or secure votes, is just as much a direct threat of physical harm as the threat of being beaten. More directly, the lack of basic shelter, nutrition, and health care directly precludes the enjoyment of rights such as political participation. (That basic needs benefits could become politicized or used as instruments of domination provides a strong argument for collapsing most social benefits schemes into a program of unconditional basic income.)* One other important right in this cluster, the right to education, is essential if for no other reason than that without at least a basic education it is difficult to understand one's rights and to navigate the system of social and legal institutions available to protect and promote them.

Finally, civil and political rights are fundamental because they provide the public means of assuring the accountability and responsibility of those who govern, including institutions and individuals responsible for secur-

---

*Unfortunately I cannot fully develop the democratic case for basic income here. For a good introduction to the debate, see Bruce Ackerman, Anne Alstott, and Philippe van Parijs, eds., *Redesigning Distribution: Basic Income and Stakeholder Grants as Cornerstones for an Egalitarian Capitalism, Real Utopias* (New York: Verso, 2005); Philippe van Parijs, *What's Wrong with a Free Lunch?* ed. Joshua Cohen and Joel Rogers (Boston: Beacon Press, 2001).

ing rights. Though far from perfect, rotation in office is the most effective mechanism yet devised for holding public officials accountable. Democratic government and rights of free speech, press, and assembly have proven the only reliable way to check the excesses of power and maintain the rule of law. In the words of Mill, "the rights and interests of every or any person are only secure from being disregarded when the person interested is himself able, and habitually disposed, to stand up for them."[22] Political and civil rights expressly guarantee people the capacity and institutional means to stand up for their rights. Shue puts a similar thought this way: "we have no reason to believe that it is possible to design non-participatory procedures that will guarantee that even basic rights are in substance respected."[23] This view tracks with the emancipatory democratic tradition's emphasis on rights to suffrage and to political participation in securing meaningful freedom and equality.

So far I have defined fundamental human rights analytically. These analytic definitions are not conclusive, however; DHR's epistemological commitment to universality requires participation in defining rights. It would obviously be impossible for me to engage in a participatory process of rights definition here; the role of theory is to make a preliminary determination of fundamental rights as a starting point for debate and discussion.* Instead, let me point out how this participatory process strengthens DHR by providing corrective mechanisms for defining rights. First, listening to and incorporating people's actual experiences of subjection helps to make certain that together the fundamental rights guarantee emancipation. Emancipation is realized through human rights, but the relationship is functional rather than definitional; that is, we know which are the fundamental human rights through learning what is needed to secure emancipation, not the other way round. This makes people's actual experience of unwarranted interference and domination crucial both to defining rights and to reforming institutions to better secure them. Second, paying close attention to actual experiences of subjection helps to ensure that rights and institutions keep pace with evolving social circumstances and with the changing salience of difference within those circumstances. For instance, being Arab or Muslim in the United States now matters more, and perhaps differently, than before September 11. Unless such changes are reflected back into our thinking about rights and the institutions that secure them, rights will not be able to do their required work. Both of these corrections help to make DHR more universal, and both reflect the fundamental right to political participation. They also remind us why fundamental human rights must be understood provisionally.

I want to stress that this participatory aspect of DHR does not mean that rights are whatever people decide they are. As in my discussion of rights

---

*I refer only to clusters of rights here, primarily due to space constraints, postponing the analytic work for another time.

clusters above, we can work out an account of fundamental rights analytically. The idea is that the adequacy, application, and interpretation of rights
must be informed by people's real experiences if the rights are actually to
ensure emancipation. This idea is like a participatory version of reflective
equilibrium: we begin with our account of fundamental rights and refine and
expand it as warranted by people's actual experiences. This way of thinking
about rights helps to address two troublesome problems in contemporary
human rights debates. First, there is a worry that human rights comprises
too much. In DHR fundamental rights, while expansively defined, are also
self-limiting (the requirements of emancipation providing the limits).

The second problem DHR helps to resolve concerns differing cultural
understandings of rights. Today most human rights theorists embrace
flexibility in interpreting rights in different cultures and contexts, a position even human rights universalists have accepted.[24] The difficulty is that
once we acknowledge that interpretations of rights can legitimately vary it
becomes hard to differentiate violations from alternative interpretations
without reintroducing the cultural or contextual criteria the flexibility was
meant to obviate in the first place. DHR offers a pragmatic approach to such
determinations grounded in the interdependence of fundamental rights; all
fundamental rights must be defined and realized in such a way that they
actually prevent threats to and interference with other fundamental rights.
Take, for example, the right to expression: certain limits on Nazi propaganda
in Germany or on incitement to ethnic violence in deeply divided societies
do not seem like unreasonable limits on expression; bans on opposition
political parties or on criticism of government policies that favor certain
ethnic groups while disadvantaging others clearly cross the line. But the
middle ground is, as usual, very muddy. DHR can differentiate between these
cases because the restrictions on Nazi propaganda do not limit expression
severely enough to jeopardize the enjoyment of other rights, while the ban
on opposition parties clearly does. Intermediate cases can be approached in
the same way, allowing variation in how rights are defined and realized while
ensuring that their basic function is unimpaired.

Fundamental rights do not guarantee people a life that is substantively
good or well-functioning or flourishing. Common objections to rights-based
theories include charges of inattention to the requirements of real freedom
and of excessive and destructive individualism. Charges of the first type typically associate rights with "negative" liberties and then show that negative
liberties alone cannot ensure that we are free to become who we would like
to be or really are.[25] In response I would reiterate that DHR is not open to
charges of this type; its emphasis on rights to an adequate standard of living, in particular, means that it goes well beyond the standard formulations
of "negative" rights, as it must do to ensure emancipation. That said, I fully

admit that DHR offers no substantive vision of the good life; one might enjoy all of one's fundamental rights and still not be happy or "free" in the positive sense invoked by Taylor and many others. I see this as an advantage of DHR; unlike theories that specify primary goods, essential human functions or capabilities, or accounts of flourishing,[26] DHR refrains from taking a position on what constitutes the good life. It specifies the conditions of emancipation—the social, economic, and political meaning of freedom and equality—that make the good life possible. What paths and projects individuals and communities pursue are limited by the obligations of reciprocal recognition of others as free and equal beings but not by any more substantive account of the good. This is an advantage because what constitutes a good or well-functioning life is invariably a value-laden and highly controversial question; to take a position on such questions seems to me beyond what a theory of democracy requires.

This leads directly to a second charge, that of an excessive individualism destructive of community.[27] DHR reflects a shared commitment to emancipation, a commitment reflected in social guarantees of fundamental rights (see next section). This shared democratic commitment constitutes a kind of community in itself, one in which political care is expressed through reciprocal recognition of others as free and equal, through social guarantees of rights, and through the concern those rights express for others.[28] Because DHR offers no substantive conception of the good life, it leaves open to people the chance to pursue, collectively or individually, those forms of it which they find most appealing. Of course, "some conceptions of rights are incompatible with some conceptions of community. . . . Likewise, some conceptions of community . . . do not recognize individuals as beings with rights. But not all conceptions of rights are at odds with all notions of community."[29] Democracy certainly rules out some kinds of group or community practices, but it is a mistake to create a false dichotomy between individuals and communities; neither can exist without the other. In fact, the point of rights is to provide for human interaction,[30] to define in part how community is possible. Individual rights sustain social relations;[31] they "establish modes of social relations of cooperation and commonality among individuals or groups of individuals."[32] Rights themselves, properly understood, form part of a broad and appealing definition of a democratic community and its values.[33]

Much more could be said to explore and respond to these worries about rights-based theories; I cannot say it here.* Rather, I shall stress again that DHR sees equal enjoyment of fundamental rights as vital to eliminating domination and subjection and thus to achieving emancipation; this aim

---

*Jones, *Rights*, chap. 8–9., offers among the most cogent and concise discussions of these questions; see also Gould, *Rethinking Democracy*.

restates the democratic promise of freedom and equality. What people do with their freedom should be left to them, individually and as members of communities, to decide. Democracy should not require people to do with their rights anything other than what they choose.

Securing a Right   DHR requires *securing the enjoyment* of rights for everyone so that everyone will be free from unwarranted interference and domination. What does it mean to secure a right? Simply, to provide social guarantees for its enjoyment. Shue argues that a social guarantee implies that correlative duties are associated with rights. As he puts it, "a right is ordinarily a justified demand that some other people make some arrangements so that one will still be able to enjoy the substance of the right even if—actually *especially* if—it is not within one's own power to arrange on one's own to enjoy the substance of the right. It is not enough," he adds, "that at the moment it happens that no one is violating the right."[34] He concludes that basic rights entail at least the following kinds of duties: to avoid depriving people of their basic rights, to aid the deprived, and to protect against deprivation by enforcing the first duty, and by designing institutions that minimize incentives to violate rights and help to promote their fulfillment.[35] An institutionally grounded approach to human rights is thus required by the duties correlated with basic rights and by the need for viable and effective social guarantees of those rights.[36]

For a right to be secured its actual enjoyment must be socially guaranteed against standard threats.[37] We can specify three conditions that must be part of such a social guarantee: first, the right in question must be generally recognized and understood. Second, the standard threats to the right must be identified and means of addressing those threats devised. Finally, those means must be incorporated into legal and social institutions which are adequately empowered to actually check the threats; they must be fully funded, must have the appropriate jurisdiction, and so on. Simply signing on to international conventions or placing laws on the books are not in themselves enough—though both can obviously be a great help. As Thomas Pogge argues, a guarantee of secure enjoyment of rights should be understood as a requirement that society be organized such that "all its members enjoy secure access to [those rights]. To be sure, no society can make the objects of all human rights absolutely secure. And making them as secure as possible would constitute a ludicrous drain on societal resources for what, at the margins, might be very minor benefits in security."[38] Pogge recommends security thresholds that would specify when rights can be considered sufficiently secure.[39] These thresholds can be determined probabilistically: the goal is not a perfect guarantee of physical security but a sufficiently low probability of violation.[40] (Chapter 8 is devoted to fleshing out such institutional requirements and to proposals for meeting them.)

The enjoyment of all of the fundamental human rights is a necessary condition of emancipation; is it also a sufficient condition? We can answer this question using counterfactuals, trying to think of situations in which an individual enjoys all of the fundamental human rights and is nonetheless susceptible to domination or interference. Let us consider three cases. First, we might imagine that some right or protection is necessary to secure emancipation but not recognized or secured. Strictly speaking, there could be no such right, since fundamental human rights are defined as those necessary to the enjoyment of all others. Unrecognized or insecure rights would represent a failure in the participatory mechanisms through which rights are identified and institutions modified to protect and enforce them. The failure of these mechanisms, however, does not invalidate the hypothesized connection between fundamental human rights and emancipation; it indicates a problem of institutional design.

A second case would involve individuals who enjoy all of their human rights under a benevolent dictator. This example highlights what it means to *secure* rights; when enjoyment of rights depends upon the good will or forbearance of another individual those rights are not secure according to our definition. The mere absence of violations is not enough; if rights can be revoked or trampled upon at the whim of an arbitrary ruler, they cannot be said to be guaranteed. Probabilistically, benevolent dictators are too likely to turn malevolent or to be succeeded by malevolent rulers. As Harrington so colorfully put it when describing the threat posed by arbitrary power, even the greatest bashaw in Constantinople was, under the seventeenth-century Turkish sultanate, merely a tenant of his head.[41] A third case concerns a people living in a democratic society characterized by respect for human rights and the rule of law and by the operation of institutions and procedures that protect fundamental rights against standard threats arising within that society. Still, these individuals might be injured, coerced, or deterred by the activities or decisions of international governance organizations (IGOs) or transnational corporations (TNCs). It seems we cannot describe this people as free from subjection. This example again highlights the demanding requirements for securing rights, though this time the issue concerns how we conceive threats. Assuming that the threats originating outside the society in question are not unforeseeable or unavoidable, it would again be wrong to describe this society as one in which the standard threats to human rights have been effectively addressed. Its members do not really enjoy their rights because foreseeable, avoidable threats are inadequately secured against. That some of the standard threats arise outside the jurisdiction of the state or community that has traditionally taken responsibility for guaranteeing rights might alter the social and political problematic but does not change the requirements of the social guarantee.

In the latter two cases, then, close examination reveals that fundamental rights are not in fact being protected or securely enjoyed. Ensuring that fundamental rights do create emancipation requires paying attention to their indivisibility and interdependence, to the adequacy of institutional guarantees, and to the full variety of threats. The last case highlights the special demands globalization and interdependence place on democratic theory and practice. In DHR, the requirement to guarantee rights against standard threats is not diminished or relaxed depending upon the threat's origins; concern with the effects of policies and activities is likewise unaffected by the location of the individuals threatened. Threats to fundamental human rights, whether posed by state governments, IGOs, TNCs, or any other actors must be neutralized by effective institutions; this imperative follows from the demands of a social guarantee of fundamental rights. Whether societies were ever sufficiently well-contained to insulate citizens' rights from "outside" threats is doubtful; today, however, there is no doubt. States cannot adequately secure citizens' rights in an interdependent world. This has important implications for DHR in the global context: the theory requires a range of governance and oversight institutions at the global level to secure human rights.[42] This case suggests how DHR will address the unique challenges globalization poses for democracy, challenges to which I return below.

Governance and Democratization

DHR understands democracy as *the political commitment to universal emancipation through securing the equal enjoyment of fundamental human rights for everyone.* Having explained and defended this theory of democracy, I now want to elaborate upon its political implications. Achieving emancipation for everyone implies a general concern with governance. In DHR, democratization means extending the social guarantees of fundamental human rights beyond the familiar limits of the "political" as it has traditionally been understood to encompass all those conceptual domains where governance occurs and where domination and interference are thus likely. The analytic and critical focus on governance facilitates democracy's "horizontal" and "vertical" extension—into the family, the workplace, and civil society and into the transnational sphere. But "democratization" on this view does not mean creating majoritarian representative institutions; it means creating secure institutional guarantees for human rights.

DHR and Governance

Governance is a more encompassing term than government. It is sometimes referred to as "government-like" activity, especially in the supranational domain, where authority is exercised in international or transnational space in the absence of sovereign governments.[43] Rosenau defines global governance as "a system of rule at all levels of human activity—from the family to the international organization—in which the pursuit of goals through the exercise of control has transnational repercussions."[44] Leaving aside the bits about levels and transnational repercussions (which simply gloss "global"), governance is a system of rule characterized by the goal-oriented exercise of control in any sphere of human activity. Governance is necessary whenever and wherever common ends and interests require cooperation and interaction among groups and individuals, but because rule involves the exercise of control, power, and coercion, it creates conditions in which domination and interference constitute significant dangers.

Focusing on governance proves particularly congenial to DHR's emancipatory project because governance encompasses systems of rule in diverse domains of human interaction. The commitment to securing emancipation means that DHR must be concerned with structures of unfreedom wherever they occur. Since governance occurs in all kinds of social activities and interactions, subjection often originates in domains outside the narrowly conceived public or political realm; indeed, the fundamental interdependence of social life makes compartmentalizing different systems of rule into separate spheres or domains arbitrary from a democratic point of view. DHR recognizes the analytic value of such conceptual boundaries but denies their political salience; it treats the fundamental interdependence of social life as a fact demanding an integrated and comprehensive account of democracy.

While subjection can occur wherever governance transpires, it takes different forms within different systems of rule, each requiring appropriate responses. In addition to providing an integrated and comprehensive response to interdependence, democracy must also provide a nuanced and flexible one. DHR is well-suited to this complex challenge for four reasons. First, it provides a single normative framework that integrates democratic responses across many domains of governance. Democracy requires that all governance activities respect and conform with the requirements of fundamental human rights. Democracy thus means the same thing in the state, the family, the economy, and in civil society; one standard of democratic legitimacy applies consistently in all domains. The second advantage of DHR is that this uniformity does not dictate institutional similarity across domains. DHR is concerned with an end, not with any particular institutional method or procedure for ensuring it. Of course, its means must be consistent with its aims, specifically with human rights themselves. Since DHR is ultimately defined by its political goal, emancipation, rather than by its method, it can accommodate a great deal of flexibility in the pursuit of that goal.

Third, DHR is flexible with respect to the territorial problems plaguing modern democratic theory; global interdependence is not fundamentally different from other forms of social interdependence, though it obviously has different manifestations and implications. Again, because DHR aims to achieve the promise of emancipation for everyone, it conceives the challenge posed by supranational systems of governance in the same way as local or national challenges. It prescribes the same remedy: governance must be subjected to institutional guarantees of fundamental rights. The institutional flexibility just described means that DHR need not pursue these guarantees in the same way at the global level that it might locally, even while pursuing the same ends. This combination of normative unity and institutional flexibility contributes to DHR's fourth advantage: its critical power. DHR aims to democratize structures of governance by identifying and eliminating subjection and securing against the threat of it. The commitment to freedom and equality implies a critique of subjection,[45] and DHR's integrated and comprehensive normative framework, institutional flexibility, and workable definition of emancipation (security of fundamental human rights) make this critical project feasible.

DHR makes no distinctions with respect to the origin of threats to rights or the physical or political location of the subjects of those threats (on this or that side of a border, in the public or the private sphere). The theory likewise makes no allowances based upon the systems of governance within which the threats arise (economic, social, familial). Democrats should be equally concerned with the activities of state and municipal governments, of IGOs and international financial institutions (IFIs), with TNCS, clubs, families, schools, churches, and corporations.

The "Horizontal" Extension of Democracy

Feminists and Marxists have offered powerful and parallel critiques of domination and oppression in traditionally "private" spheres of social relations and their impact on political equality among citizens.[46] By the "horizontal" extension of democracy I mean democratization of the economy, the family, and the associational life of civil society. Civil society comprises many domains of human interaction structured by governance but not traditionally considered appropriate sites for democracy. DHR tracks with many contemporary democratic theories in seeking greater democracy in these traditionally "private" realms. Typical approaches to democratizing civil society include enhancing deliberation, establishing economic or "workplace" democracy, promoting policies and programs to eliminate sex and gender subjection, and broadly revitalizing associational life. The merits of such reforms are by now familiar: greater inclusion, greater participation, greater collective control over decision making, and so forth. All are commendable goals, and all would certainly enhance democracy. Yet for all their benefits such schemes typically encounter three objections: they violate property rights, they invite majority tyranny by expanding public control over private concerns, and they make unrealistic demands on the time and other resources of citizens. This is not the place to consider the merits of these charges or the numerous responses that have been offered to them; here I shall use them to highlight certain advantages of DHR in extending democracy horizontally.

With respect to property rights we can begin by describing that a right to security of one's personal possessions is a fundamental right. Without such a right things like clothing, automobiles, telephones, and any number of items could be controlled, rationed, or confiscated in highly coercive ways destructive of other fundamental rights. The right to personal possessions is also interdependent with other rights—to an adequate standard of living, to safe long-term shelter, to adequate health care and nutrition, to a decent education, and so on. The real question for DHR is whether this right shields personal possessions, in the form of wealth and income, from tax, and whether it protects private, nondemocratic forms of corporate governance. It does not,[47] making it quite different from the right to private property apotheosized by libertarians and neoliberal capitalists. So long as tax is fair, predictable, nonarbitrary and general in its application, and nonconfiscatory (in relation to an adequate standard of living), it is properly a political question. As for corporate governance, like all other forms of governance it must include institutional safeguards for all fundamental rights, including rights to participation. DHR supports (and might require) market-based economic systems, and it is not opposed to large accumulations of wealth. Again, as Paine put it, "I care not how affluent some may be, provided that none be miserable in consequence of it";[48] in the terms I have been using, wealth and private ownership of the means of production are allowed insofar as they do not interfere with anyone's emancipation.

DHR survives concerns about intrusive majoritarianism because it does not call for majoritarian solutions in democratizing civil society. As I specified above, different forms of governance will generate different threats to emancipation and require different institutional responses. Instituting elections in families might lead prudent parents to adopt careful family planning practices, but it is not clear that it would lead to better compliance with human rights or to greater collective or individual good for the members of the family. That said, democrats cannot be indifferent to subjection within families; how best to guarantee the rights of all family members, including children, requires careful thought.* Similarly, there are good reasons to allow

---

*Children pose a special problem because they depend upon their parents, but this dependence is not (ideally) a form of *subjection*. From a very young age most children are capable of participating in governing themselves; I can see no reason why any of their human rights should be suspended. How these rights should be enforced is a question for another time. Similarly difficult questions arise concerning the rights of infirm elderly persons.

corporations autonomy from government control, but that autonomy cannot include violating the fundamental rights of employees, including their right to political participation. Still, that right need not mean (nor would it preclude) popular management or collective ownership of firms. DHR permits institutional flexibility in pursuit of a clear aim: securing emancipation. Participation is central to this aim, but it can take many forms.

This leads directly to the third concern regarding the demands democracy makes on people. One aspect of this concern is that inequalities in time and resources, including education, affect people's ability to be heard and to influence outcomes. DHR's response to this problem includes the guarantees of an adequate standard of living, including education, for all citizens. It also includes institutions and procedures that recognize and account for the differences that will nonetheless remain in people's ability to express themselves.[49] Another aspect of the concern about democracy's demands is that some proposals for democratizing the disparate domains of social life seem to require inordinate individual sacrifices. Specifically, the idea that all people should deliberate on every issue that significantly affects them—participating in workplaces, local assemblies, and civic associations as well as in higher levels of democratic government—imposes unrealistic burdens on people's time, resources, and enthusiasm for politics. The deliberative and participatory ideals, however noble and appealing, are impossible in practice.

They are also sometimes obnoxious. People have many legitimate personal worries and priorities that consume their time, as well as the right to participate (or not) as they choose. DHR requires that effective democratic institutions be available for people to use when they want or need them. But using them should not be required, nor should the agreement, real or in principle, of everyone affected be the standard of democratic legitimacy. Such a standard is unrealistic and reflects the lingering influence of a sovereign commitment to collective autonomy that is incoherent outside small, taken-for-granted associations. Representative political institutions are required in DHR because they are necessary for emancipation. Effective guarantees for rights do require deliberative and participatory norms and mechanisms within democratic forums and assemblies. But this requirement has to be detached from ethical accounts requiring everyone to participate all the time. Penetrating critiques of liberal democracy and its limits have obscured one of the eighteenth century's great political discoveries: electoral institutions, *properly designed, monitored, and constrained,* can relieve people of much of the burden of everyday politics while still protecting their freedom and equality.

I am fearful of being misunderstood here. My criticism is not of deliberative or participatory norms and procedures; DHR relies on both. My criticism pertains rather to democratic accounts of legitimacy that are grounded in the deliberation or participation of all affected. Effective participation certainly means more than pulling a lever every few years and paying attention in moments of constitutional crisis; it probably also means less than what many deliberative and participatory democrats seem to desire. This middle ground seems to be the ground where actual politics happens. The streets are not full of people demanding more deliberation on principle. When they are full, it is typically of people expressing their outrage about specific issues or policies, demanding that their rights be recognized, or simply insisting that their votes be counted.

The "Vertical" Extension of Democracy: Globalization

The horizontal extension of democracy through DHR includes institutionalizing social guarantees for fundamental rights in all domains where governance occurs. Similarly, DIIR requires institutional guarantees in governance systems associated with globalization. By the "vertical" extension of democracy I simply mean its extension into these supranational domains. DHR has three novel and important implications with respect to globalization. The first concerns supranational governance. Cosmopolitan theories see the need for global democracy as a function of increasing interdependence and of the resulting deficits and disjunctures. Their response is to subject global politics to traditional popular controls through extending traditional democratic institutions. DHR conceives global democracy differently, as entailed by the general requirement to democratize all structures or systems of governance. Thus nothing in DHR hinges on arguments about how advanced, unprecedented, or irreversible globalization is; everything hinges instead on realizing universal freedom and equality through institutional guarantees of human rights.

The second implication relates to borders. Borders and boundaries of various kinds serve many important and desirable functions: among many other things, they facilitate administration, define the physical places and conceptual domains in which specific needs and concerns crystallize, and make communal political action possible. The problem borders pose for democracy is that they often create and rationalize asymmetrical enjoyment of and concern for rights. These asymmetries correspond with the nature of the boundaries themselves: ethnic and national boundaries, in different ways, can grant privileges to some and exclude or even dehumanize others; boundaries between public and private can shield structures of domestic and economic oppression from democratic scrutiny. Modern democratic theory encounters problems with globalization—as it encounters problems with the democratization of civil society—because sovereignty's conceptual framework limits its scope and reach in these areas. DHR acknowledges that borders, including borders among political units, cannot and need not be eliminated. They must, however, be *democratized*; that is, prevented from affecting people's secure enjoyment of fundamental rights.

This requirement establishes demanding criteria for the validity of borders and boundaries: no borders can justify or excuse differences in the secure realization of everyone's fundamental rights. No territory, no conceptual domain, no group, class, or category, is exempt from democracy's requirements. On this view familiar elements of modern democracy, such as territorial jurisdiction and exclusive citizenship, must be thoroughly reconsidered. We must think hard about whether they remain the best ways of promoting the goal of democratic emancipation. Similarly, our acceptance that different norms govern social activity and interaction in the home or the workplace, on this side of the river or that one, on this continent or another, becomes straightforwardly invalid. Among the limits DHR will have to overcome are the psychological limits that confine our conceptions of democracy to our country, to fellow citizens, to the public sphere, to "politics." Realizing the theory will require nothing short of a transformation of political culture (a prospect I consider in more depth in chapter 9). Note that DHR does not require the elimination of boundaries or differences; all sorts of boundaries sustain cultures, religions, and traditions of all kinds. Such boundaries are in themselves neither democratic nor undemocratic; a lot hinges on how they matter and for whom. DHR is not hostile to such differences or their preservation, and it takes no principled position on what reasons should justify political boundaries.[50] It does, however, take a principled position in insisting that such boundaries cannot interfere with human emancipation.

The third important implication of DHR with respect to globalization is, once again, its institutional flexibility.* Because human rights can be secured in various ways, the institutional requirements of democracy at the supranational level need not be identical with those with which we are familiar in the democratic state, nor must they be uniform across all systems of governance. This flexibility rescues DHR from a certain rigid, "one-size-fits-all" quality in cosmopolitan schemes. Consider the prospect of electing members to the IMF's Executive Board; the influence of power and money, already decried by students of democracy everywhere, could only be more corrosive in areas where arcane policy intersects with high financial stakes. It is hard to see how a global parliament could exercise much oversight over the IMF or other IFIs, again because of the expertise involved in running them as well as the deep divisions among the world's people over how they should be run. Moreover, as complaints about the EU's democratic deficit remind us, even democratic and accountable institutions do not automatically

---

*I present specific institutional proposals in the next chapter.

generate confidence or legitimacy.* The point is neither to criticize global parliaments nor to give up on democratizing IFIs; it is rather to stress that supranational democracy need not come in the package of global elections and parliaments. Flexible and innovative institutions are likely to be more effective at securing rights and enhancing freedom than traditional democratic models in this domain. Supranational politics is not just national politics writ large; its dynamics and its challenges are different and require a differentiated approach to democratization.

DHR and Democratization

In DHR the same logic governs the horizontal and vertical extensions of democracy: the pursuit of emancipation for all through securing fundamental human rights. Conceptually there is no difference between democracy in the family, the economy, and supranational domains, although institutionally the differences will be significant. Seeing this uniformity clarifies the close connection between securing fundamental human rights and dismantling structures of oppression. It lets us understand democratization as the elimination of and protection against structures of subjection through extending guarantees of fundamental rights. This broad understanding of democratization encompasses historical struggles for rights and inclusion as well as contemporary projects for global democracy. Both represent efforts to use the logic of rights, freedom, and equality to critique and ultimately dismantle structures of subjection; both use democracy's universal promise to push it beyond its traditional limits. In this respect DHR is firmly within the emancipatory democratic tradition: it is a theory of democratization.

Four Objections

Before concluding, I want to consider several objections I have not had occasion to address directly in the preceding account. The first involves the charge of cultural and masculine bias in human rights theories.† DHR purports to be independent of metaphysical foundations, but isn't the very idea of human rights linked to particular gender and cultural biases and to a Western worldview?

---

*This is true even though, as Moravcsik argues, its institutions are as "democratic" as those of any democratic state; see Andrew Moravcsik, "In Defence of the 'Democratic Deficit': Reassessing Legitimacy in the European Union," *Journal of Common Market Studies* 40, no. 4 (2002).

†On the cultural charge, see Joanne R. Bauer and Daniel A. Bell, eds., *The East Asian Challenge for Human Rights* (Cambridge, UK: Cambridge University Press, 1999); Adamantia Pollis and Peter Schwab, eds., *Human Rights: Cultural and Ideological Perspectives* (New York: Praeger, 1979); on feminist concerns, see Hilary Charlesworth, "What Are "Women's International Human Rights"?" in *Human Rights of Women: National and International Perspectives*, ed. Rebecca J. Cook (Philadelphia: University of Pennsylvania Press, 1994); Elizabeth Kiss, "Alchemy or Fool's Gold? Assessing Feminist Doubts About Rights," *Dissent* 42 (1995).

There are two issues here, which I can only address briefly. The first concerns the origins of human rights, which, like democracy, developed historically in the West. Understanding the origins of human rights helps us understand their historical biases and limits. It is not clear, however, that this history reflects any deep cultural differences in values.[51] Moreover, while the question of origins is relevant to our practical understanding of rights, it is not determinative of questions about their validity. If the claim that human rights rely indirectly on a cultural (and perhaps by extension metaphysical) foundation is simply a call for rejecting the concept of rights as invalid (as opposed to rejecting systems or definitions of rights as flawed, because of their cultural biases), it is an instance of the organic fallacy. Human rights have been linked historically to struggles for freedom and equality all over the world, and they remain an indispensable vocabulary of democratic emancipation. Human rights' effectiveness is not a philosophical question; it is a matter of our allegiance to them as a way of being in society.[52] As Bobbio puts it, "it is not a matter of knowing which and how many of those rights there are, what their nature is and on what foundation they are based, whether they are natural or historical, absolute or relative; it is a question of finding the surest method of guaranteeing rights and preventing their continuing violation."[53]

The claim of indirect cultural and metaphysical foundations might, however, be a claim that unspecified others do not want human rights and democracy and that a theory like DHR thus entails "imposing" them. If this is an empirical claim about what people around the world want, the evidence is hardly conclusive. While authoritarian rulers and some socially privileged elites (along with some Western academics) often decry "Western" human rights and democracy, many more people invoke them in their struggles against domination and oppression.[54] One need only think of student pro- testers in China and Iran, of the new South Africa, of Burmese democracy movements or of indigenous and peasants' rights groups in Latin America to see the global appeal of human rights and democracy. I would submit that, given the choice, most people would like to enjoy democracy and human rights; DHR emphasizes participation in defining rights and flexibility in their implementation, so that people might do so on their own terms.

If the claim about "imposing" values is that not everyone accepts or en- dorses them, DHR already recognizes as much in describing democracy as a political commitment, really, a fighting creed. As to whether people should be "forced" to accept DHR, I am not sure what the question means. DHR recognizes and respects everyone's right to believe what they want, but it cannot respect the substance of those beliefs if they conflict with democracy. Democracy cannot be compatible with or allow everything; no ideology can. So does DHR force people to change their beliefs? No. (How would it?)

Does it, as a political system, constrain them when they violate the rights of others? Of course it does. Politics is about, among other things, order; democracy requires rules, power, and coercion, just like any other political system. It differs from other political systems, among other ways, in designing and constraining rules, power, and coercion so that so far as possible they promote (or do not hinder) freedom and equality and minimize subjection. Democracy is, at a minimum, less oppressive than the alternatives; so long as we think people must live under rules, imposing democracy is at least less oppressive than imposing any other system.*

The second objection concerns what polity or political community has this commitment to democracy. This is not the individualism charge I addressed above (i.e., the charge that rights undermine community). Rather, the question concerns what we might call a communitarian concern with who will support democracy, who will bear its burdens and obligations. The answer is that democratic community is self-generating; it comprises all those people who express the commitment to democracy in their treatment of others as free and equal. It is a community grounded in respect, recognition, and reciprocity. This community exists wherever social activity and interaction are *democratic*. DHR avoids the bootstrapping problem discussed in connection with cosmopolitan theories in chapter 5 because it does not rely on claims about the legitimacy of decision-making authority in any particular community. While DHR's institutions, like any systems of rule, must have some territorial extension, the universality of fundamental human rights makes the particular configuration of democratic institutions relatively inconsequential. DHR does not recognize culturally, ethnically, nationally, or religiously constituted communities as democratic subjects in themselves. The democratic community is not fixed or exclusive of other commitments such as culture or religion; nor are such commitments necessarily considered undemocratic. DHR does depend on political solidarity, but this must not be treated as a historical artifact but rather as something called forth by political institutions.[55]

The democratic community is manifest in laws, institutions, traditions, social practices, and social movements. It grows as people become convinced of democracy's value. DHR usefully reinforces a shared emancipatory vocabulary for achieving democracy while invigorating human rights discourse with an explicit and active *political* agenda. As a practical matter, democrats can deepen the commitment where it already exists by showing people how it is implicit in their beliefs and practices. Democrats can spread the commitment by persuading people of its value and appeal and by using

*In light of the American invasion of Iraq and its present justification on the grounds of "democratizing" that country, I must clarify that this discussion has nothing to do with "imposing" democracy by force: the notion strikes me as wrong and wrongheaded.

democratic principles to call power to account. To ask what community has the commitment to democracy is to assume that communities precede democracy, choose it. The real history of democratization suggests otherwise. Democracy has always been advanced in fits and starts by people and movements seeking greater freedom and equality. It has always advanced through struggle, usually against improbable odds. It has always been generative of new understandings of community.

The third objection concerns the claim that democracy and human rights are not fully compatible. As Michael Freeman agues, democracy is "the will of the people" and we can only overlook the tension between democracy and human rights by assuming that the people always will human rights; history, however, proves otherwise.[56] This theoretical worry has a publicly influential advocate in Fareed Zakaria, whose widely discussed *Foreign Affairs* article decried "the rise of illiberal democracy"; that is, democracies in which majorities elect racists, fascists, separatists, and opponents of peace and justice in free and fair elections.[57] For Zakaria, democracy simply means free and fair elections; in his view such elections frequently result in governments that violate the rights and liberties of (some of) their citizens. Given a choice between free and fair elections and protection of rights and liberties, Zakaria cautions that we should perhaps prefer the latter and reckon with the potential ineluctability of the trade-off.[58]

This objection, in various forms, applies not only to DHR but to all democratic theories; it is in essence the "liberal" objection, one liberal democrats sometimes use to justify not only constitutional guarantees of rights but also a range of other limitations on the scope of democratic rule. Of course, democrats should be concerned when populist or plebiscitary regimes trample human rights, but these regimes only appear "democratic" in the objection because democracy is reduced to elections and nothing more. The argumentative strategy is to strip democracy of everything appealing—including its moral and political foundations, reducing it to a political method—and then to show that this method does not guarantee desirable results. It is the same strategy elitist democratic theorists have employed for decades.[59] The real question, then, is whether the forensic move, defining democracy solely in terms of elections and opposing it to human rights, is valid and makes sense.

As Freeman points out, consideration of this issue requires that we revisit the moral and political foundations of majority rule.[60] Sheldon Leader, in a different context, helpfully differentiates between oligarchic and democratic justifications for majority rule. In oligarchic conceptions, the majority rules because of some inherent feature of that group.[61] This feature, I would argue, is its *sovereignty*. In sovereign democracy the sovereign rules by right; only on this understanding of majority rule can we imagine that whatever the people will is law (though even here popular rule serves the rights and interests of the citizens). Because DHR rejects sovereignty as a premise for democratic rule, this objection loses force; besides, no friend of democracy has ever seriously maintained that democracy is whatever a majority decides.[62] On the democratic or egalitarian justification of majority rule, Leader argues,

> we cannot take a statement of majority will, even a well-considered and fully-informed statement which reflects the view of far more than a bare majority, as decisive of our understanding of the dimensions of a fundamental right. . . . We must instead always match the majority's view against the standards by which it was given the mandate to rule. . . .[63]

In DHR the standards conveying the mandate to rule are the freedom and equality of all people. Thus majority decisions that violate these principles are self-contradictory and self-annulling.[64] Of course, theoretical arguments cannot prevent democracies from violating human rights; but no government conforms perfectly in practice with the principles on which it is justified. Empirical exceptions do not disprove normative theories. What *would* count against democratic theory would be evidence that democracies are *more likely* to violate human rights than other types of regime. It turns out that the opposite is the case; democracies do better at protecting human rights than any other type of regime.

The final objection I shall consider is that DHR extends democracy too far, encroaching on areas properly within the purview of justice. I cannot fully engage this question here, but in explaining why not I hope I shall answer the objection sufficiently. First let me say that I see the domain of justice as broader than the domain of democracy: justice includes questions about my duties and obligations to friends, lovers, colleagues, and others that fall outside the scope of democratic theory. That said, if we are concerned with social institutions and relationships, with politics, then it is not at all clear that "justice" is a superior conceptual frame to "democracy." The objection against DHR only makes sense if one presumes the priority of justice to democracy in politics; it is precisely this presumption, however, that is the real point at issue. Ian Shapiro has argued that "a suitably developed account of democracy affords the most attractive political basis for ordering social relationships justly."[65] Moreover, it is impossible to imagine a just society today without also imagining that it is, among other things, democratic. These points are hardly conclusive, but they indicate that the objection assumes what it ought to demonstrate. Once we abandon the presumption that justice is the first virtue of social institutions, a set of largely neglected questions opens up. While I cannot pursue those questions here, I hope my brief remarks testify to their importance. In concluding I will simply observe that one apparent advantage of a democratic approach for thinking about global social relations is its political, as opposed to metaphysical, anchor.

Conclusion: DHR and Democracy

We saw in earlier chapters that modern democracy has long been entangled with the discourse of sovereignty. Modern democratic theory looks the way it does thanks in large part to this long and complex relationship, which imposed a strange particularlism on its universal principles. I have attempted to reconstruct democratic theory by returning to these core principles, universal freedom and equality, and working out what they might prescribe once we strip them of their contingent historical association with sovereignty. The result is what I have called democracy as human rights.

DHR emphasizes universal emancipation through securing fundamental human rights for everyone. This locates it squarely within the emancipatory democratic tradition. It departs significantly from conventional democratic concerns about the rights and privileges of citizens and from traditional democratic procedures and institutions bound by territorial limits. It is not an enlightening criticism, however, to point out that DHR does not look like modern democracy. Any theoretical reconstruction would be counted a failure if judged by its similarity to the theory it set out to reconstruct. Besides, though DHR is unfamiliar and perhaps unusual, it is nonetheless consistent with a particular way of thinking about the connections among rights, freedom, equality, and emancipation in the democratic tradition. I am not claiming that DHR is the only correct or possible interpretation of what universal freedom and equality mean or require; I do think, however, that it provides a plausible and appealing interpretation of what these principles might mean and require.

The question then arises, what role is left for traditional democratic politics? The emphasis on human rights and on the variety of ways in which they might be realized and secured might seem to leave only a residual role for familiar institutions and popular politics. On the contrary, while collective decision making becomes integrated into a more comprehensive democratic framework, it remains crucially important. Collectively binding decisions are the stuff of politics, and while globalization raises profound questions about where such decisions should be taken, they must be taken somewhere.* DHR does transform the justification for representative political institutions, however. In modern democracy, popular rule within a particular territory is an artifact of sovereignty; in DHR, representative institutions are justified by

---

*I discuss the "where" problem further in the next chapter.

their role in securing fundamental rights. This justification, familiar in "protective" theories of democracy, captures the instrumental and constructive value of democratic institutions in combating oppression and formulating needs and interests.

DHR also constrains parliamentary politics in two ways: it sets an affirmative agenda for social guarantees of fundamental rights, and it negatively limits parliamentary action where such action would directly violate fundamental rights or leave them exposed to violation in foreseeable and avoidable ways. Beyond that, the human rights agenda elucidated here, while certainly robust and demanding, is not a comprehensive political program. It does not supply ready answers to many important political questions, including questions about how best to secure fundamental rights against standard threats and about what political goals to pursue beyond the protection of rights. That is not to say it is unconcerned with such questions; rather, it leaves them to the democratic political process. DHR does not exhaust popular politics or resolve conflict; it specifies the democratic core of politics and provides a framework in which political problems can be addressed and conflicts worked out. Indeed, DHR allows more room for politics—for conflict, disagreement, competing policy initiatives, and the like—than most contemporary theories of democracy based in accounts of deliberation, public reason, or discursive legitimacy, theories that somehow seem always to supply pat answers to all the difficult questions.

Undertaking a reinterpretation of democracy might seem hubristic, but reinterpretation is an important, if frequently overlooked, feature of democracy's historical development. Democracy has always been a protean concept, one whose meaning was constantly contested; Markoff observes that in the eighteenth century it was hardly clear what democracy's institutional form and requirements were; it was mainly an oppositional stance toward monarchy and inherited forms of privilege.[66] Since that time the meaning or interpretation of democracy has been constantly evolving; it "has never been a finished thing."[67] As globalization accelerates and intensifies, Markoff argues that "democracy must be reinvented if it is to continue meaningfully—as it always has been."[68] DHR is a contribution to the contemporary debate about reinvention.

CHAPTER 8

Institutionalizing Democracy
as Human Rights

Democratic theorists often try to give some account of how our normative recommendations might translate into political practice, typically through institutional proposals designed to highlight the distinctive features of those recommendations. Inevitably, however, institutional proposals are open to practical objections that can easily swamp the ideas they embody; this is especially so when those ideas are unorthodox. Why, then, risk making such proposals in the first place? I see three good reasons: to elaborate upon and refine the normative recommendations, to probe their political feasibility, and to spark further reflection about how best to reform democratic political practice. So while institutional proposals must be judged in light of their practical appeal, they should also be read as a continuation and elaboration of our normative reflections.

DHR requires that fundamental rights be secured against standard threats. As we have seen, securing rights entails providing institutional guarantees for their enjoyment. In this chapter I translate this general requirement into three specific ones and outline proposals for institutions to satisfy each. The following proposals represent preliminary sketches, not finished blueprints; they are intended to stimulate our "institutional imagination" regarding what democracy requires and how its requirements might be realized. Indeed, one aim of this exercise is "to discover and imagine democratic institutions that are at once more participatory and effective than the familiar configuration of political representation and bureaucratic administration."[1] On the terms established by DHR, the efficacy of institutions must be judged by the entire system's performance in achieving emancipation.

I begin by showing that to secure fundamental rights three types of institution are necessary: representative political institutions; direct functional institutions, such as schools, police, and social welfare agencies whose work contributes directly to implementing specific rights; and, indirect functional institutions, which are charged with policy, oversight, and enforcement functions. DHR also requires that all governance agencies adopt internal rules and procedures consistent with respect for fundamental human rights; these are fairly straightforward requirements and I shall not elaborate on them here. After briefly considering "standard threats," I discuss each of these three institutional types in turn, focusing primarily on the third. Indirect functional institutions are in many respects the most novel and most distinctive of DHR, and it is largely through them that the theory addresses issues associated with globalization. This focus therefore highlights DHR's strength and appeal relative to other "global" theories of democracy. In emphasizing this third type of institution I do not mean to diminish the importance of the other two, however; DHR depends on all of them in securing human rights.

Institutions and Standard Threats

In the previous chapter I showed that securing a right involves three steps: recognizing the right, identifying standard threats to it, and then creating institutional guarantees against those threats. Having defined fundamental human rights—or rather, having specified the process through which they are defined and redefined—it remains to consider briefly what constitutes a "standard threat" before undertaking our institutional analysis.

Standard threats are simply those that are foreseeable and preventable at an acceptable cost. This category includes recurring threats as well as those that should reasonably be anticipated. There is little sense in striving for an analytically impregnable definition of standard threats; the idea conveys an affirmative duty to take past experience and probable consequences into account in designing institutions. Life is full of novelties and seemingly random occurrences—from abnormal weather and sociopathic behavior to bizarre coincidences of innumerable kinds. Such events and actions cannot be reasonably anticipated. Moreover, as Pogge argues, reducing risk levels to zero would be astronomically expensive and often of dubious benefit (given the cost).[2] For these reasons, threats to rights can never be fully eliminated. Yet many threats, such as famine, poverty, political repression, and violence against women, are sadly commonplace. By analyzing and responding to such threats, it should in principle be possible to establish social guarantees at acceptable thresholds.[3] As Shue notes, the duties involved here are both individual and collective: not only to design institutions that provide social guarantees, but also to avoid depriving people of their rights and to aid the deprived.[4]*

To secure rights against standard threats requires three types of institution: representative political institutions, and direct and indirect functional institutions. Let us consider each in greater detail.

Representative Political Institutions

The first category includes those institutions that follow directly from the right to political participation; these are the representative political institutions, such as parliaments or assemblies, familiarly associated with the democratic political method. These institutions are overdetermined in DHR. As Jones explains, a democratic form of government is a consequence of individuals' right to participate, on terms equal with others, in the exercise of political authority to which they are subject.[5] The right to participation, as I argued in the previous chapter, is fundamental: it is a requirement of emancipation and necessary to the enjoyment of other rights. Without representative institutions it would be difficult to hold authorities accountable, express grievances, or articulate and pursue collective aims.[6] In this sense representative institutions resemble the "direct" functional institutions I shall describe in the next section. While representative political institutions are directly required by the right to participation, they do not exhaust its requirements;[7] participatory designs and procedures figure crucially wherever governance occurs.

This justification for representative government differs importantly from the traditional one that informs sovereign conceptions of democracy. In the latter, representative government provides the instrument through which the will of the people is divined and enacted into law; representative government facilitates the (collective) autonomy of the sovereign. In DHR, representative political institutions are required to secure fundamental rights; on this justification collective autonomy drops out. It is replaced by emancipation as the goal or object of representation. This change is significant because of its bearing on where to locate representative political institutions. This question ranks among the thorniest issues confronting students of globalization and global democracy. One thorn in particular snags many proposals: what group of people should decide which issues? In sovereign democracy this question did not arise, or rather, it was not pertinent because sovereignty

---

*These duties belie the frequent charge that rights-based theories ignore the obligations of individuals and communities. As sensible proponents have always maintained, rights imply and entail duties. Nettlesome questions about who in particular has duties with respect to whose rights can be largely subsumed into the idea of an institutionally satisfied social guarantee, leaving individuals with the direct duties to refrain from violating others' rights and to support the institutions.

provided the answer. Now that this answer is no longer practical or persuasive, the most common approach is to rely on some variant of the all-affected principle, substituting an empirically-based normative conception of popular sovereignty for the territorial original. This principle, as we saw in chapter 5, faces quite serious if not decisive objections.[8]

For modern democratic theory, including cosmopolitan variants like Held's, getting the location of representative institutions right is crucial because their purpose is to ensure the collective autonomy of the appropriate set of citizens. The legitimacy of political decisions is linked to the rightfulness of the "community" that takes the decisions (however it is defined). Because DHR justifies representative institutions on their role in securing emancipation, it escapes the burden of finding the "right" location for these institutions. Put differently, *where* representative institutions should be located ceases to be about locating sovereignty in DHR. There is no unique solution to the optimal location of representation because there is no link between a rightful sovereign and particular decisions or territories. Efficacy in securing rights becomes the chief criterion in designing representation; given the depressing diversity of subjection in our world this efficacy can probably only be addressed on an ad hoc basis, not resolved at the level of general principle. This way of conceiving representation gives DHR the flexibility to adapt to future political developments impossible to predict now.

Moreover, because collective decision making is just one, though a very important, mechanism for securing rights and realizing emancipation, representative institutions need not be our only or even primary means of achieving supranational democratization. Thus as a practical matter DHR can, without contradiction, take as its starting point the boundaries of existing states, though it will treat them with less reverence—particularly with respect to rules, policies, and judgments originating outside these borders—than they command today.* This is a distinct advantage, because despite the heady rhetoric often swirling around globalization, the nation-state remains, and seems likely to remain for the foreseeable future, the primary locus of politics, in both institutional and psychological terms. Even accounting for globalization's alleged acceleration effect, the evolution of a new supranational political order will be a lengthy and uneven process. As developments in the European Union have shown, people often seem more willing to accept outside determinations concerning rights and policy in clearly defined areas of regulation and cooperation than they do the legitimacy of permanent supranational legislative arrangements.

---

*How to assess democratically the merits of different configurations of borders is a complex issue I cannot address here. For a lucid account of how democratic requirements might govern the creation of *new* governmental authorities, see Thomas W. Pogge, "Creating Supra-National Institutions Democratically: Reflections on the European Union's 'Democratic Deficit'," *The Journal of Political Philosophy* 5, no. 2 (1997).

DHR does share with many other contemporary theories of democracy a local impulse; many of its direct and indirect functional institutions are ideally local in nature. Further, the principle of subsidiarity—roughly, that problems should be addressed at the most local level adequate for their effective resolution—seems consistent with DHR's participatory requirements and its justification of representation as a means of protecting human rights. Again, complexities abound concerning how local any local decisions should be; again, there is probably no unique answer. I write below of "local" and "municipal" arrangements, taking care not to specify further the referents of these vague terms. This ambiguity is intentional; it reiterates DHR's flexibility in dealing with this indeterminacy.

Direct Functional Institutions

The second category of institution required by DHR comprises all those direct functional institutions needed to secure fundamental rights against standard threats. They are *functional* institutions in that their justification is the rights-securing role they perform; they are *direct* in that they deliver services or implement policies through which people's rights are immediately protected. Direct functional institutions are distinct from *indirect* functional institutions discussed in the next section, which deal with policy, oversight, and enforcement; they are the frontline organizations through which rights are implemented and protected.

Institutions performing similar direct functions already exist in most societies; examples include schools, police forces, health care networks, social welfare agencies, and others like them. DHR, however, reconceives these institutions as *democratic* institutions and transforms them accordingly. In doing so it makes clear that democracy demands much more than representative political institutions and periodic elections. The goal of emancipation means that DHR treats a broad range of social functions as integral to democracy's realization. Incorporating them into its basic institutional framework greatly facilitates democracy's horizontal extension; as social guarantees for all the fundamental rights are institutionalized, freedom and equality become possible across a widening spectrum of social activities and interactions. In addition, direct functional institutions embody DHR's recognition of the indivisibility and interdependence of all human rights. A system can no more be democratic if it lacks adequate social guarantees of income, education, or health care than if it lacks meaningful elections. Creating institutional guarantees for all the fundamental rights translates indivisibility and interdependence into concrete political practice.

Transforming existing social institutions into democratic ones of the kind required by DHR entails organizational reorientation and structural reform. By reorientation I mean revising an organization's goals and mission.

Structural reforms—opening institutions to greater public participation, developing more deliberative methods of goal-setting, policy-making, and implementation—will in large part follow from democratization of the institutions themselves. Consider three brief examples: policing, health care, and income support programs. If police view their role as protecting everyone's basic rights, as opposed to law enforcement or "battling bad guys," policing can become an instrument for advancing democracy. Structural reforms that might follow could include shifts toward community-generated policing priorities reached through an open and participatory deliberative process. This process would be balanced by administrative checks and oversight[9] and directed toward an overhaul of training to reflect the function of policing in a democratic society. Similarly, a reorientation of health care toward guaranteeing universal care for individuals and providing strong public health protection, and away from maximizing profit for executives and shareholders, makes it more democratic. At a systemic level, a democratic reorientation might entail a move from the American model, which often reifies social inequalities, to systems along the lines of those in Canada and the Britain, which at least in principle minimize those inequalities by providing (different) social guarantees of health care for all citizens. Making the system more participatory could include efforts to involve citizens' juries in crucial decisions regarding rationing and other policies.[10] Despite some problems,[11] such innovations offer a more democratic approach to important social decision making in health care. Finally, with respect to income support provision, I suggested in the last chapter that basic income schemes might be the most democratic way to guarantee rights to subsistence.* By transforming income support from a redistributive welfare program into an unconditional democratic right, basic income eliminates unwarranted interference in the lives of "clients" and the contingency of benefits that can create conditions of domination in existing welfare programs.[12] Basic income also enhances freedom—especially women's freedom—by ensuring economic independence, by maximizing flexible and innovative employment opportunities and arrangements, and by efficiently protecting against social misfortune in its various forms.[13]

Obviously the devil lies in the details of such reforms, and the complexities involved warrant serious deliberation; my purpose is primarily to indicate what the democratic transformation of functional organizations might look like. In general, these reforms should emphasize participation and the deliberative identification of goals and needs. It is also crucial that institutions

---

*There is a wide range of social welfare services beyond income support programs, many of which will not be addressed by basic income; my focus on basic income should not be mistaken for a comment on such services.

be adequately empowered to actually secure the rights in question. Beyond these general requirements DHR does not demand any specific organizational form,[14] though decentralization, where feasible, seems to be one way of achieving responsiveness. Participatory, deliberative institutions allow people to determine their aims and to decide how to advance them. DHR has an important advantage over many deliberative models, however, in that it provides independent (not "objective") substantive criteria of democratic effectiveness (guarantees of rights) by which institutional performance can be assessed. It thus avoids the familiar deliberative democratic dilemma of pure procedural versus epistemic claims for legitimacy.[15]

Not all direct functional institutions are electoral, but this does not make them undemocratic. Plenty of independent agencies make decisions in democracies every day; so long as these agencies are open to democratic direction and participation and conform with the requirements of fundamental human rights, there is no democratic difficulty.[16] Indeed, bureaucratic and administrative agencies might counter-intuitively be *more* amenable to deliberative and participatory approaches than legislatures, because they are accustomed to conflict and unconstrained by electoral imperatives.[17]

Supranational Functional Institutions?

We began by postulating an increasingly interdependent planet—by assuming globalization. This interdependence raises the possibility that securing some rights might require supranational functional institutions. Like direct functional institutions, supranational functional institutions play a direct role in protecting a fundamental right or rights. Unlike direct functional institutions, they are primarily supranational or global (rather than local) in nature.

To see why such supranational institutions might be required, consider poverty. Securing fundamental rights against standard threats surely includes institutionalized programs to eradicate poverty. This requirement might be met in a variety of ways, yet without supranational institutions designed to promote sustained and sustainable growth, eliminating global poverty might be impossible. In such instances DHR would require supranational functional institutions to secure the rights in question. DHR only requires direct functional institutions when they are necessary to secure rights. If there are several ways to guarantee everyone's equal enjoyment of fundamental rights against standard threats, DHR is indifferent among them. Again, the principle of subsidiarity—that local institutions will, other things equal, be more participatory and responsive—creates a presumption in favor of local arrangements, but this is a presumption rather than a decision-rule; the primary object is security of rights. For supranational functional institutions to be required, it would be necessary to show both that the function they perform is necessary and that there is no equally effective alternate scheme for fulfilling it more locally.

DHR does not preclude functional international governance organizations (IGOs) dealing with economic or other important policy issues, even if they are not required; it subjects them to the same democratic regime as other governance institutions (a regime described in the next section). Determining whether such IGOs are required or merely permitted demands careful analysis immersed in the arcana of the particular issue domain in question. Such analysis is impossible here. In the following section I treat international financial institutions (IFIs) and other IGOs as permitted institutions subject to democratic oversight by indirect functional regimes. I postpone for another time the detailed study of specific functional regimes that would let us determine which of them DHR might require.

Indirect Functional Institutions

Indirect functional institutions are those responsible for oversight and enforcement of human rights in governance regimes. Their purview includes monitoring the activities of representative and direct functional institutions to ensure compliance with DHR and oversight of *all* governance systems permitted but not directly required by DHR. They are indirect because they are not immediately involved in securing specific rights; their function is nonetheless crucial in providing social guarantees of all the basic rights in two respects.

First, in connection with the two other types of democratic institution required by DHR, representative and direct functional institutions, indirect functional institutions help secure rights against foreseeable threats like error, corruption, and incompetence. They provide accountability and, when necessary, correct mistakes and reform practices that violate DHR's conditions. This oversight takes place through a variety of mechanisms (to be described below), including: municipal and supranational courts and commissions, which allow individuals to challenge policies that violate or clearly threaten their fundamental rights; and, human rights audits, which provide ongoing assessments of internal procedures and policy outcomes and mandate cooperative remediation efforts.

The second respect in which indirect functional institutions are crucial in securing human rights involves their oversight of nondemocratic actors, institutions, and systems of governance. Agents of all kinds engage in governance activities, from prisons, families, local businesses, and civic associations to IGOs, IFIs, and transnational corporations (TNCs), exercising control over people in ways that significantly impact their human rights. Although these agents are "nondemocratic" in that they are not mandated by DHR, they nonetheless have a huge bearing on whether democracy is realized. DHR's commitment to emancipation demands vigilance against threats originating in any domain or from any actors. That is the point of DHR's emphasis on governance: to extend and institutionalize democratic concern beyond the traditional sphere of politics. This commitment helps DHR steer a middle course between two equally unsatisfying extremes: ignoring nondemocratic agents and institutions (treating them as "private") or subjecting them to direct popular or bureaucratic control. Either approach can lead directly to real reductions in people's freedom and equality. So DHR calls for their *democratization* in the sense of holding them accountable for their impact on human rights.

I want to emphasize that this function applies to *all* systems of governance at *all* levels. Much of the ensuing discussion focuses on DHR's role in democratizing supranational governance arrangements of various kinds; this focus reflects our concern with globalization, but it should not obscure DHR's concern with democracy at every level. The indirect institutions anchor DHR's vertical extension of democracy, including its response to many threats associated with globalization and interdependence; they also facilitate democracy's horizontal extension, institutionalizing accountability for nongovernmental actors who exercise control and power in domains like civil society and the economy. Though I do not highlight this horizontal dimension here, it is vital to DHR's success.

Audits

The indirect approach relies heavily on audits, formalizing them through a broader network of local and supranational institutions designed to review and enforce them. Audits introduce a participatory (and thus democratic) dimension into governance conducted by nondemocratic institutions; they also allow considerable flexibility regarding how to achieve security for fundamental rights. This flexibility makes DHR adaptable to the many varieties of governance activity ranging from local decision making to IFI activity. Combined with policy-setting and enforcement institutions, audits and audit institutions represent an alternative path toward democratizing governance at all levels.

Two related but distinct processes are grouped together under the heading of audits: human rights impact assessments and human rights audits. Both assess the human rights performance of governance institutions, including direct functional and nondemocratic institutions. Impact assessments are designed to evaluate the likely effects of a policy on human rights and to preempt or modify proposals that threaten them. Actors routinely engaged in governance activities, including direct functional institutions, IGOs, and TNCs, should conduct these evaluations prior to enacting major policies.

Audits, by contrast, assess human rights performance retrospectively. They scrutinize policy outcomes as well as internal procedures like labor standards, management practices, and public accountability.

The use of both prospective and retrospective audits has been slowly attracting attention and adherents. Models for prospective audits include the Australian government's "impact on women" assessments in the early 1980s, a program transformed in 1987 through an initiative called the Women's Budget Program. This program mandated detailed accounts of each cabinet ministry's activities and their impact on women. These accounts evaluated spending and policy proposals explicitly in terms of their anticipated effects on women. The program also aimed to educate and sensitize bureaucrats to women's issues and concerns. The program-mandated reports were codified into a single document circulated on budget night, the Women's Budget Statement.[18] Initially, some ministries were resistant or smug; the Treasury insisted, for instance, that policies to promote economic growth had a uniform effect on men and women; upon further analysis, however, certain tax breaks or incentives for workers proved to have rather different effects.[19]

A similar model exists today in the City and County of San Francisco, where the Commission on the Status of Women evaluates policies using guidelines derived from the UN Convention on the Elimination of All Forms of Discrimination Against Women (CEDAW). The Commission applies gender analysis to budget, service, and employment questions. Data and reports are used to analyze these performance areas using human rights principles, to formulate and implement recommendations and action plans, and to monitor implementation.[20] The San Francisco program is particularly interesting because it operationalizes human rights principles through a straightforward application of gender analysis carried out by regular employees using available data; costly investigations and reliance on experts are avoided in favor of programs designed to change the culture of public service delivery in the city. Other experiments with prospective audits in areas like environmental planning and management are also instructive for students of democracy.[21]

Models for retrospective audits include two of particular interest to DHR. One, the Social Accountability 8000 (SA8000) system, was created by the Council on Economic Priorities Accreditation Agency to establish auditable social standards and an independent auditing process for monitoring workers' rights. The system, designed for corporate use by a group of business leaders, human rights NGOs, and trade union representatives, includes measurable human rights standards, a set of recommended management systems for implementing and monitoring those standards, documentation to assist with interpreting and implementing the standards, a system for training and certifying auditors, and a list of accredited auditors. The measures are based on International Labor Organization standards, the Universal Declaration of Human Rights, and the UN Convention on the Rights of the Child, and include guidelines for child and forced labor, health and safety, freedom of association and the right to collective bargaining, discrimination, disciplinary practices, working hours, and compensation.[22] Critics of the system object to its voluntary nature, its secretive and unaccountable audit process, its relatively lax certification requirements, and its reliance on for-profit auditing firms for certification.[23] Even assuming the merit of these charges, SA8000 shows that it is possible to develop auditable standards for human rights in a corporate setting and that such standards, if properly conceived and implemented, can benefit firms and workers alike. Problems concerning standards, auditing procedures, and enforcement are serious but can be addressed through the broader institutional framework of DHR.

The other retrospective model to consider here is the Democratic Audit of the United Kingdom. The Democratic Audit undertakes a comprehensive assessment of the status of democracy in the United Kingdom, although the method has potentially wider application.[24] This ambitious project employs indices derived from democratic theory, focusing on the electoral process, open and accountable government, political and civil rights, and civil society. The audit includes qualitative assessments of democratic performance based on these criteria along with proposals for reform. As Beetham shows, audits differ from other forms of democracy assessment in that they are critical, locally based, and normatively oriented.[25] Beetham recognizes that the standards adopted for audits can be controversial, so he emphasizes their derivation from clear democratic principles.[26] This model proves congenial to DHR, which provides readily auditable standards and is derived from a clearly articulated democratic theory. Because DHR's scope extends well beyond the traditional electoral mechanisms of representative democracy, it can encompass a variety of institutions and systems of governance within one general framework, though precise standards will vary with the type of institution being evaluated.

Human Rights Impact Assessments   The idea behind impact assessments is simple: major policies, including budgetary proposals, considered by governance organizations should be assessed for their likely impact on human rights. Conducted by the proposing agencies using standardized guidelines and following general requirements established by regional* human rights commissions and courts (see below), impact assessments would help to identify and avert adverse policy outcomes through a rights-based analysis and through an open and participatory review process conducted

---

*Here and throughout I use the term *regional* to refer to *supranational* regions—Europe, Southeast Asia, and so on.

in cooperation with local councils (see below). These assessments offer several benefits from a democratic perspective. First, as with environmental reviews, they institutionalize public participation in the early stages of policy development, helping to satisfy an important fundamental right. Second, as with gender analysis of policies and budgets, impact assessments help to educate and sensitize policymakers to human rights concerns, which it is hoped will lead to better management and to improvement in future proposals. Third, these assessments can reconcile expertise with democratic control by providing forums through which concerned individuals can question findings and assumptions and suggest alternative strategies or priorities.

Two significant problems are apparent: how to define which policies trigger an impact assessment review and how to achieve meaningful participation in such assessments undertaken by IGOs, TNCs, and other supranational entities. We can narrow the first problem by stipulating that the budgets and policies of all direct functional institutions and governmental agencies should be subject to impact assessments, as should all proposed legislation considered by representative political institutions. Similarly, a presumption in favor of audits should be made for the leading IFIs: the IMF, the WTO, and the World Bank. This high level of scrutiny is warranted for democratic institutions and for IGOs with obvious global impact, but it is probably not appropriate for other IGOs and nondemocratic institutions. With respect to TNCs, determining which to audit will involve difficult judgments, but many cases will nonetheless be clear-cut. Moreover, not all areas of corporate activity demand comparable scrutiny: environmental and employment practices probably warrant more rigorous review than policies concerning product development and marketing.* At the national and local levels, major corporate entities will also receive heightened scrutiny, with such factors as size of payroll, local monopoly status, and environmental impact factoring into the auditing decisions. As these examples indicate, the size and power of institutions tell us a lot about the likely impact of their activities, and different activities undertaken by similar institutions are unlikely to have the same degree of impact. Generating clear standards for impact assessment review should be left to regional commissions.

Institutionalizing participation in audits of supranational actors also poses difficult challenges. Where governance institutions operate locally (as with most direct functional institutions), participation can follow the environmental review model of public involvement. But because IGOs and

---

*Of course there are exceptions to every generalization: drug companies' production methods and decisions and tobacco companies' marketing strategies are good examples; the general point nonetheless holds.

TNCs have global reach, directly shaping millions of people's lives, local forums for participation seem impossible. Some remedies include modified deliberative polls, specially convened juries, and extensive consultation with local and regional human rights commissions (see below).* Because the point of impact assessments for nondemocratic institutions is to identify and avert human rights violations, not to subject those institutions to popular or bureaucratic control, these remedies, combined with the additional level of oversight provided through human rights audits, should provide adequate safeguards.

Human Rights Audits Human rights audits are periodic reviews of an organization's human rights performance conducted by independent experts. They cover the internal structures and procedures of an organization (including its human rights impact assessment process, its management systems, workplace conditions, and respect for the human rights of its employees) and its external human rights record (including the impact of its policies and activities and its mechanisms for public consultation and cooperation). All direct functional and government institutions and all major governance regimes would be subject to regular audits and impact assessments; other organizations, including small companies and certified NGOs (see below), would be randomly selected for audits on a less frequent and less formal basis. Reviews will be conducted by special auditors under the auspices of regional human rights commissions, which will review policies on internal human rights practices and impact assessments; they will audit the paper trail, conduct extensive, random, and secure interviews with employees and former employees at all levels, and perform random inspections of production facilities and other workplaces. Indices will be developed and updated by technical committees, also under the umbrella of the regional commissions, and composed of functional experts and representatives of relevant certified NGOs (e.g., trade unions, rights groups). Regional commissions will develop the audit through public consultation.

   Audit indices, which will be public, will evaluate human rights performance in four main areas corresponding with the four clusters of fundamental human rights; the job of the auditors is to make a determination of compliance, marginal compliance, or noncompliance for each index. No further action is required where compliance is found, though technical guidance

---

*Deliberative polling, roughly, is a technique through which a representative sample of the public is polled on a particular issue, then offered extensive information and opportunities to question relevant decision makers. The participants are then polled again, offering a picture of what "informed" public opinion might look like on particular issues; see James S. Fishkin, Robert C. Luskin, and Roger Jowell, "Deliberative Polling and Public Consultation," *Parliamentary Affairs* 53, no. 4 (2000); Fishkin, *Democracy and Deliberation*.

and suggestions might be appropriate. Where marginal compliance is found, organizations will be required to submit remediation plans, which will be subject to the approval of the auditors and monitored through subsequent reporting and audits where necessary. Where determinations of noncompliance are made, the same procedures should be followed, supplemented by direct monitoring and oversight of the remediation plans by the auditors. The costs and burdens associated with noncompliant findings should encourage organizations to get it right the first time. Final audit determinations will be submitted for approval to audit juries. These juries, whose selection and composition I discuss below, will question the auditor, review the evidence, and hear witnesses if necessary. Their function would be to ensure fairness and integrity in the auditing process. Jury sessions should be public and audit findings, including remediation plans, should be published and posted electronically.

Audits that find subject organizations in full or marginal compliance in all areas should, upon submission of satisfactory corrective action plans, be certified as human rights compliant; other organizations with noncompliant findings should be given either probationary or, in the case of ongoing uncorrected violations, decertified status. Decertification might entail a variety of formal and informal penalties varying with the nature of the organizations; for TNCs these could include fines, higher rates of taxation, and exclusion from markets, as well as civil and criminal penalties when warranted. Along with the negative publicity a decertified status would generate (think Nike), these penalties would provide further incentives for compliance. If audits expose gross human rights violations, the relevant information will be forwarded to the regional commissions for further investigation and action.

Audit juries introduce participation into the audit process, enhancing accountability and transparency; they are not juries in the judicial sense. With the other measures outlined here, they ensure a public accounting of all major governance functions. Audits generate important information for human rights enforcement and, with time, could come to play a key role in establishing the legitimacy of audited organizations. In the case of corporations, certification could be used as a marketing tool (as with Fair Trade Coffee), and noncompliance could lead to formal and informal sanctions ranging from fines and bad publicity to differential taxation rates and limited access to markets. Such incentives, which are often derided as window dressing, could matter considerably if an independent and publicly accountable audit system were in place. For IGOs, audits could provide much-needed legitimacy and, as the World Bank at least claims to have discovered, actually improve organizations' capacity to fulfill their functions.

Local Human Rights Commissions

Globalization, for all the hype about transformations, does not alter the local nature of much of human life; even the most cosmopolitan business executive usually keeps a home near an office. However much localities today are affected by events in other places all over the world, they remain relevant centers of important activity. Place may be in many ways less relevant than in the past, or easier to escape or transcend—not quite the same thing—but it is far from irrelevant. Threats to or violations of human rights always involve specific people in particular circumstances; though sometimes a single threat can affect thousands or even millions of people, it still typically manifests locally. Many other threats inhere in the structures of everyday life. For this reason local institutions will play a crucial part in a comprehensive human rights regime.

For example, most direct functional institutions, such as schools, police, and human service agencies, will operate locally. Even when such institutions are part of a broader administrative network, as with health care systems, their primary functions occur locally, and the presumption of subsidiarity should apply. Decentralization facilitates participation and sensitizes these institutions to local needs, customs, and concerns and subjects local systems of governance to democratic norms. To support these locally-based institutions, human rights guarantees should be codified in municipal law and enforced through municipal courts when necessary. Local assemblies and metropolitan authorities will shape policies and guide local development.[27] To handle local human rights functions beyond those entrusted to representative political institutions, local human rights commissions should be established. Local commissions will carry out audit functions, organize human rights education, and conduct local hearings. Each of these functions is important in itself and each helps strengthen the human rights system, making it more open, responsive, and participatory.

Members of local commissions will be selected by lot from pools of volunteers. Despite democratic theory's traditional emphasis on elections, volunteerism and selection by lot can be equally democratic devices and often make participation more open and varied.[28] This method of selection helps to depoliticize human rights; partisan competition, the mainstay of electoral politics, is appropriate in policy domains and for representative institutions, but not in oversight functions. Commissioners should be remunerated at the median local income, and every effort should be made to ensure that career concerns can be balanced with a period of public service. By making participation feasible for any qualified member of the community, these measures help to ensure the diversity of perspective that democratic universality requires.* They also facilitate representation of a different kind, of people, communities, and perspectives.[29]

Commissions might be organized in myriad ways, utilizing subcommittees, volunteers, or other methods. The only qualification for service should be human rights education (see below). Paid service should be limited to short, fixed terms of about two years, and members should be ineligible for repeat service for at least several terms. These measures help to support wide rotation in office and to cultivate community expertise and build grassroots support for DHR. Each commission should be audited at the end of its term by its successor; any serious misconduct would lead to disqualification from future service as well as to criminal proceedings if necessary. Such safeguards are necessary protections against corruption and are standard in public service.

Local commissions will have three primary responsibilities: audit review, human rights education, and local hearings. They should also serve in a consultative capacity for local assemblies, courts, and civic associations, providing guidance and technical assistance. Local audit responsibilities include direct oversight of direct functional institutions and other local governance institutions and participation in impact assessments of IGOs, TNCs, and other governance institutions where the local community is directly impacted (more below). The oversight function is straightforward: local commissions review the human rights impact assessments and audits of all local direct functional and governmental institutions. Local nondemocratic institutions might be audited on a random basis. Oversight need not be cumbersome for local commissions, which might tackle it in several ways. Commission members might serve as jurors for these local audits, or they might utilize volunteers or randomly selected jurors for this purpose. Commissions might also serve as auditors in smaller communities, while larger ones might prefer to hire professional staff. All audits should be open to the public and findings made easily available to the community at large. These audits should emphasize creative and cooperative problem solving, especially when they involve other local agencies; they should be closer to peer review than legal review.

In addition to helping secure rights, careful oversight of local human rights institutions (direct functional institutions) generates public confidence in them and increases their legitimacy. This is especially important for such institutions as the courts, police, and corrections services, where histories of abuse, corruption, and discrimination perpetuate hostility and public mistrust. Audits of these institutions, employing such devices as unannounced

---

*One positive spillover effect of basic income is its role in facilitating participation by providing economic security and continuity for individuals participating in government, social work, and so forth.

inspections and confidential interviews, will hasten their transformation into democratic institutions by opening them to public scrutiny and placing them firmly under democratic control. Again, involvement in the human rights process should also help to educate and sensitize staff. Local commissions, working with local assemblies, should be able to initiate major reform and even reorganization of direct functional institutions when warranted.

The other auditing function of local commissions relates to the local activities of IGOs, TNCs, and other governance institutions whose policies and activities directly impact particular communities. Through human rights impact assessments, local commissions can participate in human rights reviews of these policies and activities, which might include major public works projects funded by development agencies such as the World Bank or production decisions of corporations that involve local environmental concerns, job losses, and so on (generally, any exercise of governance with a clearly identifiable local impact).* Local participation in impact assessments figures centrally in democratizing these governance institutions. Again, this democratization does not consist of placing IGOs or their decisions under direct popular control; rather, it focuses on ensuring local input and on preventing outcomes that violate other human rights. Obviously, many decisions that might be consistent with human rights will still have controversial policy implications; the appropriate forum for debating such questions is representative political institutions. DHR does not provide answers to, or even criteria for answering, most political questions; it constrains those answers and the process through which they are determined.

The second important function of local commissions is human rights education. For DHR to work, people must know and understand their rights and the framework of institutions open to them for defining and securing them. They must understand how to participate effectively and feel certain that their participation will matter. Human rights education can also help reduce violations, especially in institutions like the family and civic associations where public intervention can be most intrusive. Knowledge and understanding of rights might make individuals better able and more willing to report problems and violations and to participate actively in other human rights functions. Ideally, human rights education should be provided through schools, contributing to their democratic transformation. Eventually, this curricular approach would ensure virtually universal coverage, though other alternatives should be available. Local commissions, working with schools, should develop and administer the curriculum, successful completion of which should be the only requirement for service on local commissions. This

---

*Note that this standard is not the same as the all-affected principle I have criticized elsewhere; it refers to local projects understood as having clear geographical implications.

minimal requirement ensures a level of basic competence owed to people affected by this particular system of governance.

The final function of local commissions is to hold public hearings. All meetings of the local commissions should be open to the public; these hearings fulfill a specialized purpose, providing a dedicated forum for debating issues relating to any of the commissions' functions. These issues could be organizational or operational or could pertain to more general human rights concerns within the community. Hearings institutionalize an opportunity for people to articulate needs and concerns regarding the definition and enforcement of rights. They are part gripe session, part town meeting, a forum for complaints, questioning, brainstorming, or wondering aloud. They should not replace legislative institutions; their role is to provide an opportunity for critically evaluating definitions of human rights and the institutions that secure them. As we saw in the previous chapter, these functions must be participatory if universality is to be achieved. Local hearings, and local commissions more generally, are valuable because in guaranteeing opportunities for participation they fulfill this important epistemological requirement of DHR.

Regional Courts and Commissions

To aid democracy's vertical extension into supranational governance arenas, DHR establishes a system of regional commissions and courts. These regional institutions will mediate and adjudicate conflicts among states, TNCs, localities, and individuals when these spill over national boundaries, where individuals or organizations have a human rights appeal against a state and have exhausted their national appeals, or when the actors in question (e.g.,TNCs) are inherently supranational in character. They might also serve as tribunals in cases of crimes against humanity. A special functional court and commission will deal with IGOs.

These institutions are modeled on the Council of Europe's human rights framework and the similar but less well-established Inter-American model under the umbrella of the Organization of American States. In these models human rights commissions and courts work together to resolve disputes amicably and, where necessary, through adjudication. In 1998, through Protocol 11 to its Convention, the Council of Europe abolished the European Commission on Human Rights and strengthened the European Court of Human Rights (European Court). It also made recognition of individual application mandatory for signatories.[30] The proposals that follow combine elements of the pre- and postreform models, retaining the division of labor between courts and commissions but adopting the provisions for individual application. One feature of the Council of Europe structure purposefully *not* incorporated here is its differential handling of social rights (through the European Committee of Social Rights). The courts and commissions described below will have competence to address questions concerning all of the fundamental rights.

Selection of commissioners and judges must balance two considerations: these important positions should be reserved for individuals of high talent, moral character, and dedication, yet these very considerations risk making the service the exclusive province of an elite group of jurists and experts. One solution would be for local commissions to select members to serve in a regional nominating congress. This congress would solicit and review nominations; all nominees receiving two-thirds support would enter pools from which vacancies would be filled by random selection until the slates were emptied (at which time the process would be repeated). This procedure would allow some (indirect) popular input into the selection of candidates but would also limit potential commissioners and jurists to highly qualified and broadly acceptable individuals.

Courts and commissions would share three primary functions: handling general complaints and advice regarding fundamental rights, overseeing audits for IGOs, NGOs, and TNCs, and serving as permanent international criminal tribunals. (Domestically, these functions will be lodged in national courts, many of which already perform similar constitutional functions.) With respect to general complaints, the system would work much the like prereform mechanism of the European Commission on Human Rights. Individuals, assemblies, and local commissions could bring complaints of human rights violations to the commission once municipal channels were exhausted. Commissions would make preliminary determinations about whether these claims were appropriate for further review. In cases deemed appropriate, the commission would initiate fact finding to determine what additional information might be needed to facilitate a conclusion to the matter. The commission would work with the parties to the dispute to find amicable resolutions where appropriate. Such resolutions might include changes to policies and practices, limited compensation for wronged parties, adoption of strict monitoring or reporting practices, or whatever other effective arrangements might be satisfactory to all the parties. If the parties could not agree, however, the commission would submit a report on the facts of the case, including a recommendation, to the regional court, which would determine the matter after appropriate review.

Additionally, regional commissions should have the power to initiate investigations in cases where they receive verifiable reports of serious violations. In cases it considered urgent a commission might appoint a special rapporteur to investigate a well-defined area of concern and to mediate where possible (one can imagine, at the time of writing, a panel on Chechnya, Sudan, or American prisoner detention policies worldwide). Launching investigations quickly might help to circumvent conflicts and deter massive violations. Special rapporteurs might also refer serious cases to the Human Rights Security Council to be described below. Finally, commissions might, at the request of appropriate parties, issue technical guidance regarding the interpretation of fundamental rights or their application in specific contexts, including audits.

The audit functions of regional commissions and courts would be similar in many ways to those of local commissions. Regional commissions would oversee all audits of TNCs and regional governance institutions. They would also review any complex matters referred by local commissions. Corps of trained and certified auditors would conduct the audits, which would be reviewed by juries comprised of commissioners, human rights experts (academics, attorneys, public officials), and volunteers with experience on local commissions. This would allow some participation in the regional audit process while ensuring a reasonable degree of technical prowess. Commissions would oversee remediation plans, monitor progress towards compliance, and refer contentious cases to the courts, which would decide questions of procedure and interpretation. Commissions, perhaps following guidelines established by a world conference (see below) would develop auditable indices for local and regional use, which would be reviewed and approved by the courts. (Again, national courts will perform parallel functions at the domestic level.)

One additional audit function of regional commissions would concern certification of international NGOs. Through a voluntary human rights audit, any NGO could receive certification as a human rights-compliant organization. This certification would require that the NGO have a written, public, and democratic constitution and bylaws and that it be internally democratic in its operations and activities, including membership. Only NGOs seeking a role within the democratic framework need obtain certification. While we typically think of NGOs like Oxfam or Amnesty in connection with human rights issues, the term itself encompasses a whole range of groups not formally involved in government: bowling leagues, poetry societies, skinhead gangs, and religious organizations are all nongovernmental. Many such groups are unlikely to seek formal involvement in democratic governance, and nothing in this requirement would apply to them (though they would of course be accountable for violations they might commit). The requirement is a safeguard designed to ensure that NGOs aspiring to a formal role in democratic governance are themselves democratic.*

---

*The Finnish government allows but does not require registration of civic associations; something like this program is what I have in mind here. See National Board of Patents and Registration of Finland, *Register of Associations* [Web Page] (2005 [cited 10 January 2005 2005]); available from http://www.prh.fi/en/yhdistysrekisteri.html; cf. Jan Aart Scholte, "Democratizing the Global Economy: The Role of Civil Society" (Coventry: 2003), 86ff.

When I began developing DHR I imagined that regional commissions and courts might assume the functions of war crimes tribunals, replacing the ad hoc arrangements like those in place for Rwanda and the former Yugoslavia. Standing institutions presumably have a greater deterrent effect, and the regional character of these institutions seemed like a potential solution to at least some of the charges, like politicization and victor's justice, frequently leveled against such tribunals. These tribunals also serve as an important expression of global commitment to upholding human rights norms. Since then, the International Criminal Court has become a reality, surviving (for now) bitter American government objections. While I do think regional arrangements offer some advantages, existing institutions have perhaps more potential than even the best conceived proposal; efforts in this area are probably best directed at present toward strengthening the International Criminal Court

In addition to the regional institutions, some sort of functional court will be needed for cases involving IGOs, terrorism, pollution, migration, and other issues and institutions that do not map neatly into regional compartments (perhaps including some TNCs). This court would not be an appeals court; it would rather resemble a regional court with a functional docket (similar to the United States Court of Appeals for the District of Columbia, which handles cases involving United States government agencies regardless of the jurisdiction in which they arise). Perhaps several such courts, with particular expertise in the economy, the environment, and other functional domains, would prove expedient. Functional courts would have compulsory jurisdiction over cases involving global IGOs and IFIs like Interpol and the WTO; like regional courts, they should be paired with commissions charged with investigative and other duties. These courts might also appoint special rapporteurs to address functional concerns like structural adjustment programs or human trafficking.

One significant obstacle to these proposals is the problem of enforcement. Because regional courts and commissions do not match up with already existing political jurisdictions, they cannot rely on their own administrative and judicial institutions for enforcement. Over time they might gain valuable moral authority, but cooperation with governments and governance agencies will be essential. Once again, the lesson of the European Union is instructive, and in this case encouraging as well. The European Court of Justice (the EU's primary judicial organ) relies on national courts and institutions to enforce its rulings, and it is thus subject in principle to a sort of national veto. Nonetheless, it has moved aggressively and successfully to assert its primacy over national courts and has gestured toward direct incorporation of the European Convention on Human Rights into EU law. The European Court of Justice has also expanded its powers considerably through preliminary or advisory rulings to which national courts generally adhere.[31] Given the relative youth of the European system, these developments have been rapid and surprisingly uncontroversial. Large-scale reform cannot be instantaneous, but it need not be written off as utopian either.

Especially in the early phases of its implementation, DHR would benefit tremendously from a regionally based approach to democratizing global governance. It would help to allay fears about the potential abuse of human rights doctrines as weapons of regional neocolonialism or strategic big-power interference. Regional institutions might also facilitate culturally sensitive applications of human rights norms in local contexts and prove better able to relate to their constituents in a variety of ways (language, tradition, procedure). I do not mean to suggest that different standards should apply in different regions, nor to imply that cultural traditions or practices should be allowed to trump human rights. I have in mind something more like the European Court's "margin of appreciation," which grants considerable deference to national prerogative. Skeptics have warned that sometimes the Court grants too much deference, and that this trend could undermine its legitimacy, the universality of human rights standards, and the consensus surrounding them.[32] These are valid concerns. DHR provides a check against making the margin too wide, however; as we discussed in the previous chapter, the democratic validity of any interpretation of rights can be assessed with respect to its adequacy for securing other rights. The margin of appreciation, with this check in place, sets the limit at reasonable variations, which should be expected and embraced, and which bolster, rather than undermine, universality.

World Conferences

Despite its emphasis on local and regional monitoring, oversight, and accountability, DHR's universal scope necessitates some mechanisms for global coordination. Matters ranging from definitions of human rights to the powers and organization of regional human rights organs and episodic issues or crises are best addressed through global institutions. Unlike many cosmopolitan theories, DHR does not require (nor does it rule out) global parliaments, strengthened UN or People's Assemblies, or other global representative institutions. Instead, DHR achieves global coordination of human rights functions through modifying an existing model which has proven surprisingly effective in addressing global human rights issues: the world conference.

World conferences on the environment (Rio), on population (Cairo), on women (Beijing), and on human rights (Vienna) have generated a great deal of attention because of their success in addressing major issues through cooperation and consensus among participants. Relying on preliminary meetings, circulation of draft position papers, and informal negotiations, the conferences often manage to set ambitious goals and to shape world opinion and policy on potentially divisive issues. World conferences have also stimulated concrete reform and spurred innovation and creative consensus in a variety of policy domains. Moreover, these conferences serve as focal points for NGOs and other activists; recently, opportunities for more formal participation by such actors have been expanded. Of course, these meetings have also been criticized for, among other things, refusing full and equal status to nongovernmental participants and maintaining secrecy around certain sensitive negotiations. More worryingly, from a democratic perspective, delegates to these meetings are appointed by national governments. The conferences thus retain the flavor of traditional international relations. National and sectional interests impede progress, and large powers exert disproportionate influence, a problem magnified by the limited resources available to poorer countries. On these measures (and perhaps others as well) past world conferences have fallen short of democratic standards. Many of these problems can be resolved, however, through institutional redesign.

I shall discuss some proposed changes in a moment. First I want to stress the general advantages of this model. Because the world conferences are ad hoc, they avoid the numerous hazards of permanent global assemblies or parliaments. These hazards include cost, bureaucracy, and the potential for institutional entrenchment and arrogation of power. Further, because the conferences are not legislatures, their purview is restricted to human rights matters, an admittedly broad domain on the definition of human rights operationalized here, but nonetheless a clearly delimited one. Moreover, world conferences, by operating on principles of consensus, can help to build legitimacy and minimize politicization of human rights issues at the supranational level, reinforcing and guiding the sometimes fractious global consensus on human rights. Their independence from national or political constituencies is consistent with removing basic human rights guarantees from the fray of partisan politics.

Needed modifications to the present model include methods for selecting delegates, setting the agenda, and formalizing NGO and IGO participation. Delegate selection might be initiated by regional commissions, which would nominate slates of candidates to stand for election or face votes of confidence. These nominations would be based on criteria such as expertise, strength of character, and demonstrated commitment to human rights. Nominations might also be topped up through petitions or other means. Each region would select its delegates through elections wherein individuals cast multiple votes. Campaigns would be brief, publicly funded, and nonpartisan. Representatives would serve in their individual capacity rather than as representatives of states or groups and would serve only for the particular conference to which they were elected. Conferences could be convened periodically or on the recommendation of the regional commissions. Agenda selection would depend in part on how conferences are convened; they might deal with one pressing issue or problem, as on the past model, or they might meet periodically to address a range of issues. Techniques like referenda and deliberative polling might allow for some public input into the agenda as well.

Conferences themselves would be organized along the same lines as now, though with a clearly delineated and formalized status for audit-compliant IGOs and certified NGOs. Conferences could draw on the expertise and investigative and administrative capacities of regional commissions. Preliminary meetings, white papers, and extensive public consultation should precede the conference itself—elections might even occur after these preliminaries. This consultation period would allow for a broad spectrum of views and experiences to inform the deliberations and would help promote understanding and build legitimacy for decisions made by delegates. Those decisions should reflect broad consensus, a norm which might be institutionalized through qualified majority voting—say, two-thirds of delegates and majorities in two-thirds of regional delegations for substantive decisions.

Of course, the technical and administrative details remain daunting. Still, past conferences have succeeded under less desirable circumstances, and rapidly developing information and communication technologies might be used in innovative ways to make these conferences even more open and participatory than in the past. On past experience I see no reason to succumb to undue pessimism about the potential for reformed world conferences to resolve many global human rights problems in a consensual and cooperative fashion.

Human Rights Security Council

The institutions described so far mainly provide for the implementation, oversight, and enforcement of DHR. This emphasis reflects a concern with structures of subjection and threats to rights common in everyday life. But threats posed by war and famine are equally common and perhaps more devastating than those on which we have been focusing. I have postponed discussion of these grave issues until now for two reasons. First, in developed countries, associating human rights with issues like war and famine can inadvertently reinforce the notion that human rights have to do with other people elsewhere, not with us, here. Second, war and famine evoke an intervention paradigm in which the primary focus is on immediate alleviation of dire human rights crises. Such intervention is unfortunately necessary in many instances, but thinking of securing rights as crisis intervention diverts our attention from the important measures that create stable and enduring guarantees for all fundamental rights. The appropriate metaphor for the human rights protections recommended by DHR is public health as opposed to emergency medicine; we are concerned with broad preventive measures that reduce the need for urgent intervention, though that need will never disappear.* Still, something must be said about dire crises, which remain a predictable and all too likely threat to many people's basic rights.

I have already discussed the possible organization of a permanent tribunal or tribunals to investigate and prosecute crimes against humanity. Whatever institutions do evolve should be supplemented by greater efforts to deter and punish war, violence, and coup attempts through careful institutional design and creative policy-making.[33] Stifling the shameful global arms trade, cutting off funds for warlords and dictators, and guaranteeing swift and severe punishment for violators of human rights could help deter violence and stabilize existing democratic regimes. Still, violence will erupt, bringing massive rights violations and undermining democratic institutions, and natural disasters (like the 2004 Tsunami in the Indian Ocean region) will generate human rights crises as well. I propose a Human Rights Security Council to address such concerns. The Council would monitor conflicts and trouble spots, determine when intervention is required and set terms for its implementation, and oversee reconstruction efforts. It might also try to mediate long-running conflicts and intervene constructively to preclude imminent ones. Each regional commission could select two or three of its members to serve on the Council, which could designate special rapporteurs for specific conflicts and be presided over, on a rotating basis, by a representative from the region where a particular conflict is unfolding. A world conference might decide the criteria for legitimate intervention.† Since the Council deals with human security crises of all kinds, famines and potential famines, natural disasters of broad scope, and other calamities threatening rights could be addressed under its auspices. Because members of the HRSC would not be state representatives, realpolitik and jealous insistence on sovereignty and nonintervention might give way to decisions based on urgent human needs in grave situations.

Many students of global democracy and UN reform call for an international military force to be placed at the disposal of some agency similar to the Council proposed here.[34] Clearly some kind of force must be available if the HRSC is to be effective; however, a global army, even one dedicated to protecting human rights, seems risky. An alternative would be for states to "lend" forces to the HRSC, on short notice and under HRSC command, to carry out authorized interventions on short notice according to the guidelines and objectives it establishes. A ready-reserve force of this kind is far more

---

*I am grateful to George Andreopoulos for suggesting this metaphor to me.
†For stimulating discussion of the difficult questions of when and how to intervene, see Jonathan Moore, ed., *Hard Choices: Moral Dilemmas in Humanitarian Intervention* (Lanham, MD: Rowman & Littlefield, 1998).

likely to be established in the near term and far less likely to be regretted in the future. Perhaps in addition to these measures, the HRSC might oversee force reductions in national armies and establish a corps of trained "nation-builders" who could meet humanitarian needs and coordinate reconstruction on the ground once situations stabilized.

Undoubtedly, the best way to reduce violence within and among states is to promote genuine democratization, removing authoritarian rulers and alleviating the grinding poverty that feeds instability and violence.* DHR sets out a template for providing immediate and appreciable improvements in people's lives by focusing on securing fundamental rights. When democracy delivers tangible results it stands a much better chance of survival. In the utopian long run, intervention will become obsolete as democracy takes root and flourishes.

Paying the Bills

How to pay for the institutions and programs proposed here deserves a moment's reflection; cost is frequently raised as an objection to comprehensive social guarantees and ambitious schemes for international development. I give this problem only a moment's reflection because I take the objection to be primarily ideological rather than genuinely practical: the resources are available. Adequate funding for a meaningful program of democratic development is primarily a question of political will.

Perhaps the best known proposal for generating revenues for global development is the Tobin tax, first unveiled in 1972 by Yale economist and Nobel Laureate James Tobin. The Tobin tax is a levy on foreign exchange transactions; Tobin first proposed it as a way of slowing and reducing speculative capital flows,† though recent advocates have also focused on its revenue-generating potential.[35] Other options include taxes on foreign trade and exchange, carbon-based and pollution taxes, and various user fees, such as taxes on international air travel . Some revenues would also be generated through fines on TNCs found to be noncompliant in human rights audits. My point is less to advocate a particular method of revenue creation than to note that possibilities abound. Many of these taxes, like the original Tobin

---

*Sen's remarkable work on famine and democracy remains the most persuasive testimony for democratization in this regard; see Sen, "Freedoms and Needs."

†Overseas Development Institute, *New Sources of Finance for Development* [Briefing Paper] (Overseas Development Institute, 1996 [cited 2000]); available from www.oneworld.org/odi/odi_briefing196.html. The tax dampens capital flows because the margins on currency speculation are quite small; a tax of .01 percent of turnover would add 20 percent to the costs of transactions, wiping out margins on many deals and thus deterring speculation and stabilizing currency markets. At this level the tax would have generated between $12 and 24 billion annually (based on turnover rates of about $1 trillion a day).

proposal or a tax on carbon-based fuel use, can simultaneously serve desirable policy aims. Critics frequently allege that such imposts would be impossible to collect because of the international economy's complexity; evasion, enforcement, and investor displeasure are often cited, though these same objections apply at the national level, where taxation is effectively implemented in many countries. Moreover, the computerization of most large-scale financial transactions today should facilitate easier collection.[36]

Another possibility for funding democratic development would be something like a global Marshall Plan. Such a fund, sponsored by developed countries and perhaps philanthropies and even individual donations, would represent an investment in peace, security, and prosperity for everyone. At present such a program might seem highly utopian, but as I shall argue in the next chapter, building popular support for global human rights development must become a political priority for democrats. Such a fund might be a useful and politically popular way to begin; like the original Marshal Plan it would symbolize a proud commitment to a more democratic future.

Conclusion

I have discussed three types of institution required by DHR: representative political institutions, direct functional institutions involved in providing services and guaranteeing specific rights, and indirect functional institutions charged with policy, oversight, and enforcement for human rights in direct functional institutions, government agencies, and other systems of governance. These varied mechanisms constitute a comprehensive, participatory framework institutionalizing social guarantees of fundamental human rights against standard threats.

This democratic framework is likely to encounter three general criticisms, each of which I want to address briefly by way of conclusion. The first concerns an excessive legalism, allegedly characteristic of human rights discourse and frequently attributed to a particularly American or Anglo-Saxon litigiousness and an obsession with rights more generally. There is a grain of truth in this objection, but one that actually supports the reforms DHR advocates. The excessive legalism of the contemporary human rights regime does betray a serious limitation: the current regime reflects a punitive, and thus retrospective, bias. Human rights activities today are often directed toward the prosecution of violators rather than the preemption of violations. As a comprehensive human rights framework, DHR combines enforcement functions with preventative mechanisms designed to secure human rights and to create opportunities for political participation in the entire process. This shift from punishment to prevention through institutionalized social guarantees of rights subordinates the legal discourse of human rights to a political one. While legal mechanisms are a necessary part of any effective democratic regime, they should be a progressively smaller part of an effective democratic human rights regime.*

The second likely objection is that many of the institutions proposed here, especially the supranational ones in the third category, do not follow the familiar democratic parliamentary model. They are not democratic institutions, the objection would go, because they are not representative, and the system is not democratic because it does not allow people an equal role in making all the decisions that affect them. This objection is misplaced; it applies the criteria of sovereign democracy to DHR, criteria DHR is designed to replace. As Rosenau has written, "the test of whether democracy is evolving in globalized space is not whether the institutions of representation and responsibility conform to those to be found in territorial polities."[37] DHR indicates that a more appropriate test is whether more people enjoy secure guarantees of their fundamental rights, including, but not solely, their right to political participation.

Democracy's promise of freedom and equality for all is a substantive promise, not merely a procedural one; while representative institutions are essential for realizing democracy, they are insufficient. In moving away from modern democracy's strict reliance on electoral mechanisms, DHR joins company with other promising trends in contemporary democratic theory, including efforts to theorize "real utopias," to institutionalize deliberation in practical decision-contexts, and through innovative devices like polls, audits, and juries. DHR's flexibility lets it incorporate and accommodate such efforts while remaining open to evolving representative arrangements. Such flexibility recommends DHR as a conceptual and institutional framework, one well-adapted to the tremendous uncertainty surrounding globalization and our possible democratic futures.

The final objection is complexity: the network of overlapping institutions and mechanisms, and the variety of duties with which they are charged, might seem overly, even harmfully, complicated. My response to this objection has three parts. First, while complex, these arrangements are still probably less onerous than the global federations or parliamentary systems some cosmopolitan democrats propose. Besides, as I discuss in the next chapter, many already existing institutions could be transformed to serve many of the functions outlined here. Second, because DHR is concerned with emancipation, it favors reducing government of all kinds to the minimum possible level compatible with secure enjoyment of human rights. This is because governmental institutions can themselves too easily become sources of domina-

---

*Of course, criminalizing human rights violations in municipal law, while "legalistic," is vitally important to successful human rights protection and enforcement and to the rule of law generally.

tion or unwarranted interference. Moreover, undue complexity makes the system harder for people to use and understand, damaging their enjoyment of rights. Thus DHR has a conceptual preference for as much simplicity as possible. That said, and this is my third point, there is no reason to think global democracy will be easy; even at the national level effective democracy is probably more cumbersome than other forms of rule and damnably difficult to achieve. So we must avoid confusing complexity with unnecessary complexity, keeping in mind that the democratic criterion for *necessity* here is secure enjoyment of human rights.

In conclusion, I want to reiterate that the institutions proposed here are just that, proposals, designed to further flesh out the normative requirements of DHR and to promote discussion of how its goals can be realized. DHR's primary commitment is to developing effective means of guaranteeing human rights, not to any particular institutional scheme. In the next chapter, I consider how such institutions, and the normative ideals animating them, might be cultivated and implemented globally.

CHAPTER 9

Implementing Democracy
as Human Rights

In the last chapter we surveyed the institutions through which democracy as human rights might be realized; this chapter concludes the presentation of democracy as human rights (DHR) by considering how it might be implemented. Too often proposals for democratization pay insufficient attention to implementation. Bracketing or ignoring questions about how the recommended institutions might be put into place makes it difficult to assess a proposal's plausibility and to know how we might get from here to there. Consider two examples. First, many critics of globalization lament the state's capture by corporate and financial interests or its helplessness before powerful forces of globalization. They call for global regulatory institutions and a global democratic constitution and parliament to rein in transnational corporations (TNCs), make international governance organizations (IGOs) and international financial institutions (IFIs) accountable, and manage the world economy and environment. Given the hypothesized corruption or impotence of states, however, it must fall to other agents to carry out reform. Who are these agents? How will they succeed in creating global democracy when states are too weak or unwilling to do so? Second, proponents of UN reform hope to achieve many similar aims through strengthening and democratizing the UN system: an empowered General Assembly, reformed and restructured Security Council, and so on. But how will a system predicated upon its members' sovereignty address problems of global governance for which solutions entail weakening or abolishing traditional sovereignty in many areas? Why should permanent Security Council members in particular agree to changes that would reduce their power within the UN system? Why should nondemocratic governments want to democratize the UN?

My point in emphasizing plausible implementation is not that we should evaluate reform proposals by their chances of becoming reality; we have to accept that reform will be difficult to achieve under even the best circumstances.* My point is rather that ignoring implementation invites sloppy thinking, allowing us to overlook that our proposed solutions might rely on assumptions invalidated by our original assessment of the problem. Such inattention risks reducing theorizing about global democracy to mere navel gazing. I shall try to avoid these problems by specifying how DHR might be achieved. I first address the transition to a democratic human rights regime, outlining an incremental approach to implementation grounded in the activities of transnational civil society. In the second part of the chapter I look at how DHR might work in connection with the WTO, among the most controversial and bitterly despised institutions associated with globalization. I consider general democratic criticisms of the WTO, then focus on its contentious intellectual property regime as it pertains to agriculture. The general criticisms let us revisit key differences between DHR and cosmopolitan and state reinforcement approaches in a practical context, while the case study involving agriculture allows us to demonstrate how key institutions and procedures in DHR might work.

Democratization Through Transnational Civil Society?

In chapter 5 I criticized global civil society (GCS) as an inadequate and inappropriate model for global democracy, arguing that GCS theory mistakes activity supportive of democracy with the thing itself. In making this critique I was careful to acknowledge the important role civil society actors and movements play in positively affecting specific issues and in shaping certain supranational policy domains. I also differentiated transnational networks promoting democratization of national political regimes from the question of GCS as a global democratic model. These distinctions are crucial because, as I shall argue here, supranational social and political activity can play a pivotal role in democratizing global governance. While proponents of GCS see it as constitutive of democracy, I maintain that we need to focus instead on its instrumental role in bringing about democracy. To help make this distinction clear, I shall use the term *transnational* civil society (TCS) in referring both to the supranational activity discussed by GCS theorists and to the role of transnational networks in facilitating domestic democratization.

To begin, we can emphasize that in addition to the issue networks and movements surveyed in chapter 5 there is a substantial degree of cooperation

---

*Besides, as Held observes, those chances can be difficult to assess: significant institutional change can take place remarkably rapidly in the wake of a major crisis in the international system; David Held, *Democracy and the Global Order: From the Modern State to Cosmopolitan Governance* (Stanford, CA: Stanford University Press, 1995), 281.

between principled domestic opposition groups and TCS actors. This activity is described by the "spiral model" developed by Risse and Sikkink.[1] This model describes not democracy but democratization, explaining how relatively weak movements for human rights and democracy in authoritarian countries managed to have such profound transformative effects on entrenched and intransigent regimes. Dissident and opposition groups proved amazingly successful in highlighting governments' failure to abide by their public commitments to democracy and human rights. Their success undermined those governments' credibility and legitimacy and helped spur diplomatic, economic, and political pressure for change. In exploring what he calls the "Helsinki Effect," Thomas has recently shown that even when governments and diplomats on all sides dismiss initial commitments as mere window dressing, as many did the human rights provisions of the Helsinki Final Act of 1975, principled social movements can nonetheless have a very powerful effect.[2] Similar processes were at work in antiauthoritarian and human rights campaigns in Latin America.[3] As the spiral model makes clear, then, transnational networks' success in initiating domestic democratization and ending human rights abuses depends crucially on effective targeting of domestic actors and institutions.

This model cannot be directly applied to democratization of *global* governance, as Markoff observes, without specification of the points of leverage for transnational movements in the international system, points which today are hardly obvious.[4] In the domestic context, such groups were able to use economic disruption, political protest, international diplomatic and media pressures, and other familiar tactics to leverage regime change. Such tactics, and the underlying sense of national cohesion and shared experience that held sometimes fissiparous opposition movements together, do not translate easily to the supranational context and global governance regimes. IGOs are not obviously vulnerable to the same kinds of tactics and pressures, in part because of their intergovernmental nature and in part because they·lack a clear and constant "constituency." Indeed, it is not even clear what "the regime" comprises: when we talk about democratizing global governance, do we mean the International Labor Organization and the International Criminal Court as well as the IMF and the WTO? While more acceptable to many critics, the former institutions are *institutionally* quite similar to the latter.

Second, because different regimes affect different countries and groups within them differently, there is unlikely to be much natural solidarity for or against "the regime"—although consensus remains possible on specific issues. Even when agreement does coalesce, however, it is likely to be oppositional and issue-specific; less a form of "solidarity" than a temporary alignment of interests. Solidarity around substantive political issues is barely conceivable given existing economic and political differences. Opposition to the WTO is a good example: many protesters in the rich Western countries oppose the WTO because in their view it undercuts popular sovereignty, strains postindustrial economies, and undermines human rights and sustainable development in poorer countries. But many critics in poorer countries oppose the WTO mainly because the trade rules and the decision and dispute systems are unfair to developing countries. So while some opponents want less trade, others want more, and on better terms.

Nonetheless, there are reasons for optimism regarding the transformative potential of TCS. Recent evidence suggests that transnational networks and social movements can effectively target specific global institutions.[5] The networks derive their influence from their ability to shape the international agenda, to negotiate within various international forums, to strengthen and support local organizations and coalitions, and to use their moral authority to pressure officials and raise public consciousness.[6] Transnational networks also frequently draw on well-established norms of democracy and human rights to construct frames for collective action and opposition to oppressive regimes.[7] The movement opposing the construction of big dams in India's Narmada River Valley was particularly effective in drawing on widely recognized norms of democracy and human rights.[8] Similarly, while strategies for influencing the World Bank vary across specific issue domains, appeals to the right of participation in decision making have been very effective in persuading the Bank to reconsider its policies and approach.[9]

Critics will note that much of this activity is quite similar to that cited by proponents of GCS, whose arguments I have criticized; they will suspect some legerdemain, the tendentious enlistment of all things good about transnational activity into the service of my own preferred account of democracy. One part of this objection is right on the mark: I am describing much of the same activity cited by proponents of GCS. The difference, and the point must be underlined, lies in how this activity is conceived. While theorists of GCS treat it as tantamount or ultimately adding up to global democracy, I understand it as vital in bringing about democratization. The difference is like conceiving regular exercise as equivalent with good health versus as an essential means of achieving it.

One advantage of conceiving global democratization through TCS is that it makes room for the normative commitment to democracy and human rights, and in a context where political and institutional support for those values is lacking. Given the panoply of fragmented governance regimes at the global level, virtually none of which is democratic, this approach seems fitting. One aim of TCS is to reconnect politics with the moral purpose and values associated with democracy.[10] Making such connections is vital because, given the improbability of substantive political agreement cited above, substantive normative agreement about the logic of global governance seems the best basis for cooperation toward democratization. By joining the normative commitments and institutional program of DHR with the networks of principled political action described by TCS, we can begin to discern a plausible path from here to there.

Effecting the Transition to a Democratic Human Rights Regime

Even if TCS can effectively target undemocratic regimes at the supranational level, mobilizing networks and alliances to bring pressure for reform through asserting values like democracy and human rights, Markoff's criticism remains troubling: will there be effective points of leverage from which to push for democracy and human rights? In targeting the World Bank, does one protest at its Washington headquarters, in the capitals where governments appoint its governors and formulate its policy, or in the localities where its projects are executed? How does one concentrate popular pressure on entities whose constituency is a tiny group of national leaders but whose activities potentially affect billions? What kind of sanctions can one impose, what kind of unrest can be stirred, to affect organizations that conduct no trade, control no territory, rule no population? How can one enlist states to transform the regimes they fund and direct?

I want to suggest that points of leverage from which to press for democracy and human rights in the supranational arena can and must be *constructed*. Much of the initial work does not require states' involvement or the cooperation of the targeted regimes. Social and political movements can strengthen existing institutions and create new ones. Efforts to strengthen existing institutions might focus on established regional human rights commissions and courts. Although many of these regional organizations are weak and ineffective (the European Court of Human Rights is an exception), many nonetheless possess at least a modicum of funding and legitimacy. Perhaps more importantly, their formal powers are often impressive, especially when optional protocols and other arrangements are considered. If these powers could be actualized and augmented, regional institutions could become formidable redoubts in the battle for global democracy. The efforts of prosecuting judge Baltasar Garzón in the Pinochet case are instructive: using only powers already recognized but rarely invoked under Spanish and international law, he managed almost alone to strengthen the human rights enforcement regime considerably. Though he is a controversial figure, and though the results of that particular case were disappointing, the example demonstrates how much can be done within the existing framework to enhance global enforcement of human rights and generate popular sympathy and support for the effort.

Another advantage of targeting regional institutions is the potential for exploiting governments' existing democratic and human rights commitments. Many governments are already formally pledged to relatively strict regimens of monitoring and mediation through regional human rights institutions. The gap between these paper commitments and present practice provides a textbook opportunity for creating leverage to drive reform. Bolstered by human rights NGOs and activist networks, regional institutions and their member states might be encouraged or embarrassed into undertaking more energetic utilization of their existing powers. Greater publicity would heighten awareness about these institutions, and TCS could cajole them to responsible use of their revivified powers, initiating a virtuous spiral.

Other efforts targeting established institutions could include local initiatives demanding human rights policy and budgetary analysis as implemented by the San Francisco Committee on the Status of Women. Such initiatives could be pursued through petition, referenda, and election of supportive candidates to local office or be launched by civil society groups directly, giving institutional substance to the idea of a "parallel polis" advocated by some early proponents of civil society's democratizing potential in authoritarian regimes.[11] Developing local political parties or movements to push for a democratic human rights agenda would cultivate grassroots support for DHR and help build transnational networks. None of these initiatives requires unreasonable resources and none faces depressingly long odds.

With respect to new institutions, DHR can begin from the bottom up. Many of the functions proposed in the previous chapter could be implemented without state approval or cooperation from the targeted regimes. Audits and oversight of local government and DFIs can be conducted, albeit imperfectly, by citizen watch-dog groups and publicized in and beyond communities; larger-scale audits, such as the Democratic Audit of the United Kingdom, might be conducted through foundations or universities in conjunction with local and TCS networks. Local councils might begin as parallel or shadow governmental organizations rather than as direct governmental entities. Formal and informal human rights education could be initiated through schools, universities, and community groups, all of which can form networks through Internet and telecommunications technologies.[12]

Corporations might be similarly targeted by movements. Campaigns for corporate compliance with human rights standards similar to those used so successfully against authoritarian regimes might also be initiated through NGOs and global networks of locally dispersed activists. Campaigns of this kind—Nestlé and Nike come to mind—have been effective, though they have not carried over into more systematic or sustained efforts. Still, these and other cases show that bad publicity about human rights practices can be costly and damaging. Other strategies include the threat of boycotts and picketing to persuade retailers like the ubiquitous Starbucks coffee chain to sell so-called Fair Trade Coffee, which returns more of the profit directly to growers.

Such decisions by market-leading firms can create positive ripple effects: Starbucks' decision to sell Fair Trade Coffee has many analysts persuaded that other major coffee retailers will follow suit. The Fair Trade movement, though in its infancy, is growing quickly and provides another example of a decentralized and popularly driven alternative to formal reform.[13] Although we should not be too sanguine about the policies or priorities of TNCs, the proper mix of persuasion and pressure could help make respect for human rights a crucial component of good business practice.

Eventually, even IGOs might become targets, with networks of associations joining to bring coordinated pressure on the institutions themselves and on their political masters through carefully coordinated protests and through regional commissions and courts. In many instances these institutions are already committed on paper to lofty goals and ideals: the Preamble to the WTO Agreement* calls for "positive efforts designed to ensure that developing countries, and especially the least developed among them, secure a share in the growth in international trade commensurate with the needs of their economic development." Again, points of political leverage exist wherever rhetoric does not match reality.

As these examples illustrate, a great deal of the auditing and oversight activity envisioned by DHR could be carried on independently, without the cooperation of the targeted entities. Obviously, without that cooperation and without enforceable mandates, the performance and effectiveness of these institutions will be severely limited and some of their functions will be impossible. Still, activities such as those described here could help build crucial momentum and legitimacy for DHR. Numerous public monitoring and watchdog groups operate today, and though their effectiveness is undoubtedly constrained by a lack of cooperation with governance agencies and by limited access to information, they have nonetheless effectively publicized serious wrongs and undemocratic activities, embarrassed governments and corporations, and catalyzed demands for change. The best examples of such groups are in the field of human rights monitoring and advocacy, where such organizations as Amnesty International and Human Rights Watch have been enormously successful in this regard.[†]

---

*By "Agreement" I refer to the Final Act of the Uruguay Round of Multilateral Trade Negotiations and the associated legal instruments incorporated in its Annexes, including the Agreement on Trade-Related Aspects of Intellectual Property Rights (TRIPS). These documents are available from the WTO at http://docsonline.wto.org/gen_home.asp?language=1&_=1. For an overview see John H. Jackson, *The World Trade Organization: Constitution and Jurisprudence* (London: Royal Institute of International Affairs, 1998).

†On the limits of their approach, see below and David Rieff, "The Precarious Triumph of Human Rights," *The New York Times Magazine*, August 8, 1999; Michael Ignatieff, "Human Rights: The Midlife Crisis," *The New York Review of Books* 46, no. 9 (1999).

Incremental realization of procedures like audits and local hearings cannot be overemphasized; informal, popular efforts can play a significant role in conditioning the behavior of key actors at all levels of governance, operating as informal adjuncts to existing governance structures. Bottom-up democratization and democratic innovation are plausible and consistent with DHR, unlike proposals reliant upon global institution-building and global law, which seem to rely implicitly on state action. Still, DHR must make the transition from this informal stage to full implementation. This victory might come about through a global political party committed to DHR,[14] via state-based or regional parties that adopt DHR as their core platform, or through campaigns to integrate DHR into the manifestos of all major political parties. The key is to nurture organized political support for democratic reform at the global level, to build a global democratic community to support not just worthy causes but a programmatic transformation of global governance. Such a political movement, instead of contesting policy issues within existing democratic states, would focus instead on constructing global democratic institutions. The odds are long, but the course is clear and eminently democratic: grassroots support must ultimately be translated into victory in the battle of the ballot box. This approach would mark a major development in the Western human rights movement, which despite enormous successes has never evolved into a *political movement* of any kind; human rights in the West has been more a moral than a political commitment. The antiglobalization movement, by contrast, puts boots on the pavement but lacks political coherence; as noted earlier, it is defined by common opposition to specific aspects of the emerging global governance regime rather than by shared commitment to a principled alternative. DHR envisions a sustained global political movement unified around democratic principles as necessary for achieving systemic transformation.

As these brief remarks attest, I endorse an incrementalist approach to developing a robust democratic human rights regime. This approach reflects pragmatism coupled with the belief that authoritative and legitimate governance regimes must evolve over time. Incrementalism should not be confused with quietism, however: DHR calls for an activist and participatory program for implementation consistent with its universal commitments and with historical patterns of democratization, including those instigated through the efforts of TCS. What I take to be crucial is its explicit recognition and utilization of democracy and human rights' unparalleled moral and political potency. Too many contemporary political theorists have doubted or rejected this power.[15] These norms enjoy truly global legitimacy, offering hope for a better life and indicating a clear, though for that no less arduous, way forward toward that life.[16] DHR, in turn, provides a core normative framework that reconnects TCS with the moral purpose and values of democracy, to repeat Falk's phrase. DHR also furnishes an institutional program around which TCS might organize and direct its energies and activities in the supranational domain.

Two potential problems deserve brief mention here, one concerning sovereignty, the other, indifference. One of the most significant obstacles to ambitious supranational reform is the jealously guarded sovereignty of states. As I have repeated several times, states remain the most powerful international political actors and look likely to remain so for a long time. Many would certainly object to and resist some of the reforms advocated here, including many democratic ones. Democratization will be achieved by social forces demanding and ultimately creating global democracy, not through states embarking on their own on an enlightened program of institutional construction and reform. If states are to cooperate in democratization they will have to be brought to do so through political necessity, which only a strong, coordinated, and cohesive political movement can generate. Some writers and activists have described this goal as the creation of a "human rights culture," a social awareness and understanding of human rights, how they work, what respect for them entails, and a positive commitment to their realization. Building a human rights culture means nurturing a political discourse informed by and concerned with democratic human rights—not just in headline-grabbing atrocities and disasters but in our homes, our communities, our schools and clubs, our governments, and around the world. It means expanding that political commitment through which DHR generates democratic community.

The second problem concerns just this kind of politics: is it reasonable to hope for such a transformation, given the apathy and indifference many of us witness daily? As Geras asks,

> what . . . are the implications for normative political theory of the bystander phenomenon: that is, of the depressing but widespread fact that so many people do not come to the aid of others under attack, whether fellow citizens or merely human beings, and also do not come to the aid of them in dire need or great distress?[17]

His own sobering conclusion is that modern liberal society rests on a "contract of mutual indifference" in which we all abnegate our rights by failing to defend the rights of others in need.[18]

Among the subtle tragedies of two decades of neoliberal rhetoric and "reform" is that many people have lost faith in politics to do good and to limit evil, to make us and the world better. Geras sees some hope in the possibility of a rule-governed normative system that constrains its members as well as benefiting them, a system that curbs evil in addition to promoting good.[19] In many respects DHR is such a system. It empowers individuals and imposes clear individual and collective duties on them. Its social guarantees against threats to human rights institutionalize concern for others in a sort of collective undertaking of obligations that we might as individuals omit or ignore. This kind of politics can and should give us hope, renewing and reinvigorating our commitment to democracy.

How Would it Work: Democratic Critique of the WTO

We have seen how DHR might be implemented; how would it work? To demonstrate the general approach, I use three broad democratic criticisms of the WTO to contrast DHR with other alternatives. I then demonstrate how DHR's procedures and institutions would work by focusing on WTO rules governing intellectual property and their effects on agriculture.

The main democratic complaints about the WTO are that it is undemocratic in its conception, its internal procedures, and its aims and powers. The WTO's proposed creation stirred controversy and attracted criticism even before the Agreement took effect. Opponents objected to the secrecy surrounding the negotiations and to the ratification processes in member states. The treaty was negotiated in secret, and debate on it was stymied by the unavailability of relevant documents, part of a plan, Ralph Nader has alleged, to mislead the public and its representatives.[20] The organization is also viewed as procedurally undemocratic, violating norms of transparency and accountability with its tight secrecy in dispute resolution proceedings, lack of external appeals, and apparent conflicts of interest.[21] Poorer countries find it difficult to maintain adequate delegations in Geneva to ensure that their interests are represented; compounding this problem, the rich countries, meeting behind closed doors, and outside of the rules, often work out deals and force them on other members.[22]

Finally, critics assert that the WTO pursues undemocratic ends using antidemocratic powers. The undemocratic ends include everything from trade liberalization leading to growing economic inequality to a "race to the bottom" in labor and environmental standards and even American-led economic imperialism. On this view the WTO is an instrument to be "used by the developed countries of the North to neo-colonize the countries of the poor South and find solutions to their own mounting problems at the cost of these countries.... The WTO, in short, [lays] the foundation of the total annihilation of the South."[23] The antidemocratic powers allegedly include the right of unelected bureaucrats in Geneva to "overrule democratic decision-making ..." on a host of issues, from preserving dwindling virgin forests to banning carcinogenic products from food.[24]* In sum, critics of the WTO see it as an "oligarchy" protecting and presiding over a system that destroys standards of living for most people in the world, both in developed and developing countries, increases worldwide unemployment, leads to endemic business criminality and to the collapse of legal order, to environmental degradation, political chaos, and global despair about the future.[25]

In November 1999 popular concern over the substance of WTO rules and decisions and anger about its secretive and unaccountable procedures boiled over in massive protests at the organization's ministerial meeting in Seattle. The so-called Battle of Seattle witnessed tens, perhaps hundreds of thousands of demonstrators taking to the streets in peaceful protest of "what they [saw] as the trade organization's role in worsening air pollution, killing animals, and undermining national sovereignty."[26] The protesters hoped their actions could forestall further liberalization of trade rules and pressure the WTO to impose minimum standards on labor conditions and environmental responsibility. Widespread use of heavy-handed tactics by the police did little to improve the organization's battered public image.[†] Since the Battle of Seattle, mass protests of IGOs and IFIs, even of the meetings of leaders of major industrialized economies, have become routine. While the WTO has revamped its public relations machine in the wake of these events, its agenda and procedures have changed little; it convened its subsequent meeting in Qatar, well out of protesters' geographical and political reach.

The WTO makes an excellent subject for reflection on global democracy because it nicely illustrates what I have called the paradox of sovereign democracy. In cases where freedom and equality demand reform or policy action outside the state, traditional democratic theory seems to require both that supranational governance be put to democratic purposes and that it be rejected as undemocratic. This tension was evident in Seattle, as a *New York Times* reporter perceptively observed:

> While environmental activists and labor rights groups briefly exulted that their "Stop the WTO" marches had helped do exactly that, they are likely to be angry again, too. The ferocity of the arguments here—both

---

* Decisions in high-profile cases concerning sea turtles caught in shrimp nets and clean air standards for gasoline have reinforced these worries, despite the protestations of WTO officials who allege, with some justice, that their decisions have been (innocently or willfully) misconstrued; see World Trade Organization Appellate Body, "United States—Import Prohibition of Certain Shrimp and Shrimp Products—AB-1998-4—Report of the Appellate Body" (Geneva: World Trade Organization, 1998); World Trade Organization Appellate Body, "United States—Standards for Reformulated and Conventional Gasoline —AB 1996-1—Report of the Appellate Body" (Geneva: World Trade Organization, 1996).

† In one memorable picture worth at least a thousand words, fully armored riot police are shown standing guard in front of a gleaming Niketown outlet.

in the street and in the conference rooms—made it abundantly clear that it would be a long time before the trade group would be empowered to impose trade sanctions against countries that allow children to work in factories, that do not protect sea turtles from fishing nets, or that clear-cut virgin forests.[27]

Protesters wanted to stop the WTO because they opposed its power to "overturn" domestic law and policy and what they saw as the inevitable race to the bottom in labor and environmental standards that power would trigger.* In succeeding, however, they eliminated any realistic chance for improving or enforcing those standards globally in the near future, a goal that paradoxically requires some supranational agency with the power to overturn "bad" decisions but unable to reverse "good" ones. The scare quotes indicate the further paradox implicit in trying to determine what "good" and "bad" mean: a Western factory worker's race to the bottom might be a Chinese peasant's chance at a better life.

This paradox concerning trade issues demonstrates the futility of strategies of democratic state reinforcement. Even if one cares only about democracy at home, ensuring it will sometimes require multilateral action in an interdependent world: enforcing domestic environmental standards, for instance, demands global cooperation. Less obviously, the trade paradox also points to difficulties with cosmopolitan approaches. Held's reconceptualized sovereignty solves the problem of democratic legitimacy by ensuring that those affected (or their representatives) decide, preserving the autonomy at the heart of his account of democracy and supplying democratic legitimacy. Trade is (unevenly) global, so (nearly) everyone is affected, so the global parliament decides and its decisions are democratically legitimate by hypothesis. Formally there is no difficulty, but in practice substantive disagreements about trade would simply be transposed into formal disputes over who decides. Take labor standards: people in many developing countries, including democratic ones, reject such standards as disguised protectionism. They might argue that labor standards are a domestic concern and, invoking subsidiarity, opt to decide them at home. Unionized workers in the developed world might counter (sincerely or instrumentally) that labor standards are questions of democracy and human rights and insist that these standards be set globally. Controversy over who decides would thus replace substantive controversies without rendering them more susceptible of solution. There is no democratic

---

*I place *overturn* in quotation marks to signal that the charge is not, strictly speaking, true. Upon finding that certain laws or regulations, as applied, constitute nontariff barriers to trade, the WTO requires that member nations bring the offending regulations into compliance. Article XXII of the Agreement provides for extensive sanctions, including suspension of trade concessions and compensation, if the violation is not corrected. In effect, Members have a choice: change or rescind the offending measures or accept sanctions.

way to decide who decides: once the democratic community is no longer a given, sovereign forms of democratic legitimacy become unworkable.

How Would it Work? DHR and the WTO

How would DHR address these issues? Does it provide a reasonable and workable alternative? In addressing these questions I shall leave aside criticisms of the WTO's creation for an eminently practical reason: the WTO exists. Insofar as secrecy and deception were part of its design or ratification, the process was undemocratic; this conclusion seems so straightforward as to render further discussion of it moot. Besides, we now confront the challenge of democratizing the WTO (or abolishing it), not founding it anew. How to create governance institutions democratically is an interesting and important question, but it is not my question here.[28] Rather, I am concerned with showing how my democratic human rights approach might democratize organizations like the WTO.

To begin, let us consider in more detail WTO rules governing Trade-Related Aspects of Intellectual Property Rights (TRIPS) and their impact on agriculture and human rights. Article 27.1 of the TRIPS Agreement (an annex to the WTO Agreement) "requires Members to provide for patents 'for all inventions, whether products or processes, in all fields of technology.'"[29] TRIPS rules (Article 27.3(b)) allow Members to exclude plants and animals, but not microorganisms, from patentability but require Members to provide protection for new plant varieties using patents, an "effective *sui generis* system," or both.[30] The rules also require that nonbiological and microbiological processes for producing plants and animals be patentable.[31] These controversial provisions have huge implications for the pharmaceutical and agricultural sectors, among others; I shall restrict my remarks to agriculture.

The TRIPS agreement arouses great hostility because of its implications for seed use and availability and for protection of traditional knowledge and farmers' rights. Seed use and availability involves two core concerns. The first has to do with genetic use restriction technologies (GURTS).[32] These are of two kinds: "terminator" technologies, seeds engineered to yield crops producing sterile seeds, and "traitor" technologies, seeds engineered to require chemicals for germination and healthy growth to yield crops whose seeds also require such chemicals. The former technology threatens to make farmers dependent on seed companies, the latter on agrochemical concerns.[33] Such dependency is extremely risky and has significant implications for food rights and food security. "For most small-scale farmers access to land and water, seeds and tools are [sic] the basis of their food security. For many, complete dependence on the market for their inputs or to buy their food needs is simply too risky and is likely to be so for the foreseeable future."[34] In Tanzania, for example, 80 percent of the population depends on agriculture, and 90 percent of that group relies on saved seeds. By making seed saving useless or unaffordable, GURTS could wreak mass devastation on Tanzanian agriculture and society.[35] Proponents of GURTS maintain that the increased yields derived from modified seeds would outweigh the costs of annual seed or chemical purchases, leading to greater production and higher returns. This argument rests on faulty assumptions, however: many small farmers lack the resources for initial investments in genetically modified seeds and most have little or no control over market prices for their crops;[36] while the technology might benefit large commercial farmers, it could destroy independent and subsistence farmers.*

Worries about GURTS are compounded by rules that inadequately protect traditional knowledge and the rights of farmers, concerns sometimes described in terms of "biopiracy."[37] The TRIPS model of property rights, informed by Western scientific paradigms stressing experimental research and individual invention, copes poorly with traditional knowledge, which is often informal, rarely codified, and frequently understood as the common property or shared inheritance of a group of people rather than of a single author.[38] TRIPS also protects farmers' rights poorly. Most farmers' innovation is environmentally based rather than experimental; adaptation and mutation are managed within a specific ecosystem to maintain equilibrium rather than to reach an optimal point. Such innovations are difficult to patent or protect under the TRIPS regime.[39] Further, seeds are commonly developed and shared over time, becoming widely diffused; corporations can acquire these seeds and patent them, guaranteeing themselves future compensation while ignoring the contributions of "upstream" cultivators.[40] This problem is exacerbated because TRIPS protects "essential derived varieties" of seeds, meaning that further modifications of GM seeds, even those made by farmers using traditional methods, are covered by the original patents.[41]

Unless altered, some observers fear this regime could lead to a few companies controlling seed production for all major commercially important crops in a few years.[42] Patent concentration of this kind would drastically alter the economics of small-scale agricultural production, pricing poor people out of subsistence farming and putting independent local agriculture under the thumb of Western seed and chemical conglomerates.[43] The result would be the wholesale transformation of traditional agronomic practices, with profound

---

*No one can "force" farmers to use genetically engineered seeds, but trade pressures brought by rich-country governments home to the TNCs holding patents on GURTS make it difficult for developing countries to resist their introduction; once these seeds make their way into a market, fewer natural seeds are subsequently available for saving, triggering a vicious cycle toward dependence on the patented seeds.

effects on the rights and livelihood of local producers: as James Boyle of Duke Law School describes it, "a new round of enclosures in what were the global commons."[44] Compounding these problems, many groups most impacted by TRIPS rules on agriculture doubt whether plants, as part of creation, should be patentable at all. Their views on ownership of knowledge and custom, like their agricultural practices, differ profoundly from Western beliefs. Because intellectual property questions are decided in undemocratic forums, however, these alternative views never receive adequate consideration.[45] Because WTO rules mandate that only member states can participate in trade negotiations, possessors and users of traditional knowledge are unrepresented, except perhaps, poorly, by national trade negotiators.[46] And true to form, rich countries reached agreements on TRIPS behind closed doors and presented them to less-organized developing countries as accomplished facts, further diluting traditional groups' already weak representation.[47]

DHR, like other proposals for global democracy, would remedy the internal deficiencies of the WTO by mandating greater participation, deliberation, transparency, and responsiveness or accountability. The right to political participation requires involvement in deliberation at the stages of policy formation, implementation, and review. Its social guarantee requires more than simply making officials' deliberations open to the public; it creates an affirmative obligation for the WTO to seek and respect input from individuals and groups whose rights would be affected by the proposed policies. Full transparency, including access to information and to decision makers, is a necessary part of meaningful participation and deliberation. Accountability would not require making the WTO answerable to a global parliament or to a global electorate (though it would not preclude such arrangements). The primary focus of democratic responsiveness or accountability in DHR is compliance with fundamental human rights. This compliance would be enforced through audits and through regional commissions and courts.

Trade's aims and effects would also be democratized through DHR, negatively, through limits on permissible activities, and positively, through transformation of the trade regime itself. First, DHR imposes demanding requirements on all governance agencies, including IFIs like the WTO. Compliance with fundamental rights implies duties not to directly threaten or violate rights and to ensure that policies and programs do not create or lead to violations. All governance agencies must take appropriate measures to meet these obligations both with respect to their internal procedures and their programs and policies. So the WTO would have to guarantee fairness and participation internally and show that its policies had no adverse effect on rights to security or to an adequate standard of living (as well as others). Trade rules, like those governing intellectual property, would be assessed for their likely impact in areas like traditional agriculture.[48] In this respect

DHR would in essence place negative constraints on the global trade regime. Audits and participatory planning, backed by regional commissions and courts, would be the key tools for achieving compliance. It is important to note that neither national interests nor conflicting treaty obligations would shield states or their representatives from their obligations under DHR.[49]

In addition, a fully democratized WTO would have the positive obligation to redesign the trade regime to promote human rights.* Such an initiative would begin with the recognition that human rights have largely been omitted from the rules and objectives of IGOs.[50] Under TRIPS, for instance, human rights concerns register only as exceptions to the rules; a democratic WTO would have to treat human rights as *guiding principles* for intellectual property and for the trade regime generally.[51] This human rights approach to WTO law[52] would insist that the intellectual property regime support the social and economic welfare of the poor (in developed and developing countries) and promote economic development.[53] To be democratically acceptable, the WTO and global integration law more generally should "pursue not only 'economic efficiency' but also 'democratic legitimacy' and 'social justice' as defined by human rights."[54] To put the difference more concretely, a democratic intellectual property regime would seek to maximize human welfare rather than profits or asset values.[55]

This does not mean rejecting intellectual property rights outright. Such rights are recognized in Article 27 of the Universal Declaration of Human Rights. They are neither unimportant nor undesirable from a democratic perspective.[†] But they would have to be defined and interpreted to facilitate the realization of fundamental human rights. Their impact would have to be assessed not primarily at the level of trade flows and GDP, but at the level of human rights, of individuals and groups whose rights were directly affected by the proposed regime.[56] We can better understand DHR's general approach and specific requirements by systematically working through the intellectual property example.

Audits (Impact Assessments and Human Rights Audits)

Both types of audit would be applied to the WTO. We can imagine impact assessments of the WTO's current TRIPS regime covering plants and agricul-

---

*One question that arises under DHR is whether IGOs and IFIs should be considered *necessary* for the realization of rights (considered "direct" in the parlance of chapter 8). The question turns on how we conceive their role in realizing human rights; ironically the best case for conceiving them in this way, and thus subject to the more stringent requirements discussed below, is made by proponents of neoliberalism who insist that development and democracy are impossible without a certain kind of global economic infrastructure (about which I shall have more to say in the book's conclusion).

[†]There are plausible reasons to think that intellectual property rights, properly formulated, could promote development; see Correa, "Traditional Knowledge and Intellectual Property"; UN High Commissioner for Human Rights, "Impact of Trips on Human Rights."

ture: an assessment would analyze the likely effects of TRIPS not just on trade and intellectual property but also on the practices of small-scale and subsistence agriculture.* Issues the impact assessment might cover include:

- how the anticipated change in the cost and availability of seeds would disrupt small-scale and subsistence agriculture, and by how much;
- how the new regime would impact access to food and food security in developing countries;
- how the anticipated changes in crop yields, food supply stability, and consumer prices would affect the well-being of the larger community;
- whether the proposed rules give adequate recognition to the traditional rights of farmers and adequate reward for their stewardship and cultivation of plant genetic resources;
- whether the regime provides adequate rewards to promote further scientific research in agricultural production;
- whether patents, if granted, would eliminate or prevent the use of local or traditional seed stock (for example, through rules about essentially derived varieties);
- whether the regime makes adequate allowances for the sharing and diffusion of new innovations;
- whether patents would preclude or interfere with traditional cross-breeding practices and the use of locally developed seed stocks;
- whether the new regime would allow local farmers to retain discretion in their production methods;
- whether mechanisms are included to compensate those displaced by the anticipated or unanticipated effects of the proposal.

Normally impact assessments should be conducted before a policy is implemented, though in this case and others where IGOs are democratized, retrospective audits in all major policy areas would be required.

In addition to these assessments, the WTO itself would be subject to human rights audits conducted by regional commissions and reviewed by audit juries. These audits would assess such questions as whether the right to participation was adequately protected by an organization's established internal mechanisms and procedures.† The audit would also include review of the organization's impact assessment process. For instance, for the TRIPS rules governing plants and agriculture, compliance with the right to participa-

---

*Note that the audits do not undertake a cost-benefit analysis *of rights*; rather, they analyze how different trade rules might affect the enjoyment of rights on balance. On the difficulties of cost-benefit analyses of rights see Amartya Sen, *Development as Freedom* (New York: Alfred A. Knopf, 1999).
†The World Bank's recent efforts to improve participation in all aspects of its projects and to enhance cooperation with civil society are instructive; see http://www.worldbank.org/participation/.

tion would at a minimum require consultation with traditional farmers and economic and agricultural experts representing diverse social and economic systems. These same constituents should be involved in reviewing the rules following their implementation to evaluate their effects and consider how they might be improved.

Local Councils

Two related functions of the local councils would be relevant in our example: hearings and local review panels. Hearings would provide a forum for people to express concerns about the human rights impact of policies such as rules governing trade and genetically modified seeds. These hearings would be wide-ranging, canvassing local concerns and suggestions on all aspects of the issue. They would also serve a valuable educative function; participants might discuss environmental impacts, sustainability, and overall costs and benefits to the community in human rights terms. Hearings, unlike traditional representative institutions, allow minority voices and viewpoints to be heard and help people to formulate their needs and concerns deliberatively.

Local councils would also assist the WTO in conducting impact assessments and working out effective transitional programs for communities and populations affected by its activities. The hope is that genuine cooperation might develop; IGOs and localities working together could be much more successful in meeting their respective goals and protecting their respective interests than they would be in an antagonistic setting. Such cooperation will not always be possible; real conflicts, including disagreements about basic questions of rights and guarantees, will arise, and in such instances more adversarial interaction is to be expected. Still, cooperation will frequently benefit all parties, even in cases of disagreement. By ensuring a role for public input at early stages of planning and implementation, local involvement can prevent future problems.

Commissions and Courts

The role of commissions and courts in democratizing the WTO would follow from the audit activities described in the previous sections. Recall that in addition to conducting audits, commissions develop the specific criteria and indices for use in all human rights audits. They might also assist the parties in technical matters relating to impact assessments and policy formulation generally (much like the role the UN High Commissioner has played).[57] Should audits reveal problems in the formulation or implementation of policies or in their effects, the commissions would work to develop remediation plans satisfactory to the parties involved. Commissions would also handle appeals from local councils or from the WTO in cases of noncompliance.

Only when efforts at friendly remediation failed would courts become involved. Regional courts might also hear appeals of decisions by WTO dispute resolution panels when those decisions involved human rights matters. This arrangement would help answer charges about the WTO's lack of external or independent appeal mechanisms, but since the courts' jurisdiction would be restricted to cases involving human rights, there should be little risk of "forum shopping." Alternatively, or in conjunction with this plan, regional court judges might sit on dispute panels. Such changes would provide additional layers of review to ensure ongoing compliance with human rights requirements. One can imagine a case concerning whether a communal seed bank violated rules protecting patents on genetically modified seeds, where considerations of intellectual property protection would run up against traditional agricultural practices linked to food access and security. Courts alone could not adequately resolve such matters, but in the broader context of requirements governing policy formation, implementation, and review they could well play an instrumental role.

World Conferences

World conferences would be involved in this case indirectly, in helping to determine the parameters of a democratic global economy. This task would include consideration of the trade regime, to be sure, but would extend to even broader questions concerning sustainable development and democratic control over economic decision making. It would be inappropriate to speculate here about what these parameters might be. World conferences would also define standards for fundamental rights to be audited and enforced by through regional mechanisms.

Transnational Civil Society

Seattle and subsequent protests demonstrated the oppositional power of TCS; within a human rights framework it would be enabled to play a constructive role as well. Independent groups and networks would support the functions just described, including everything from assisting in audits and writing policy papers to mobilizing pressure, shaping moral and political debate, and providing technical and practical assistance on the ground. Universities, NGOs, "new social movements," all could contribute in innumerable ways. DHR would thus strengthen TCS in many respects, providing it with permanent points of access and leverage and giving credibility and teeth to the democratic norms animating it.

Problems and Objections

By way of conclusion, let me consider two possible objections to DHR's approach to the WTO as just outlined. The first concerns the WTO's power to "overturn" or severely constrain domestic laws and policies on questions like labor and environmental standards. It is this "antidemocratic" power of the WTO that enrages many of its opponents. Nothing in the foregoing discussion indicates mechanisms for restricting or eliminating this power. What does DHR have to say about it?

Little critics will be pleased to hear. Two issues are involved: the line between human rights questions and policy or political questions, and the meaning of "democratic" decisions in the context of globalization. With respect to human rights and political questions, DHR tries to draw as bright a line as possible between them (though obviously they are intimately related). This line is plotted by reference to fundamental human rights. DHR aims to eliminate subjection and requires whatever steps are necessary to achieve that objective. Still, it leaves a very broad range of policy and political questions unresolved, or rather, it leaves them to the political process. The reasoning is that consensus on basic human rights will be easier to reach and clearer than political consensus on the myriad of policy issues raised in the context of globalization. To achieve and preserve this consensus, DHR's institutions must remain narrowly focused on securing fundamental human rights. This is because human rights and related issues will already have tremendous policy implications; attempts to use these institutions to decide controversial partisan issues would destroy their credibility and violate the demands of universality.

Consider once more intellectual property rights. DHR is concerned with whether rules governing patents are compatible with fundamental human rights. Whether there are such rules in the first place, and their precise nature, are questions about which DHR should remain agnostic, unless it could be shown that these rules are necessary to guarantee fundamental rights. Whether the WTO should have the power to overturn municipal legislation regarding patents is similarly a question about which DHR has little to say: again, so long as such fundamental rights as political participation are guaranteed. This is not to say such issues fall outside of democracy; they should appropriately be addressed through representative political institutions, which are themselves required to secure rights and which provide the only forum for collective decision making consistent with DHR. But if democratic governments subject themselves to binding dispute settlement mechanisms, whether of the WTO or the International Criminal Court, DHR cannot object. Such arrangements appear antidemocratic only if we persist in equating democracy with the decisions of a sovereign. Moreover, as noted above, without some process for overturning domestic policies and practices, successful promotion of human rights and democratization will be impossible.

The second objection concerns trade itself. The WTO's critics allege that competition with low-wage countries adversely affects wages and employment in developed countries, leading to the immiseration of unskilled workers and to rising inequality within those countries. They argue further that trade contributes to inequality within and among all countries, with the rich and corporations reaping all of its benefits. Doesn't DHR allow globalization to run amok? Isn't that inherently undemocratic? A full assessment of this complex question would require a book of its own. It seems that trade does have some adverse impact on the wages and employment prospects of unskilled workers in developed countries, though it also seems that competition is neither the sole nor the principal cause of their declining fortunes.[58] Further, there is no clear link between increased trade, integration, or foreign investment and increased inequality either within or among countries, though there is no evidence of convergence either.[59] This is not to say that inequality is not increasing within and among states; most evidence suggests that it is. The rise within states seems to be due to demographic change and to declining levels of government transfers, which have a significant and positive effect on inequality and standards of living.[60] Among states, rapidly growing populations in least developed countries mean that gaps in per capita GDP are increasing even though differences in GDP have shrunk slightly.[61]

In the recent past, greater openness to global trade was accompanied in developed countries by a stronger social safety net;[62] Ruggie coined the phrase "embedded liberalism" to describe this phenomenon.[63] This higher level of social provision was consistent with the observation that those who might suffer from liberalization could be "bought off" with promises of greater benefits.[64] Today, greater openness to trade and increased capital mobility are occurring simultaneously with cuts in the provision of social protections.[65] Given the important role of state transfers in stabilizing welfare in developed countries,[66] these reductions would contribute to growing inequality even as GDP rises.[67] While these are independent phenomena, their joint occurrence is hardly random; together they are key pillars in a neoliberal ideological consensus permeating the IFIs. This ideology, not globalization itself, should concern democrats most.

One thing does emerge clearly from this debate: political choices play a significant role in mediating the effects of trade. Tax policies, job training, income support, and other transfers all have a huge role in determining how workers fare under a more open trade regime. More importantly, the specific policies used to create and regulate global markets and to distribute the gains from trade make a tremendous difference. That gains from trade suffice to compensate those who lose from it is an economic shibboleth; whether such compensation is ever made is a political question. Trade's impact on welfare varies considerably according to the structure of the trade regime. My point is that under neoliberal rules and policies currently in place, economic globalization has abetted growing economic injustice, but it need not do so if different rules and policies were implemented.

To see why this matters, consider one final example involving trade and agriculture. This time, however, imagine a requirement to phase out subsidies for certain agricultural products. An impact assessment concludes that the policy would destroy the livelihoods of certain communities wholly dependent on the crop subsidies. Through consultation with local actors and reviews commissioned as part of the assessment, policymakers conclude that a remote location and a dearth of infrastructure mean that no viable economic alternatives currently exist for the community. In these circumstances, proceeding with the planned subsidy rollback would lead directly and predictably to the violation of community members' human rights. Under DHR the policy might at this point be scrapped, or an exception made for this subsidy or for this and similarly affected communities.

Or, with the consent of the affected population, the policy might be implemented along with a plan to address the human rights problems it raises. Among the strategies for remediation might be safety nets including (re)employment programs, targeted good supplies, and a program of food price stabilization, all of which are allowed under present WTO rules.[68] More imaginatively, we might envision investments in new economic infrastructure guided by locally devised development strategies. Skeptics might assert that the cost of these plans would doom them from the start. But under DHR the alternative is to scrap the proposal because of its adverse human rights implications. The economic motivation for supporting these plans would be the desire to carry out the broader subsidy reduction; the costs would include allocating some of the anticipated gains from the proposed subsidy reduction to the affected communities for a fixed period. Note that this is not a *redistribution* of wealth but a political decision about the *initial* distribution of expected benefits. This example, while far from exhaustive, shows DHR's flexibility and creative potential.

Implementing DHR will not be easy; it requires a political will and global commitment to democracy that will have to be constructed through the labors of networks of individuals and associations striving to realize a shared vision of a global democratic future. Democratic change, if it happens, will happen slowly and unevenly, in fits and starts. Old institutions will have to be painfully transformed, new ones patiently built. But lasting democratization has always been achieved more or less in this way, through righting real and immediate wrongs and through incremental reform of existing institutions. It has always been the product of a principled commitment to making the promise of freedom and equality real and meaningful for everyone.

Conclusion

Globalization, Neoliberalism, and Democratization

In this book I have used globalization as a lens to help in clarifying the confusions and limitations of modern democratic theory. In this brief conclusion I want to reverse my perspective, to consider the argument's implications for neoliberal globalization and democratization.

Globalization is frequently regarded as a threat to democracy, a force that undermines popular sovereignty. While this study confirms that globalization erodes sovereignty, it also finds reason to view globalization less negatively and monolithically than democratic critics are wont to do. Epistemologically, globalization helps us to appreciate the conceptual limits and limitations of modern democracy; understanding and addressing them is essential for reconstructing democratic theory. Normatively, globalization forces democratic theory to confront uncomfortable questions about what its universality means and requires. Let me give two examples.

First, despite its ostensibly universal principles, democratic theory has had almost nothing to say about how the wealth of the developed Western democracies was generated in part through and still depends in part upon injustice and exploitation among peoples and states. That generous levels of social welfare provision associated with democracy in the West might be impossible outside the parameters of this perverse system where the vast majority of wealth is concentrated in a handful of rich "democracies," does not register as a problem within traditional democratic theory. While cosmopolitan democratic theorists have addressed problems associated with democratic deficits and disjunctures, few have tackled questions of global economic injustice directly. This is unfortunate, because democracy's universal logic and emancipatory promise offer an appealing political alternative to liberal and utilitarian approaches. Globalization makes such questions difficult for democrats to ignore.

Second, consider common "democratic" objections to trade. One familiar fear concerns the "export" of manufacturing jobs to developing countries. Critics decry this development both because of job losses and because of its potential to increase domestic inequality by hurting workers in sectors competing with low-cost imports. Protecting the social and economic emancipation of workers displaced by changing patterns of trade is certainly an issue with which democrats must be concerned, but framing such changes as a threat to democracy skews our understanding of their broader effects. Greater openness to trade can also have an equality-enhancing effect in globally competitive export sectors; in addition, spillover effects from the lower prices that come with cheaper imports effectively increase disposable income, which can directly assist individuals and families and stimulate overall demand, boosting employment in some domestic sectors.* Further, not all trade is alike; increased openness in the service sector, for instance, can have positive effects even on low-wage and unskilled workers because this sector typically utilizes local labor. Cleaning services, for instance, can be opened to trade, but the jobs cannot be "exported." Finally, emphasizing job losses in developed countries shows a disconcerting one-sidedness; whether jobs "exported" or "outsourced" to low wage countries lift workers there out of poverty or significantly improve their quality of life is uniformly ignored in discussions of the "race to the bottom." One fears that race may be *at* the bottom of this disregard, much as it seems to be at the bottom of many democrats' convenient innocence of the global geopolitical prerequisites of the "democratic" welfare state. These are not merely questions about how we understand trade; they raise broader issues to do with global interdependence and with what a genuinely democratic approach to those issues might look like. Again, globalization makes such questions clear and urgent.

Of course, it is no more responsible to treat trade as an unmitigated good than it is to treat it as an unmitigated evil. Startlingly low wages by Western standards might be good wages elsewhere; they might be the wages of sweatshops, exploitation, and forced labor. Trade generates economic benefits more than sufficient to compensate the losers; powerful corporate interests

---

*Take the case of a heavily subsidized, unionized auto manufacturing sector. While trade liberalization might lead to the loss of high-paying jobs in this sector, the savings to consumers on automobiles might be significant (a car is a big ticket item). Increases in disposable income might generate higher demand in other sectors and perhaps improve local levels of employment. Plus, the state saves the cost of the subsidy. The loss of a job, especially a well-paid one, is painful and unfortunate, but if one is concerned with the general welfare, it is hard to know how to balance that loss against significant, if more diffuse, gains.

might capture all of those gains for executives and investors, immiserating those whose livelihoods disappear. Some service and low-skill sectors might expand in developed countries under more open trade; the jobs created in these sectors might not outstrip job losses in others and might not pay a living wage. Again, my point is neither that globalization is a wholly good thing nor that it is a wholly bad thing; it is rather that we have to recognize that a great deal of how good or bad it ultimately is depends on politics.

That politics matters, and matters a lot, suggests that we need a more nuanced view of globalization's political or ideological character. Globalization is often identified with the set of neoliberal economic policies known as the "Washington Consensus," which comprises:

> fiscal discipline; a redirection of public expenditure priorities toward fields offering both high economic returns and the potential to improve income distribution, such as primary health care, primary education, and infrastructure; tax reform (to lower marginal rates and broaden the tax base); interest rate liberalization; a competitive exchange rate; trade liberalization; liberalization of inflows of foreign direct investment; privatization; deregulation (to abolish barriers to entry and exit); and secure property rights.[1]

Much opposition to globalization arises from these objectionable policies, which is understandable. They often don't work, with short bursts of rapid economic growth followed hard by financial crises, growing inequality, and economic stagnation. These failures are always somehow attributed to corruption, mismanagement, or insufficient zeal in implementing the policies, never to the policies themselves.[2] Even when they do "work," however, they often do so at the expense of the most vulnerable members of a society; women, the poor, children, the uneducated, the old and infirm fall through or beyond ever-shrinking social safety nets. It is hardly surprising in this light that globalization appears as a threat to democracy.

While many critics have recognized these antidemocratic aspects of globalization, they frequently attribute them to the wrong source. Globalization, I have argued, is the universalization of social relations and interactions, including but not limited to economic ones; it is ancient, uneven, multifaceted, and ineluctable. These material processes must be kept distinct from neoliberalism, the ideology currently driving and shaping globalization.[3] Globalization's social, economic, and political significance results from a complex mediation of its material processes by neoliberal ideology. Failure to distinguish adequately between these dimensions leads to two debilitating analytic confusions. First, when the ideology becomes conflated with the processes, the ideology seems to take on their natural and irresistible qualities. The rhetoric of neoliberalism uttered by economists and politicians accentuates this confusion; globalization gets described as if it were some sort of socioeconomic storm people should try to weather as best they can. This aura of inevitability fosters political apathy and cultivates a zero-sum mentality pitting most against most in a latter-day Hobbesian scramble for whatever crumbs fall from the opulent tables of a wealthy few. The ceaseless competition between rich and poor, North and South, winners and losers, stokes a political conflagration that consumes our hopes and our energies

Failure to distinguish globalization's material and ideological aspects also confuses us about what exactly democrats ought to oppose and what we ought to do in opposing it. Globalization runs over, around, and through established borders and boundaries, transforming familiar understandings of social life. It is easy to mistake this universalization as a threat to democracy. Many democratic critics do just that, seeking to counter globalization by reasserting democratic control at the state level or by replicating it on a cosmopolitan scale. In either case the intuition is the same: the universalization of social activity creates deficits and disjunctures which must be closed up by re-creating spatial parity among social and economic phenomena and the political instrumentalities that govern them. I have already addressed the significant (though different) normative limitations of these approaches. Remarkably, however, we can now see that they both originate in the same analytic mistake: conceiving universalization as the threat to democracy.

The real threat, I submit, comes not from universalization but from neoliberalism. Neoliberalism is antithetical to democracy: it subjects economic activity to the discipline of the market rather than the forum; it gives precedence to the rights of capital and investors over the rights of women and men; it serves the imperatives of profit and growth before those of emancipation. It sacrifices individuals and communities at the altar of an economic orthodoxy deifying the mythically "free" markets of global capitalism. This neoliberal fundamentalism is as menacing to freedom and equality as any afoot in the world today, and opposing it is an urgent democratic priority. Still, it would be wrong, and probably futile besides, to oppose or reject globalization. It has to be democratized.

Global democratization must begin, can only begin, with the thorough transformation of globalization's ideological matrix, with the substitution of freedom, equality, and human rights for the values and priorities of neoliberalism. This task is primarily political. At the outset, it is less about building institutions than about building political will by articulating appealing values and persuading people to fight for them. In this respect, the logic of democratization remains quite simple: people will support democracy when they realize that their freedom and equality depend on yours and mine and everyone's, when they see global human rights as an entitlement securing emancipation for all. Democratic theory loses its way when it strays from this logic.

I do not want to deny that universalization poses a significant *challenge* for democracy, but it is a challenge democrats should welcome; after all, democratization has always been about dismantling familiar boundaries, tearing down barriers to inclusion, and tearing up social contracts that define social, economic, and political independence too narrowly. Globalization is a potentially democratic development precisely because its own universalizing dynamic invites us to reconceive democracy's universal logic and embrace its universal promise. Whether that potential is fulfilled is a question for democrats: what will we do with the challenges and opportunities globalization presents?

One of my central arguments throughout this book has been that political values and ideas are closely connected with the broader social and economic contexts in which they take shape and mature. When those contexts change radically, some values and ideas will evolve; some will become incoherent; still others will slip into irrelevance. I do not see globalization as a complete break with the past, although I do think that the changes it has wrought in the configuration of rule are lasting and significant. I do not think that democratic principles have become outmoded or irrelevant; nonetheless, I believe they must be rethought. As I have indicated, this entails questioning many of our most basic political assumptions, including assumptions about what democracy is, how it works, and how it is justified. Such questioning is never easy, especially when the values with which we are concerned are so cherished and so deeply ingrained in our political consciousness.

We can take courage from Constant who, faced with a similar challenge, remained undaunted. After poignantly describing how no reader could be left unmoved by the beauty and power of classical ideals of liberty, Constant implored: "let us mistrust ... this admiration for certain ancient memories.... Since we live in modern times, I want a liberty suited to modern times."[4] We need democracy suited to modern times; I hope this book has helped us toward it.

Notes

Introduction

1. The details of this account are from University of Washington Libraries, *History of the Tacoma Narrows Bridge* [Web page] (University of Washington Libraries: Manuscripts, Special Collections, University Archives, October 25, 2002 [cited July 15, 2003]); available from http://www.lib.washington.edu/specialcoll/tnb/.
2. Larry Siedentop, "Two Liberal Traditions," in *The Idea of Freedom: Essays in Honor of Isaiah Berlin*, ed. Alan Ryan (Oxford: Oxford University Press, 1979). My approach also has similarities with that outlined in James Tully, "Political Philosophy as a Critical Activity," *Political Theory* 30, no. 4 (2002), 533-55.
3. Benjamin Constant, "On the Liberty of the Ancients, Compared with That of the Moderns," in *Political Writings*, ed. Biancamaria Fontana (Cambridge, UK: Cambridge University Press, 1988).
4. Ibid., 312–20.
5. I have expressed my reservations about the Cambridge approach in Michael Goodhart, "Theory in Practice? Quentin Skinner's Hobbes, Reconsidered," *The Review of Politics* 62, no. 3 (2000), 531–61.
6. Michael Ignatieff, "Human Rights: The Midlife Crisis," *The New York Review of Books* 46, no. 9 (1999), 58–62; Michael Ignatieff, "Is the Human Rights Era Ending?" *The New York Times*, February 5 2002, A25; David Rieff, "The Precarious Triumph of Human Rights," *The New York Times Magazine*, August 8 1999, 36–41.

Chapter 1

1. John R. Bolton, "Should We Take Global Governance Seriously?" *Chicago Journal of International Law* 1, no. 2 (2000), 205-21; Ralph Nader and Lori Wallach, "GATT, NAFTA, and the Subversion of the Democratic Process," in *The Case against the Global Economy*, ed. Jerry Mander and Edward Goldsmith (San Francisco: Sierra Club Books, 1996); Jeremy Rabkin, *Why Sovereignty Matters* (Washington, D.C.: AEI Press, 1998).
2. John Dunn, "Democracy, Globalization, and Human Interests" (Denver, CO, April 1998); John Dunn, "Capitalism, Socialism, and Democracy: Compatibilities and Contradictions," in *The Economic Limits to Modern Politics*, ed. John Dunn (Cambridge, UK: Cambridge University Press, 1990).
3. Susan Strange, *The Retreat of the State: The Diffusion of Power in the World Economy* (Cambridge, UK: Cambridge University Press, 1996), xiii; cf. Paul Hirst and Grahame Thompson, *Globalization*

223

in Question: The International Economy and the Possibilities of Governance (Cambridge, UK: Polity Press, 1996), 1–2.

4. John Williamson, "What Should the World Bank Think About the Washington Consensus?" *The World Bank Research Observer* 15, no. 2 (2000), 251–64.

5. Ricardo Petrella, "Globalization and Internationalization: The Dynamics of the Emerging World Order," in *States against Markets: The Limits of Globalization*, ed. Robert Boyer and Daniel Drache (London: Routledge, 1996).

6. Hirst and Thompson, *Globalization in Question*; Kenneth N. Waltz, "Globalization and Governance," *PS: Political Science and Politics* 32, no. 4 (1999), 693–700.

7. David Held, *Democracy and the Global Order: From the Modern State to Cosmopolitan Governance* (Stanford, CA: Stanford University Press, 1995), 99.

8. Roland Axtmann, *Liberal Democracy into the Twenty-First Century: Globalization, Integration, and the Nation-State* (New York: Manchester University Press, 1996); cf. Frank Decker, "Governance Beyond the Nation-State: Reflections on the Democratic Deficit of the European Union," *Journal of European Public Policy* 9, no. 2 (2002), 256–72; Michael Zürn, "Democratic Governance Beyond the Nation-State: The EU and Other International Institutions," *European Journal of International Relations* 6, no. 2 (2000), 183–221.

9. See Carole Pateman, *Participation and Democratic Theory* (Cambridge, UK: Cambridge University Press, 1970), and the essays excerpted in Henry Kariel, ed., *Frontiers of Democratic Theory* (New York: Random House, 1970).

10. The 2004 figure is from Freedom House, *Freedom in the World 2005: Civic Power and Electoral Politics* [Online Report]. (New York: Freedom House, 2005 [cited 31 March 2005]); available from http://www.freedomhouse.org/research/freeworld/2005/charts2005.pdf. The 1974 figure is from Larry Diamond, "Universal Democracy?" *Policy Review Online*, no. 119 (2003.[cited 31 March 2005]); available from http://www.policyreview.org/jun03/diamond.html.

11. Stephen Gill, "Globalization, Democratization, and the Politics of Indifference," in *Globalization: Critical Perspectives*, ed. James H. Mittelman (Boulder, CO: Lynne-Rienner, 1996).

12. Phillip G. Cerny, "Paradoxes of the Competition State: The Dynamics of Political Globalization," *Government and Opposition* 32, no. 2 (1997), 251–74; John W. Meyer et al., "World Society and the Nation-State," *American Journal of Sociology* 103, no. 1 (1997), 144–81; Waltz, "Globalization and Governance."

13. Jack Donnelly, *Universal Human Rights in Theory and Practice* (Ithaca, NY: Cornell University Press, 1989). Donnelly is writing about human rights regimes, but this excellent definition captures the nature of international policy and regulatory regimes generally.

14. Peter Malanczuk, *Akehurst's Modern Introduction to International Law*, 7th rev. ed. (New York: Routledge, 1997), 17ff.

15. Cerny, "Paradoxes of the Competition State," 253; cf. Saskia Sassen, *Losing Control? Sovereignty in an Age of Globalization* (New York: Columbia University Press, 1996).

16. Thanks to Michael Mann for reminding me of their importance.

17. For a comprehensive look at this process see Ronald H. Linden, ed., *Norms and Nannies: The Impact of International Organizations on the Central and East European States* (New York: Rowman & Littlefield, 2002).

18. David Beetham, "Market Economy and Democratic Polity," *Democratization* 4, no. 1 (1997), 76–93; David Beetham, "Four Theorems About the Market and Democracy," *European Journal of Political Research* 23 (1993), 187–201.

19. Oscar Arias Sanchez, Address delivered at Hunter College, City University of New York, April 20, 1999.

20. Such concerns have been made the explicit focus of the "Doha Round" of negotiations; see World Trade Organization, *Ministerial Declaration* (Wt/Min(01)/Dec/120 November 2001[cited June 9, 2003]); available from http://www.wto.org/english/thewto_e/minist_e/min01_e/mindecl_e.htm. There are, of course, exceptions: workers in highly protected or state-run sectors will typically be opposed to greater liberalization; see Jeffry A. Frieden and Ronald Rogowski, "The Impact of the International Economy on National Policies: An Analytical Overview," in *Internationalization and Domestic Politics*, ed. Robert O. Keohane and Helen V. Milner (Cambridge, UK: Cambridge University Press, 1996); Ronald Rogowski, *Commerce and Coalitions: How Trade Affects Domestic Political Alignments* (Princeton, NJ: Princeton University Press, 1989).

21. John Markoff, "Globalization and the Future of Democracy," *Journal of World-Systems Research* 5, no. 2 (1999): 300.

22. P.J. Taylor, "Embedded Statism and the Social Sciences: Opening up to New Spaces," *Environment and Planning A* 28 (1996), 1917–28; Cerny, "Paradoxes of the Competition State."

23. See, e.g., Charles R. Beitz, "Sovereignty and Morality in International Affairs," in *Political Theory Today*, ed. David Held (Stanford, CA: Stanford University Press, 1991); Held, *Democracy and the Global Order*; Michael Walzer, *Spheres of Justice: A Defense of Pluralism and Equality* (New York: Basic Books, 1983), 281.

24. Pierre Manent, "Democracy without Nations?" *Journal of Democracy* 8, no. 2 (1997): 94–6.; Robert Dahl, *Democracy and Its Critics* (New Haven, CT: Yale University Press, 1989); Walzer, *Spheres of Justice*.

25. Robert O. Keohane, "Sovereignty, Interdependence, and International Institutions," in *Center for Social Theory and Comparative History Colloquium Series* (Los Angeles: 1991), 25.

26. Yael Tamir, *Liberal Nationalism* (Princeton, NJ: Princeton University Press, 1993); David Miller, *On Nationality* (Oxford: Clarendon Press, 1995); on the shared sacrifices needed for democracy see Charles Taylor, "No Community, No Democracy, Part I," *The Responsive Community* 13, no. 4 (2003), 17–28; Charles Taylor, "No Community, No Democracy, Part II," *The Responsive Community* 14, no. 1 (2003/4), 15–25.

27. Will Kymlicka, *Politics in the Vernacular: Nationalism, Multiculturalism and Citizenship* (Oxford: Oxford University Press, 2001); Will Kymlicka, "Citizenship in an Era of Globalization: Commentary on Held," in *Democracy's Edges*, ed. Ian Shapiro and Casiano Hacker-Cordón (Cambridge, UK: Cambridge University Press, 1999).

28. Kymlicka, *Politics in the Vernacular*; Will Kymlicka, *Multicultural Citizenship: A Liberal Theory of Minority Rights* (Oxford: Clarendon Press, 1995); Charles Taylor, *Multiculturalism: Examining the Politics of Recognition*, ed. Amy Gutmann (Princeton, NJ: Princeton University Press, 1994).

29. Miller, *On Nationality*, 89–90.

30. Tamir, *Liberal Nationalism*, Bernard Yack, "Popular Sovereignty and Nationalism," *Political Theory* 29, no. 4 (2001), 514–36.

31. David Miller, *Citizenship and National Identity* (Cambridge, NJ: Polity Press, 2000), 53; cf. Benjamin Barber, *A Place for Us: How to Make Society Civil and Democracy Strong* (New York: Hill & Wang, 1998); Benjamin Barber, *Strong Democracy: Participatory Politics for a New Age* (Berkeley: University of California Press, 1984).

32. Miller, *Citizenship and National Identity*, 53; cf. Jürgen Habermas, "Three Normative Models of Democracy," in *Democracy and Difference: Contesting the Boundaries of the Political*, ed. Seyla Benhabib (Princeton, NJ: Princeton University Press, 1996).

33. Miller, *Citizenship and National Identity*, 83.

34. Ibid., 1.

35. Ibid., 93.

36. See Decker, "Governance Beyond the Nation-State," 263.

37. See, e.g., Esref Aksu and Joseph A. Camilleri, eds., *Democratizing Global Governance* (New York: Palgrave Macmillan, 2002); Richard Falk and Andrew Strauss, "On the Creation of a Global People's Assembly: Legitimacy and the Power of Popular Sovereignty," *Stanford Journal of International Law* 36, no. 2 (2000), 212–20; Albert J. Paolini, Anthony P. Jarvis, and Christian Reus-Smit, eds., *Between Sovereignty and Global Governance: The United Nations, the State, and Civil Society* (New York: St. Martin's Press, 1998); Jamie Mayerfield, "The Mutual Dependence of External and Internal Justice: The Democratic Achievement of the International Criminal Court," *Finnish Yearbook of International Law* 123 (2001), 71–107.

38. Ronnie D. Lipschutz, "Reconstructing World Politics: The Emergence of Global Civil Society," *Millennium: Journal of International Studies* 21, no. 3 (1992): 393; cf. Mustapha Kamal Pasha and David L. Blaney, "Elusive Paradise: The Promise and Peril of Global Civil Society," *Alternatives* 23, no. 4 (1998), 417–50.

39. Jackie Smith, "Global Civil Society? Transnational Social Movement Organizations and Social Capital," *American Behavioral Scientist* 42, no. 1 (1998): 104; cf. John S. Dryzek, "Transnational Democracy," *Journal of Political Philosophy* 7, no. 1 (1999), 30–51.

40. Smith, "Global Civil Society?" 104.

41. Dryzek, "Transnational Democracy," 46; cf. John S. Dryzek, *Democracy in Capitalist Times: Ideals, Limits, Struggles* (New York: Oxford University Press, 1996), 146.

42. Richard Falk, "Global Civil Society and the Democratic Prospect," in *Global Democracy: Key Debates*, ed. Barry Holden (New York: Routledge, 2000), 171.

43. Held, *Democracy and the Global Order.*
44. Ibid., 231.
45. Ibid., 233.
46. Michael Mann, "Has Globalization Ended the Rise and Rise of the Nation-State?" *Review of International Political Economy* 4, no. 3 (1997), 472-96; Michael Mann, "Neither Nation-State nor Globalism," *Environment and Planning A* 28 (1996), 1960–64.
47. Cf. John Markoff, "Who Will Construct the Global Order?", in Bruce William Morrison, ed., *Transnational Democracy in Critical and Comparative Perspective: Democracy's Range Reconsidered* (London: Ashgate Publishing, 2004), 4.
48. See, e.g., Michael Mann, *The Sources of Social Power,* vol. 1, *A History of Power from the Beginning to A.D. 1760* (Cambridge, UK: Cambridge University Press, 1986).
49. James N. Rosenau, "The Complexities and Contradictions of Globalization," *Current History* 96, no. 613 (1997): 361; cf. Markoff, "Who Will Construct the Global Order?"; Zürn, "Democratic Governance."

Chapter 2

1. Nicholas Greenwood Onuf, "Sovereignty: Outline of a Conceptual History," *Alternatives* 16, no. 4 (1991): 425.
2. Jens Bartelson, *A Genealogy of Sovereignty* (Cambridge, UK: Cambridge University Press, 1995); John Hoffman, *Sovereignty* (Minneapolis: University of Minnesota Press, 1998); cf. Stephen D. Krasner, *Sovereignty: Organized Hypocrisy* (Princeton, NJ: Princeton University Press, 1999).
3. Kenneth N. Waltz, "Globalization and Governance," *PS: Political Science and Politics* 32, no. 4 (1999), 693–700; Jeremy Rabkin, *Why Sovereignty Matters* (Washington, D.C.: AEI Press, 1998).
4. Jörg Friedrichs, "The Meaning of New Medievalism," *European Journal of International Relations* 7, no. 4 (2001), 475–502; David Held, *Democracy and the Global Order: From the Modern State to Cosmopolitan Governance* (Stanford, CA: Stanford University Press, 1995); Saskia Sassen, *Losing Control? Sovereignty in an Age of Globalization* (New York: Columbia University Press, 1996).
5. Krasner, *Sovereignty,* 3–10.
6. Michael Goodhart, "Sovereignty: Reckoning What Is Real," *Polity* 34, no. 2 (2001), 241–57.
7. J. Samuel Barkin and Bruce Cronin, "The State and the Nation: Changing Norms and the Rules of Sovereignty in International Relations," *International Organization* 48, no. 1 (1994): 107. "Legitimate authority" is technically a redundancy—though given the ubiquity of unjust and unscrupulous rulers who claim authority, it is a useful (and thus forgivable) one. Authority, when not misused as a synonym for mere control, signifies rightful rule. Legitimacy, when not confused with popularity, means being entitled to allegiance. Authority (rightful rule) presumes legitimacy (the recognition of rule's rightfulness). They are overlapping concepts, "kissing cousins"; Richard Flathman, "Legitimacy," in *A Companion to Contemporary Political Philosophy,* ed. Robert E. Goodin and Philip Pettit (Oxford: Blackwell, 1993), 527.
8. F.H. Hinsley, *Sovereignty* (Cambridge, UK: Cambridge University Press, 1986).
9. See Bartelson, *A Genealogy of Sovereignty,* 57.
10. Daniel Philpott, *Revolutions in Sovereignty: How Ideas Shaped Modern International Relations* (Princeton, NJ: Princeton University Press, 2001); cf. Daniel Philpott, "Sovereignty: An Introduction and Brief History," *Journal of International Affairs* 48, no. 2 (1995), 353–68.
11. Alexander B. Murphy, "The Sovereign State System as Political-Territorial Ideal: Historical and Contemporary Considerations," in *State Sovereignty as Social Construct,* ed. Cynthia Weber and Thomas J. Biersteker (Cambridge, UK: Cambridge University Press, 1996).
12. Krasner, *Sovereignty.*
13. Bartelson, *A Genealogy of Sovereignty.*
14. Ibid., 23.
15. Kenneth N. Waltz, "Theory of International Politics," in *Neorealism and Its Critics,* ed. Robert O. Keohane (New York: Columbia University Press, 1986), 53. The ensuing summary is drawn from this account.
16. John Gerard Ruggie, "Continuity and Transformation in the World Polity: Toward a Neorealist Synthesis," in *Neorealism and Its Critics,* ed. Robert O. Keohane (New York: Columbia University Press, 1986), 141. Hereafter I shall simply refer to "the medieval–modern transition."

17. Ibid., 142., italics in original. Cf. John Gerard Ruggie, "Territoriality and Beyond: Problematizing Modernity in International Relations," *International Organization* 47, no. 1 (1993): 168; Alexander Wendt, *Social Theory of International Relations* (Cambridge, UK: Cambridge University Press, 1999), chap. 6.
18. Ruggie, "Territoriality and Beyond," 148.
19. Niklas Luhmann, *The Differentiation of Society*, trans. Stephen Holmes and Charles Larmore (New York: Columbia University Press, 1982), 245.
20. Cf. Friedrich Kratochwil, "Of Systems, Boundaries, and Territoriality: An Inquiry into the Formation of the State System," *World Politics* 39, no. 1 (1986), 27–52.
21. Ruggie, "Territoriality and Beyond," 151.
22. Ibid., 150, Ruggie, "Continuity and Transformation," 143.
23. Ruggie, "Continuity and Transformation," 142ff.
24. Hendrik Spruyt, *The Sovereign State and Its Competitors: An Analysis of Systems Change* (Princeton, NJ: Princeton University Press, 1994), 12.
25. Ruggie, "Continuity and Transformation," 142. The internal quotations are from Joseph R. Strayer, *On the Medieval Origins of the Modern State* (Princeton, NJ: Princeton University Press, 1970), and Perry Anderson, *Lineages of the Absolutist State* (London: Verso, 1974), respectively.
26. Ruggie, "Continuity and Transformation," 143; cf. Spruyt, *The Sovereign State and Its Competitors*, 5, 13.
27. Anderson, *Lineages of the Absolutist State*, 37.
28. John A. Agnew, "Timeless Space and State-Centrism: The Geographical Assumptions of International Relations Theory," in *The Global Economy as Political Space*, ed. Stephen J. Rosow, Naeem Inayatullah, and Mark Rupert (Boulder, CO: Lynne-Rienner, 1994), 105.
29. James Anderson, "The Shifting Stage of Politics: New Medieval and Postmodern Territorialities," *Environment and Planning D: Society and Space* 14 (1996): 141.
30. Stephen Kobrin, "Back to the Future: Neomedievalism and the Postmodern Digital World Economy," *Journal of International Affairs* 51, no. 2 (1998): 370ff. ; cf. Mary Kaldor, "European Institutions, Nation-States, and Nationalism," in *Cosmopolitan Democracy: An Agenda for a New World Order*, ed. Daniele Archibugi and David Held (Cambridge, UK: Polity Press, 1995).
31. Walter Ullmann, *Principles of Government and Politics in the Middle Ages* (London: Methuen, 1961).
32. Luhmann, *The Differentiation of Society*, 236ff.
33. Otto Gierke, *Political Theories of the Middle Age*, ed. F.W. Maitland (Cambridge, UK: Cambridge University Press, 1900); Cary Nederman, "Freedom, Community, and Function: Communitarian Lessons of Medieval Political Theory," *American Political Science Review* 86, no. 4 (1992), 977–86; Ullmann, *Principles of Government and Politics in the Middle Ages*.
34. Anderson, *Lineages of the Absolutist State*, 38.
35. See Hinsley, *Sovereignty*, 98ff.
36. The following account does not purport to explain or even to survey the medieval–modern transition, but merely to put the reader in mind of certain relevant and familiar facts. I draw on numerous sources, including Agnew, "Timeless Space"; Anderson, "Shifting Stage"; Anderson, *Lineages of the Absolutist State*; Marc Bloch, *Feudal Society: The Growth of Ties of Dependence*, trans. L.A. Manyon, 2 vols., vol. 1 (Chicago: University of Chicago Press, 1961); Marc Bloch, *Feudal Society: Social Classes and Political Organization*, trans. L.A. Manyon, 2 vols., vol. 2 (Chicago: University of Chicago Press, 1961); Kurt Burch, "The "Properties" of the State System and Global Capitalism," in *The Global Economy as Political Space*, ed. Stephen J. Rosow, Naeem Inayatullah, and Mark Rupert (Boulder, CO: Lynne-Rienner, 1994); Brian M. Downing, *The Military Revolution and Political Change: Origins of Democracy and Autocracy in Early Modern Europe* (Princeton, NJ: Princeton University Press, 1992); R. G. Hawtrey, *Economic Aspects of Sovereignty* (London: Longmans, Green, 1952); Edward Jenks, *Law and Politics in the Middle Ages* (New York: Holt, 1908); Michael Mann, *The Sources of Social Power*, vol. 1, *A History of Power from the Beginning to A.D. 1760* (Cambridge, UK: Cambridge University Press, 1986); Barrington Moore, *Social Origins of Dictatorship and Democracy: Lord and Peasant in the Making of the Modern World* (Boston: Beacon Press, 1966); J. G. A. Pocock, "The Ideal of Citizenship since Classical Times," in *Theorizing Citizenship*, ed. Ronald Beiner (Albany: State University of New York Press, 1995); Ruggie, "Territoriality and Beyond"; Ruggie, "Continuity and Transformation"; Strayer, *On the Medieval Origins of the Modern State*; Brian Tierney, *The Crisis of Church and State: 1050–1300* (Englewood Cliffs, NJ: Prentice-Hall, 1964); Charles Tilly, "Reflections on the

History of European State-Making," in *The Formation of National States in Western Europe*, ed. Charles Tilly (Princeton, NJ: Princeton University Press, 1975); Richard Tuck, *Natural Rights Theories: Their Origin and Development* (Cambridge, NJ: Cambridge University Press, 1979); Ullmann, *Principles of Government and Politics in the Middle Ages*; Immanuel Wallerstein, *Historical Capitalism* (London: Verso, 1983); Lynn Jr. White, *Medieval Technology and Social Change* (Oxford: Oxford University Press, 1962); Neal Wood, *John Locke and Agrarian Capitalism* (Berkeley, CA: University of California Press, 1984).

37. Burch, "Properties of the State System," 47–53.
38. Anderson, *Lineages of the Absolutist State*, 45–46.
39. Agnew, "Timeless Space," 97.
40. R. B. J. Walker, *Inside/Outside: International Relations as Political Theory* (Cambridge, UK: Cambridge University Press, 1993), 62.
41. Ibid., 41; cf. Quentin Skinner, *The Foundations of Modern Political Thought: The Renaissance*, 2 vols., vol. 1 (Cambridge, UK: Cambridge University Press, 1978).
42. See also Bartelson, *A Genealogy of Sovereignty*.
43. Quentin Skinner, "The State," in *Contemporary Political Philosophy: An Anthology*, ed. Robert E. Goodin and Philip Pettit (Oxford: Blackwell,1997), esp. 6–11.; Skinner, *Foundations I*.
44. Hinsley, *Sovereignty*, 130–31.
45. Quentin Skinner, *The Foundations of Modern Political Thought: The Age of Reformation*, 2 vols., vol. 2 (Cambridge, UK: Cambridge University Press, 1978), 349.
46. Ibid.
47. See Bartelson, *A Genealogy of Sovereignty*, 101–2; Hinsley, *Sovereignty*, 70–6.
48. Hinsley, *Sovereignty*, 75.
49. Skinner, *Foundations 2*, 351. This latter development was "precluded in medieval Europe by the legal assumptions underpinning the feudal organization of society, and by the Church's claims to act as a law-making power coeval with rather than subordinate to the secular authorities." (Ibid.)
50. Hinsley, *Sovereignty*, 121–22.
51. Jean Bodin, *On Sovereignty: Four Chapters from the Six Books of the Commonwealth*, ed. Julian H. Franklin, trans. Julian H. Franklin (Cambridge, UK: Cambridge University Press, 1992), 1.
52. Thomas Hobbes, *Leviathan*, ed. C.B. Macpherson (New York: Penguin Books, 1968), 227.
53. Bodin, *On Sovereignty*, 3.
54. Ibid., 46.
55. Ibid., 56.
56. Ibid., 58–9.
57. Hobbes, *Leviathan*, 227.
58. Cited in Jean Bethke Elshtain, *Sovereignty at Century's End* [Web Page] (1999 [cited June 27, 2003]); available from http://sacred-sovereign.uchicago.edu/jbe-sovereignty.html.
59. Stephen J. Rosow, "Nature, Need, and the Human World: "Commercial Society" and the Construction of the World Economy," in *The Global Economy as Political Space*, ed. Stephen J. Rosow, Naeem Inayatullah, and Mark Rupert (Boulder, CO: Lynne-Rienner, 1994), 26.
60. Onuf, "Outline," 435.
61. Tuck, *Natural Rights Theories*.
62. See Hinsley, *Sovereignty*.
63. Spruyt, *The Sovereign State and Its Competitors*.
64. Christian Reus-Smit, "Constructivism," in *Theories of International Relations* (New York: Palgrave, 2001); Wendt, *Social Theory of International Relations*; Philpott, *Revolutions in Sovereignty*.
65. Cf. Murphy, "Sovereign State System."
66. Charles R. Beitz, *Political Theory and International Relations* (Princeton, NJ: Princeton University Press, 1979), 36.
67. Wendt, *Social Theory of International Relations*, 279ff.
68. Martin Wight, "Why Is There No International Theory?" in *Diplomatic Investigations: Essays in the Theory of International Politics*, ed. Herbert Butterfield and Martin Wight (Cambridge, MA: Harvard University Press, 1966).
69. Naeem Inayatullah and Mark Rupert, "Hobbes, Smith, and the Problem of Mixed Ontologies in Neorealist IPE," in *The Global Economy as Political Space*, ed. Stephen J. Rosow, Naeem Inayatullah, and Mark Rupert (Boulder, CO: Lynne-Rienner, 1994).
70. Hobbes, *Leviathan*, 188.

71. Emmerich de Vattel, *The Law of Nations: Or, Principles of the Law of Nature Applied to the Conduct and Affairs of Nations and Sovereigns* (HTML edition by Jon Roland of the Constitution Society, 1758; reprint, 1999).; cf. Wight, "Why Is There No International Theory?"
72. Cited in Onuf, "Outline," 426.
73. Hinsley, *Sovereignty*, 26.

Chapter 3

1. Cf. David Held, *Models of Democracy*, 2nd ed. (Stanford, CA: Stanford University Press, 1996).
2. Jean L. Cohen, "Changing Paradigms of Citizenship and the Exclusiveness of the Demos," *International Sociology* 14, no. 3 (1999): 246.
3. Charles Taylor, "No Community, No Democracy, Part I," *The Responsive Community* 13, no. 4 (2003): 24.
4. Bernard Yack, "Popular Sovereignty and Nationalism," *Political Theory* 29, no. 4 (2001), 514–36; cf. Jürgen Habermas, *Between Facts and Norms: Contributions to a Discourse Theory of Law and Democracy*, trans. William Rehg (Cambridge, MA: MIT Press, 1996).
5. Anthony Arblaster, *Democracy*, 2nd ed. (Minneapolis: University of Minnesota Press, 1994), 29; cf. F. H. Hinsley, *Sovereignty* (Cambridge, UK: Cambridge University Press, 1986); Nicholas Greenwood Onuf, "Sovereignty: Outline of a Conceptual History," *Alternatives* 16, no. 4 (1991), 425–46; Quentin Skinner, *The Foundations of Modern Political Thought: The Age of Reformation*, 2 vols., vol. 2 (Cambridge, UK: Cambridge University Press, 1978).
6. The latter in particular influenced conciliarist thinking; see Quentin Skinner, *The Foundations of Modern Political Thought: The Renaissance*, 2 vols., vol. 1 (Cambridge, UK: Cambridge University Press, 1978); Skinner, *Foundations 2*. Cf. Antony Black, "Communal Democracy and Its History," *Political Studies* 45, no. 1 (1997), 5–20.
7. Cf. Perry Anderson, *Lineages of the Absolutist State* (London: Verso, 1974), 45ff.; James Tully, *Strange Multiplicity: Constitutionalism in an Age of Diversity* (Cambridge, UK: Cambridge University Press, 1995).
8. Robert Filmer, *Patriarcha and Other Writings*, ed. Johann P. Sommerville (Cambridge, UK: Cambridge University Press, 1991), 184.
9. John Bowle, *Hobbes and His Critics* (London: Frank Cass, 1969), 132.
10. Richard Ashcraft, *Revolutionary Politics and Locke's Two Treatise of Government* (Princeton, NJ: Princeton University Press, 1991); Peter Laslett, "Introduction," in *Locke's Two Treatises of Government* (Cambridge, UK: Cambridge University Press, 1960).
11. Carole Pateman, *The Sexual Contract* (Stanford, CA: Stanford University Press, 1988), 39–40.
12. James Tully, *An Approach to Political Philosophy: Locke in Contexts* (Cambridge, UK: Cambridge University Press, 1993), 117.
13. "Universal" does not exhaust the meaning of "natural" in these theories, however; see John Dunn, *The Political Thought of John Locke* (Cambridge, UK: Cambridge University Press, 1969); Richard Tuck, *Natural Rights Theories: Their Origin and Development* (Cambridge, UK: Cambridge University Press, 1979).
14. Several readers of this chapter have raised this objection; for a recent statement of the case and a comprehensive bibliography see John T. Scott, "The Sovereignless State and Locke's Language of Obligation," *American Political Science Review* 94, no. 3 (2000), 547–61.
15. This claim is hard to square with Locke's simultaneous insistence that man has a property in his own person; Ibid., 550ff.; cf. Kirstie M. McClure, *Judging Rights: Lockean Politics and the Limits of Consent* (Ithaca, NY: Cornell University Press, 1996), 84. On how Locke's religious views affect his political theory, see Dunn, *The Political Thought of John Locke*.
16. Daniel Philpott, *Revolutions in Sovereignty: How Ideas Shaped Modern International Relations* (Princeton, NJ: Princeton University Press, 2001), 18–19.
17. Hinsley, *Sovereignty*, 152ff.; John Stuart Mill, "Considerations on Representative Government," in *Utilitarianism, on Liberty, and Considerations on Representative Government*, ed. H. B. Acton (Cambridge, UK: Cambridge University Press, 1972), 246.
18. See McClure, *Judging Rights*, 111.
19. See Yack, "Popular Sovereignty and Nationalism."
20. E.g., Ashcraft, *Revolutionary Politics*; Laslett, "Introduction"; Tully, *Locke in Contexts*.

21. Hinsley, *Sovereignty*, 154.

22. Ashcraft, *Revolutionary Politics*; Laslett, "Introduction."

23. Paul Hirst and Grahame Thompson, *Globalization in Question: The International Economy and the Possibilities of Governance* (Cambridge, UK: Polity Press, 1996); cf. W. Michael Reisman, "Sovereignty and Human Rights in Contemporary International Law," *American Journal of International Law* 84, no. 4 (1990), 866–76.

24. Andrew Hurrell, "Global Inequality and International Institutions," in *Global Justice*, ed. Thomas W. Pogge (Oxford: Blackwell, 2001), 39.

25. Hirst and Thompson, *Globalization in Question*.

26. John Rawls, *A Theory of Justice* (Cambridge, MA: Harvard University Press, 1971), 17–22, 121; Pateman, *The Sexual Contract*, 41–43.

27. Scott, "The Sovereignless State," 550–51.

28. Arblaster, *Democracy*, 29.

29. Pateman, *The Sexual Contract*, 58.

30. John Locke, *A Letter Concerning Toleration*, ed. James Tully (Indianapolis, IN: Hackett, 1983), 34; cf. Susan Moller Okin, "Gender, the Public, and the Private," in *Political Theory Today*, ed. David Held (Stanford, CA: Stanford University Press, 1991).

31. Pateman, *The Sexual Contract*, 60.

32. John Stuart Mill, "The Subjection of Women," in *On Liberty and Other Writings*, ed. Stefan Collini (Cambridge, UK: Cambridge University Press, 1989), 147.

33. Carole Pateman, "Self-Ownership and Property in the Person: Democratization and a Tale of Two Concepts," *Journal of Political Philosophy* 10, no. 1 (2002), 20–53.

34. See Pateman, *The Sexual Contract*.

35. Ibid., passim.

36. Jean Bethke Elshtain, *Public Man, Private Woman: Women in Social and Political Thought* (Princeton, NJ: Princeton University Press, 1981); Pateman, *The Sexual Contract*.

37. Patricia Springborg, "Republicanism, Freedom from Domination, and the Cambridge Contextual Historians," *Political Studies* 49, no. 5 (2001): 870.

38. Okin, "Gender, the Public, and the Private," 70.

39. John Dunn, "Conclusion," in *Democracy: The Unfinished Journey 508 B.C to A.D. 1993*, ed. John Dunn (Oxford: Oxford University Press, 1992), 247–49.; David Held, *Democracy and the Global Order: From the Modern State to Cosmopolitan Governance* (Stanford, CA: Stanford University Press, 1995), 38.

40. Filmer, *Patriarcha and Other Writings*, 189.

41. Yack, "Popular Sovereignty and Nationalism," 522–23.

42. Emmerich de Vattel, *The Law of Nations: Or, Principles of the Law of Nature Applied to the Conduct and Affairs of Nations and Sovereigns* (HTML edition by Jon Roland of the Constitution Society, 1758; reprint, 1999), I.203; cf. Frederick G. Whelan, "Vattel's Doctrine of the State," *History of Political Thought* IX, no. 1 (1988): 75.

43. See Whelan, "Vattel's Doctrine of the State."

44. Duncan Ivison, "Property, Territory, Sovereignty" (paper presented at the American Political Science Association Annual Meeting, San Francisco, CA, 2001), 7–8; cf. Kurt Burch, "The "Properties" of the State System and Global Capitalism," in *The Global Economy as Political Space*, ed. Stephen J. Rosow, Naeem Inayatullah, and Mark Rupert (Boulder, CO: Lynne-Rienner, 1994); Whelan, "Vattel's Doctrine of the State."

45. See, e.g., Benedict Anderson, *Imagined Communities: Reflections on the Origins and Spread of Nationalism*, rev. ed. (New York: Verso, 1998); Ernest Gellner, *Nationalism* (New York: New York University Press, 1997); Yack, "Popular Sovereignty and Nationalism."

46. See, e.g., Yael Tamir, *Liberal Nationalism* (Princeton, NJ: Princeton University Press, 1993); David Miller, *On Nationality* (Oxford: Clarendon Press, 1995). As a practical matter, national self-determination was strongly associated with the democratic aspirations of peoples throughout the twentieth century.

47. Tamir, *Liberal Nationalism*, 117–22.

48. Ibid., 117.

49. On international constitutions see Philpott, *Revolutions in Sovereignty*.

50. R.B.J. Walker, *Inside/Outside: International Relations as Political Theory* (Cambridge, UK: Cambridge University Press, 1993), 41–42.

51. Wendt, *Social Theory of International Relations*, 279ff.
52. Rousseau, "Abstract and Judgment of Saint-Pierre's Project for Perpetual Peace" in Chris Brown, Terry Nardin, and Nicholas Rengger, eds., *International Relations in Political Thought: Texts from the Ancient Greeks to the First World War* (Cambridge, UK: Cambridge University Press, 2002), 425–27.
53. Charles W. Mills, *The Racial Contract* (Ithaca, NY: Cornell University Press, 1997). My argument here largely follows Mills.
54. See ibid., 67, and Tully, *Locke in Contexts*, chap. 2.
55. Mills, *The Racial Contract*, 68–69.
56. Ibid.
57. See, e.g., Uday Singh Mehta, *Liberalism and Empire: A Study in Nineteenth-Century British Liberal Thought* (Chicago: University of Chicago Press, 1999); Sankar Muthu, *Enlightenment against Empire* (Princeton, NJ: Princeton University Press, 2003).
58. Walker, *Inside/Outside*, 63, 41–42. Walker is one of the few theorists to grasp the significance of the close connection between sovereignty and democracy: "Rethinking the meaning of democracy cannot be separated from a fundamental rethinking of the principle of state sovereignty as the key practice through which a specifically modern reification of spatio-temporal relations affirms a specifically modern answer to all questions about who we could possibly be" (154).

Chapter 4

1. Peter Malanczuk, *Akehurst's Modern Introduction to International Law*, 7th rev. ed. (New York: Routledge, 1997), 17.
2. James N. Rosenau, "The Complexities and Contradictions of Globalization," *Current History* 96, no. 613 (1997): 361.
3. Friedrich Kratochwil, "Of Systems, Boundaries, and Territoriality: An Inquiry into the Formation of the State System," *World Politics* 39, no. 1 (1986): 42; Niklas Luhmann, *The Differentiation of Society*, trans. Stephen Holmes and Charles Larmore (New York: Columbia University Press, 1982), 245; Mark W. Zacher, "The Decaying Pillars of the Westphalian Temple: Implications for International Order and Governance," in *Governance without Government: Order and Change in World Politics*, ed. James N. Rosenau and Ernst-Otto Czempiel (Cambridge, UK: Cambridge University Press, 1992).
4. See Christoph Görg and Joachim Hirsch, "Is International Democracy Possible?" *Review of International Political Economy* 5, no. 4 (1998): 588, who argue that "the political form of the nation-state is a necessary condition of the present form of economic globalization."
5. Anthony P. Jarvis and Albert J. Paolini, "Locating the State," in *The State in Transition: Reimagining Political Space*, ed. Joseph A. Camilleri, Anthony P. Jarvis, and Albert J. Paolini (Boulder, CO: Lynne-Rienner, 1995), 15.
6. James N. Rosenau, "Governance, Order, and Change in World Politics," in *Governance without Government: Order and Change in World Politics*, ed. James N. Rosenau and Ernst-Otto Czempiel (Cambridge, UK: Cambridge University Press, 1992); David Held et al., *Global Transformations: Politics, Economics, and Culture* (Stanford, CA: Stanford University Press, 1999), 50ff.
7. Held et al., *Global Transformations*, 53.
8. Ibid., 55.
9. Phillip G. Cerny, "Globalization and Other Stories: The Search for a New Paradigm for International Relations," *International Journal* 51 (1996): 623.
10. Susan Strange, *The Retreat of the State: The Diffusion of Power in the World Economy* (Cambridge, UK: Cambridge University Press, 1996).
11. Saskia Sassen, *Losing Control? Sovereignty in an Age of Globalization* (New York: Columbia University Press, 1996), 5.
12. Kenneth N. Waltz, "Globalization and Governance," *PS: Political Science and Politics* 32, no. 4 (1999): 694.
13. E.g., Paul Hirst and Grahame Thompson, *Globalization in Question: The International Economy and the Possibilities of Governance* (Cambridge, UK: Polity Press, 1996); Stephen D. Krasner, *Sovereignty: Organized Hypocrisy* (Princeton, NJ: Princeton University Press, 1999); Stephen D. Krasner, "Westphalia and All That," in *Ideas and Foreign Policy: Beliefs, Institutions, and Politics*, ed. Judith Goldstein and Robert O. Keohane (Ithaca, NY: Cornell University Press, 1993).

14. For a good general survey of the traditionalist and transformationalist views, see Held et al., *Global Transformations*.
15. See Hedley Bull, *The Anarchical Society: A Study of Order in World Politics* (New York: Columbia University Press, 1977); Alexander Wendt, *Social Theory of International Relations* (Cambridge, UK: Cambridge University Press, 1999).
16. Immanuel Kant, " Idea for a Universal History with a Cosmopolitan Purpose" in *Kant's Political Writings*, ed. Hans Reiss, trans. H.B. Nisbet (Cambridge, UK: Cambridge University Press, 1970), 45–53.
17. Immanuel Kant, "On the Common Saying: 'This May be True in Theory, but it does not Apply in Practice,'" in ibid., 90.
18. Immanuel Kant, "Perpetual Peace: A Philosophical Sketch," in ibid., 99.
19. Ibid., 103, emphasis added.
20. Cf. John Gerard Ruggie, "Territoriality and Beyond: Problematizing Modernity in International Relations," *International Organization* 47, no. 1 (1993), 139–74.
21. Stephen Kobrin, "Back to the Future: Neomedievalism and the Postmodern Digital World Economy," *Journal of International Affairs* 51, no. 2 (1998): 384.
22. Charles Beitz thought this was true in the late 1970s; see Charles R. Beitz, *Political Theory and International Relations* (Princeton, NJ: Princeton University Press, 1979).
23. See Joseph E. Stiglitz, *Globalization and Its Discontents* (New York: W.W. Norton, 2002).
24. Jeffry A Frieden and Ronald Rogowski, "The Impact of the International Economy on National Policies: An Analytical Overview," in *Internationalization and Domestic Politics*, ed. Robert O. Keohane and Helen V. Milner (Cambridge, UK: Cambridge University Press, 1996).
25. Cited in Robert O. Keohane, "Sovereignty, Interdependence, and International Institutions," in *Center for Social Theory and Comparative History Colloquium Series* (Los Angeles: 1991), 19.
26. Held et al., *Global Transformations*, 9.
27. The earliest suggestion of this parallel of which I am aware is Bull, *The Anarchical Society*; cf. Ruggie, "Territoriality and Beyond," 149; Kratochwil, "Systems, Boundaries, and Territoriality."
28. Robert D Kaplan, "The Coming Anarchy," *The Atlantic Monthly*, February 1994, 44–76.
29. Jörg Friedrichs, "The Meaning of New Medievalism," *European Journal of International Relations* 7, no. 4 (2001), 475–502; cf. Kobrin, "Back to the Future"; David Held, *Democracy and the Global Order: From the Modern State to Cosmopolitan Governance* (Stanford, CA: Stanford University Press, 1995), 135ff. The idea has even made its way into popular print media; see Paul Lewis, "As Nations Shed Roles, Is Medieval the Future?" *The New York Times*, January 2 1999, 7.
30. Held et al., *Global Transformations*, 9.
31. Michael Mann, "Nation-States in Europe and Other Continents: Diversifying, Developing, Not Dying," *Dædalus: Journal of the American Academy of Arts and Sciences* 12, no. 3 (1993): 137.
32. Gidon Gottlieb, *Nation against State* (New York: Council on Foreign Relations Press, 1993); Kratochwil, "Systems, Boundaries, and Territoriality"; Ruggie, "Territoriality and Beyond"; Susan Strange, "The Erosion of the State," *Current History* 96, no. 613 (1997), 365-9; Strange, *The Retreat of the State*.
33. John W. Meyer et al., "World Society and the Nation-State," *American Journal of Sociology* 103, no. 1 (1997), 144–81; Cerny, "Paradoxes of the Competition State."
34. Held, *Democracy and the Global Order*, 135.
35. P.J. Taylor, "Embedded Statism and the Social Sciences: Opening Up to New Spaces," *Environment and Planning A* 28 (1996), 1917–28; F. H. Hinsley, *Sovereignty* (Cambridge, UK: Cambridge University Press, 1986).
36. Mann, "Nation-States in Europe and Other Continents," 137.
37. Held, *Democracy and the Global Order*, 224.
38. Görg and Hirsch, "Is International Democracy Possible?" 598.
39. Fritz Scharpf, "Interdependence and Democratic Legitimation," (Cologne: Max Planck Institute for the Study of Societies, 1998), 13.
40. Robert E. Goodin, Carole Pateman, and Roy Pateman, "Simian Sovereignty," *Political Theory* 25, no. 6 (1997): 821–23.
41. Held, *Democracy and the Global Order*, 145–46.
42. Rousseau was already aware of this problem; he maintained that a robust democracy was only possible in small, homogenous political communities where face-to-face meetings are feasible and representation unnecessary. "I do not see how the sovereign can possibly continue to exercise its rights among us unless the republic is very small"; *Social Contract*, III.16.xiv.

43. Cf. Carole Pateman, *Participation and Democratic Theory* (Cambridge, UK: Cambridge University Press, 1970), 109. Rousseau solved the problem by conceiving the social contract as the means through which citizens realize the general will, which is identical with justice and the common good. Thus the "citizen consents to all laws, even those that pass against his will. When the opinion contrary to my own prevails, this merely proves that I was mistaken, and that what I considered to be the general will was not so. If my private opinion had prevailed, I would have done something other than what I had willed; it is then that I would not have been free" (SC IV.2.viii). The genius of this solution is that it turns disagreement into agreement without denying the reality of conflict. It is convenient for Rousseau that the general will reliably manifests itself in the majority; he acknowledges as much when he states that should it cease to do so, liberty is dead (SC IV.2.ix).
44. E.g., James Bohman, "Deliberative Democracy and Effective Social Freedom: Capabilities, Resources, and Opportunities," in *Deliberative Democracy: Essays on Reason and Politics*, ed. James Bohman and William Rehg (Cambridge, MA: MIT Press, 1997).
45. John Dunn, "Democracy, Globalization, and Human Interests" (Denver, CO, April 1998), 23.
46. Ibid., 15.

Chapter 5

1. Charles Taylor, "No Community, No Democracy," pt. 1, *The Responsive Community* 13, no. 4 (2003): 17 (emphasis in original); see also Charles Taylor, "No Community, No Democracy," pt. 2, *The Responsive Community* 14, no. 1 (2003/4). Taylor collapses two phases of the popular sovereignty revolution into one; the first phase, represented by Locke, transfers sovereignty to the people without establishing the people qua sovereign as a collective entity with a will of its own; this entity emerges during the revolutions of the eighteenth century, under the influence of Rousseau and the *Declaration of the Rights of Man and Citizen*.
2. Taylor, "No Community, No Democracy," pt. 1, 17–18.
3. Ibid., passim.
4. Will Kymlicka, "Citizenship in an Era of Globalization: Commentary on Held," in *Democracy's Edges*, ed. Ian Shapiro and Casiano Hacker-Cordón (Cambridge, UK: Cambridge University Press, 1999), 115.
5. Ibid., 122.
6. See Jürgen Habermas, "Three Normative Models of Democracy," in *Democracy and Difference: Contesting the Boundaries of the Political*, ed. Seyla Benhabib (Princeton, NJ: Princeton University Press, 1996); Yael Tamir, *Liberal Nationalism* (Princeton, NJ: Princeton University Press, 1993); Taylor, "No Community, No Democracy," pt.1.
7. David Miller, *On Nationality* (Oxford: Clarendon Press, 1995), 81ff.; Tamir, *Liberal Nationalism*, 90.
8. Fareed Zakaria, "The Rise of Illiberal Democracy," *Foreign Affairs* 76, no. 6 (1997), 22–43; Michael Freeman, "The Perils of Democratization: Nationalism, Markets, and Human Rights," *Human Rights Review* 2, no. 1 (2000), 33–51.
9. Taylor, "No Community, No Democracy," pt. 1, 20.
10. Miller, *On Nationality*, 79–80.
11. Chris Brown, *International Relations Theory: New Normative Approaches* (New York: Columbia University Press, 1992), 24.
12. The argument in this section draws on Michael Goodhart, "Civil Society and the Problem of Global Democracy," *Democratization* 12, no. 1 (2005), 1–21.
13. Mustapha Kamal Pasha and David L. Blaney, "Elusive Paradise: The Promise and Peril of Global Civil Society," *Alternatives* 23, no. 4 (1998): 418.
14. Ronnie D. Lipschutz, "Reconstructing World Politics: The Emergence of Global Civil Society," *Millennium: Journal of International Studies* 21, no. 3 (1992): 393.
15. Jackie Smith, "Global Civil Society? Transnational Social Movement Organizations and Social Capital," *American Behavioral Scientist* 42, no. 1 (1998): 102.
16. Ronnie D. Lipschutz, *After Authority: War, Peace, and Global Politics in the 21st Century* (Albany: State University of New York Press, 2000), 174; cf. John S. Dryzek, "Transnational Democracy," *Journal of Political Philosophy* 7, no. 1 (1999): 44.
17. Smith, "Global Civil Society?" 104.

18. Sanjeev Khagram, James V. Riker, and Kathryn Sikkink, "From Santiago to Seattle: Transnational Advocacy Groups Restructuring World Politics," in *Restructuring World Politics: Transnational Social Movements, Networks, and Norms*, ed. Sanjeev Khagram, James V. Riker, and Kathryn Sikkink (Minneapolis: University of Minnesota Press, 2002), 7–8.

19. Thomas Risse, "The Power of Norms Versus the Norms of Power: Transnational Civil Society and Human Rights," in *The Third Force: The Rise of Transnational Civil Society*, ed. Ann M. Florini (Tokyo/Washington, D.C.: Japan Center for International Exchange and Carnegie Endowment for International Peace, 2000), 185ff.

20. Khagram, Riker, and Sikkink, "From Santiago to Seattle," 15; see also Sanjeev Khagram, "Restructuring the Global Politics of Development: The Case of India's Narmada Valley Dams," in *Restructuring World Politics: Transnational Social Movements, Networks, and Norms*, ed. Sanjeev Khagram, James V. Riker, and Kathryn Sikkink (Minneapolis: University of Minnesota Press, 2002).

21. Elisabeth Mann Borgese, "Global Civil Society: Lessons from Ocean Governance," *Futures* 31, no. 9/10 (1999), 983–91; Robert O'Brien et al., *Contesting Global Governance: Multilateral Economic Institutions and Global Social Movements* (Cambridge, UK: Cambridge University Press, 2000); Scott Turner, "Global Civil Society, Anarchy and Governance: Assessing an Emerging Paradigm," *Journal of Peace Research* 35, no. 1 (1998), 25–42.

22. Pasha and Blaney, "Elusive Paradise," 426.

23. Dryzek, "Transnational Democracy," 46ff.

24. Richard Falk, "Global Civil Society and the Democratic Prospect," in *Global Democracy: Key Debates*, ed. Barry Holden (New York: Routledge, 2000), 171; Barry K. Gills, "'Globalization' and the 'Politics of Resistance'," *New Political Economy* 2, no. 1 (1997), 11–15.

25. Ann M. Florini and P. J. Simmons, "What the World Needs Now?" in *The Third Force: The Rise of Transnational Civil Society*, ed. Ann M. Florini (Tokyo/Washington, D.C.: Japan Center for International Exchange and Carnegie Endowment for International Peace, 2000); Jan Aart Scholte, "Democratizing the Global Economy: The Role of Civil Society" (Coventry: 2003); Jan Aart Scholte, "Civil Society and Democracy in Global Governance," *Global Governace* 8, no. 3 (2002): 281–304.

26. See, e.g., Thomas Risse and Kathryn Sikkink, "The Socialization of International Human Rights Norms into Domestic Practices: Introductions," in *The Power of Human Rights: International Norms and Domestic Change*, ed. Thomas Risse, Stephen C. Ropp, and Kathryn Sikkink (Cambridge, UK: Cambridge University Press, 1999); Risse, "The Power of Norms"; Kathryn Sikkink, "Human Rights, Principled Issue-Networks, and Sovereignty in Latin America," *International Organization* 47, no. 3 (1993), 411–41; Daniel C. Thomas, *The Helsinki Effect: International Norms, Human Rights, and the Demise of Communism* (Princeton, NJ: Princeton University Press, 2001).

27. Lipschutz, *After Authority*, 172.

28. Georg Wilhelm Friedrich Hegel, *Philosophy of Right*, trans. T. M. Knox (Oxford: Oxford University Press, 1967), 124ff.; Neera Chandhoke, *State and Civil Society: Explorations in Political Theory* (New Delhi: Sage, 1995).

29. Michael Walzer, "The Concept of Civil Society," in *Toward a Global Civil Society*, ed. Michael Walzer (Providence, RI: Berghahn Books, 1995), 24.

30. Pasha and Blaney, "Elusive Paradise," 422.

31. See Nancy L. Rosenblum, *Membership and Morals: The Personal Uses of Pluralism in America* (Princeton, NJ: Princeton University Press, 1998).

32. R. B. J. Walker, "Social Movements/World Politics," *Millennium: Journal of International Studies* 23, no. 3 (1994): 683.

33. Frederick G. Whelan, "Prologue: Democratic Theory and the Boundary Problem," in *Liberal Democracy; Nomos XXV*, ed. J. Roland Pennock and R. W. Chapman (New York: New York University Press, 1983).

34. See David Held, "Democracy, the Nation-State, and the Global System," in *Political Theory Today*, ed. David Held (Stanford, CA: Stanford University Press, 1991).

35. See David Beetham, *Democracy and Human Rights* (Cambridge, UK: Polity Press, 1999), chap. 1.

36. Nicholas Greenwood Onuf, "Sovereignty: Outline of a Conceptual History," *Alternatives* 16, no. 4 (1991): 426.

Chapter 6

1. This approach is very much in the spirit of James Tully, "Political Philosophy as a Critical Activity," *Political Theory* 30, no. 4 (2002), 533–55.
2. E.g., Richard Tuck, *Natural Rights Theories: Their Origin and Development* (Cambridge, UK: Cambridge University Press, 1979).
3. David Zaret, "Tradition, Human Rights, and the English Revolution," in *Human Rights and Revolutions*, ed. Jeffrey N. Wasserstrom, Lynn Hunt, and Marilyn B. Young (Lanham, MD: Rowman & Littlefield, 2000); cf. Kenneth Minogue, "The History of the Idea of Human Rights," in *The Human Rights Reader*, ed. Walter Laquer and Barry Rubin (New York: New Amsterdam Library, 1979).
4. Albert Soboul, *A Short History of the French Revolution: 1789–1799*, trans. Geoffrey Symcox (Berkeley: University of California Press, 1977), 160–61.
5. See Olympe de Gouges, "The Rights of Women" [Web Page] (Paris: 1791 [cited 31 March 2005]); available from http://www.pinn.net/~sunshine/book-sum/gouges.html; Mary Wollstonecraft, *A Vindication of the Rights of Men* and *a Vindication of the Rights of Woman*, ed. Sylvana Tomaselli (Cambridge, UK: Cambridge University Press, 1995); C. L. R. James, *The Black Jacobins: Toussaint L'Ouverture and the San Domingo Revolution*, 2nd ed. (New York: Vintage Books, 1989).
6. Georges Lefebvre, *The Coming of the French Revolution: 1789*, trans. R. R. Palmer (New York: Vintage Books, 1957), 184.
7. Lynn Hunt, "The Paradoxical Origins of Human Rights," in *Human Rights and Revolutions*, ed. Jeffrey N. Wasserstrom, Lynn Hunt, and Marilyn B. Young (Lanham, MD: Rowman & Littlefield, 2000), 12.
8. Carole Pateman, "Democracy and Democratization," *International Political Science Review* 17, no. 1 (1996): 7.
9. Ian Shapiro, *Democratic Justice* (New Haven, CT: Yale University Press, 1999), 30.
10. Michael Walzer, *Spheres of Justice: A Defense of Pluralism and Equality* (New York: Basic Books, 1983), xii.
11. Ibid., xiii.
12. See Richard Ashcraft, "Liberal Political Theory and Working-Class Radicalism in Nineteenth-Century England," *Political Theory* 21, no. 2 (1993), 249–72.
13. Philip Pettit, *Republicanism: A Theory of Freedom and Government* (Oxford: Oxford University Press, 1997), 6; Anne Phillips, *Engendering Democracy* (University Park, PA: Pennsylvania State University Press, 1991), 46ff.; Iris Marion Young, *Justice and the Politics of Difference* (Princeton, NJ: Princeton University Press, 1990), 117.
14. I stress *classical* republicans, as many contemporary proponents do see nondomination as a universal political ideal.
15. See Gregory Claeys, "The Origins of the Rights of Labor: Republicanism, Commerce, and the Construction of Modern Social Theory in Britain, 1796–1805," *Journal of Modern History* 66, no. 2 (1994), 249–90. Unfortunately I will not be able to pursue this possibility further here.
16. Michael B. Levy, "Freedom, Property and the Levellers: The Case of John Lilburne," *The Western Political Quarterly* 36, no. 1 (1983): 116.
17. See Iain Hampsher-Monk, "The Political Theory of the Levellers: Putney, Property and Professor Macpherson," *Political Studies* 24, no. 4 (1976), 397–422, for an overview and review of the literature on the Levellers and suffrage in the English Commonwealth.
18. Andrew Sharp, "Introduction," in *The English Levellers*, ed. Andrew Sharp (Cambridge, UK: Cambridge University Press, 1998), xii. Sharp ultimately concludes that it is safest to call them Leveller democrats, a moniker whose advantage is that it can hardly be wrong.
19. Hampsher-Monk, "Political Theory of the Levellers," 412–13.
20. Andrew Sharp, ed., *The English Levellers* (Cambridge, UK: Cambridge University Press, 1998), 31.
21. Sharp, "Introduction," xviii.
22. Hampsher-Monk, "Political Theory of the Levellers," 420.
23. Levy, "Freedom, Property, and the Levellers," 118.
24. Hampsher-Monk, "Political Theory of the Levellers," 420.
25. Sharp, ed., *The English Levellers*, 136–37, 61ff., 74–75.
26. Ibid., 55.

27. Ibid., 57; on subsistence see Levy, "Freedom, Property, and the Levellers," 122.
28. Sharp, ed., *The English Levellers*, 103.
29. Ibid., 109.
30. Ibid., 118.
31. Ibid., 137, 61, 75.
32. Thomas Paine, "Declaration of Rights," in *The Writings of Thomas Paine*, ed. Moncure Daniel Conway (New York: G.P. Putnam's Sons, 1894), 128.
33. Thomas Paine, *The Rights of Man* (Mineola, NY: Dover, 1999), 91.
34. E.g., Joseph Dorfman, "The Economic Philosophy of Thomas Paine," *Political Science Quarterly* 53, no. 3 (1938), 372–86.
35. Paine, "Declaration of Rights," 130, emphasis mine.
36. Thomas Paine, "Agrarian Justice," in *The Writings of Thomas Paine*, ed. Moncure Daniel Conway (New York: G.P. Putnam's Sons, 1894), 337.
37. See Claeys, "Origins of the Rights of Labor."
38. Paine, "Agrarian Justice," 328.
39. Paine, *The Rights of Man*, 151.
40. Ibid., 172., emphasis mine; Paine, "Agrarian Justice," 331.
41. Paine, "Declaration of Rights," 130.
42. Ibid., 129.
43. Paine, "Agrarian Justice," 325.
44. Paine, "Declaration of Rights," 131.
45. Wollstonecraft, *Vindications*, 61.
46. See Virginia Sapiro, "A Woman's Struggle for a Language of Entitlement and Virtue: Mary Wollstonecraft and Enlightenment 'Feminism'," in *Perspectives on Feminist Political Thought in European History: From the Middle Ages to the Present*, ed. Tjitske Akkerman and Siep Stuurman (London: Routledge, 1998).
47. Wollstonecraft, *Vindications*, 68–69.
48. Ibid., 69,13.
49. Ibid., 29ff.
50. Ibid., passim.
51. Ibid., 236.
52. Ibid., 59, emphasis mine.
53. Ibid., 230.
54. Ibid., 294.
55. Ibid.
56. See, e.g., ibid., 239.
57. She calls this a revolution in "manners,"; see ibid., 117. On Wollstonecraft's appropriation of the language of manners and morals, see Daniel I. O'Neill, "Shifting the Scottish Paradigm: The Discourse of Morals and Manners in Mary Wollstonecraft's *French Revolution*," *History of Political Thought* 23, no. 1 (2002), 90–116.
58. Elizabeth Cady Stanton, "The Seneca Falls Declaration" (1848) in *AMODOCS: Documents for the Study of American History* [Web site] (Lawrence, KS: University of Kansas [accessed 12/31/04]).
59. O'Neill, "Shifting the Scottish Paradigm," 115.
60. Ellen C. DuBois, *The Elizabeth Cady Stanton—Susan B. Anthony Reader: Correspondence, Writings, Speeches* (Boston: Northeastern University Press, 1992), 83, 27.
61. Ibid., 81.
62. Ibid., 116.
63. Ibid., 135. This theme was stressed even more emphatically by Stanton's friend and collaborator Susan B. Anthony.
64. Ibid., 247.
65. Ibid., 32.
66. Ibid., 132.
67. Douglass, *The Meaning of July Fourth for the Negro* [Web page] (1852 [cited January 2 2005]); available from http://www.pbs.org/wgbh/aia/part4/4h2927.html.
68. Lucy Stone, Remarks to the meeting of the American Equal Rights Association [Web Page] (1869 [cited 31 March 2005]); available from http://www.sscnet.ucla.edu/history/dubois/classes/995/98F/doc30.htm).

69. Cf. Brooke Ackerly, "Women's Human Rights Activists as Cross-Cultural Theorists," *International Journal of Feminist Politics* 3, no. 3 (2001), 1–36.
70. Cited in Ashcraft, "Liberal Political Theory," 262.
71. Cited in Samuel Bowles and Herbert Gintis, *Democracy and Capitalism: Property, Community, and the Contradictions of Modern Social Thought* (New York: Basic Books, 1986), 9.
72. Ashcraft, "Liberal Political Theory," 262–63. Ashcraft calls the political vocabulary in which democratic empowerment is expressed "natural rights liberalism"; as noted above, I prefer to see the commitment to human rights as a point of overlap between distinct liberal and radical democratic traditions.
73. In Karl Marx and Friedrich Engels, *The Marx-Engels Reader*, ed. Robert C. Tucker (New York: W.W. Norton, 1978), 40ff.
74. Minogue, "The History of the Idea of Human Rights," 12.
75. Bowles and Gintis, *Democracy and Capitalism*, 9n.
76. Ibid., 25.
77. Aung San Suu Kyi, *Freedom from Fear and Other Writings*, ed. Michael Aris, rev. ed. (New York: Penguin Books, 1995), 269.
78. Robert E. Goodin, Carole Pateman, and Roy Pateman, "Simian Sovereignty," *Political Theory* 25, no. 6 (1997): 821-23.
79. John Hoffman, *Sovereignty* (Minneapolis: University of Minnesota Press, 1998), 99.
80. Hedley Bull, *The Anarchical Society: A Study of Order in World Politics* (New York: Columbia University Press, 1977), 152.
81. James N. Rosenau, *Turbulence in World Politics: A Theory of Change and Continuity* (Princeton, NJ: Princeton University Press, 1990), 437.
82. See Reus-Smit, "Human Rights and Sovereignty"; Daniel Philpott, *Revolutions in Sovereignty: How Ideas Shaped Modern International Relations* (Princeton, NJ: Princeton University Press, 2001).

Chapter 7

1. Carol C. Gould, *Rethinking Democracy: Freedom and Social Cooperation in Politics, Economy, and Society* (Cambridge: Cambridge University Press, 1988), 26; Carol C. Gould, "Feminism and Democratic Community Revisited," in *Democratic Community: Nomos XXXV*, ed. John W. Chapman and Ian Shapiro (New York: New York University Press, 1993).
2. John Rawls, *Political Liberalism* (New York: Columbia University Press, 1993) 143ff.
3. Michael Goodhart, "Origins and Universality in the Human Rights Debates: Cultural Essentialism and the Challenge of Globalization," *Human Rights Quarterly* 25, no. 4 (2003), 935–64.
4. Ken Booth, "Three Tyrannies," in *Human Rights in Global Politics*, ed. Tim Dunne and Nicholas J. Wheeler (Cambridge, UK: Cambridge University Press, 1999), 40–41.
5. Quentin Skinner, *Liberty before Liberalism* (Cambridge, UK: Cambridge University Press, 1998), 84; cf. Philip Pettit, *Republicanism: A Theory of Freedom and Government* (Oxford: Oxford University Press, 1997). As Pettit rightly notes, nondomination is not a "positive" conception of freedom or liberty in Berlin's sense; Pettit, *Republicanism*, 27.
6. Pettit, *Republicanism*, 22.
7. Steven Wall, "Freedom, Interference and Domination," *Political Studies* 49, no. 2 (2001): 223.
8. Ibid.; for a possible way out of this dilemma see Pettit, *Republicanism*, 103–6; for a rebuttal, see Wall, "Freedom, Interference and Domination," 224ff.
9. Amartya Sen, "Human Rights and Economic Achievements," in *The East Asian Challenge for Human Rights*, ed. Joanne R. Bauer and Daniel A. Bell (Cambridge, UK: Cambridge University Press, 1999), 7.
10. Charles R. Beitz, "Human Rights as a Common Concern," *American Political Science Review* 95, no. 2 (2001): 280, makes this argument for human rights.
11. Cf. ibid., 274.
12. Iris Marion Young, *Inclusion and Democracy* (Oxford: Oxford University Press, 2000).
13. Jean Bethke Elshtain, *Democracy on Trial* (New York: Basic Books, 1995).
14. Iris Marion Young, *Justice and the Politics of Difference* (Princeton, NJ: Princeton University Press, 1990), 105.
15. Susan Mendus, "Losing the Faith: Feminism and Democracy," in *Democracy: The Unfinished Journey 508 B.C to A.D. 1993*, ed. John Dunn (Oxford: Oxford University Press, 1992), 23.

16. Cf. Michael Walzer, *Spheres of Justice: A Defense of Pluralism and Equality* (New York: Basic Books, 1983), xii.
17. Michael Ignatieff, *Human Rights as Politics and Idolatry*, ed. Amy Gutmann (Princeton, NJ: Princeton University Press, 2001), 54; cf. Beitz, "Human Rights as a Common Concern."
18. See, e.g., Seyla Benhabib, *Situating the Self: Gender, Community and Postmodernism in Contemporary Ethics* (New York: Routledge, 1992); James Bohman and William Rehg, "Deliberative Democracy: Essays on Reason and Politics" (Cambridge, MA: MIT Press, 1997); John S. Dryzek, *Deliberative Democracy and Beyond: Liberals, Critics, Contestations* (New York: Oxford University Press, 2000).
19. Abdullahi Ahmed An-Na'im, ed., *Human Rights in Cross-Cultural Perspectives: A Quest for Consensus* (Philadelphia: University of Pennsylvania Press, 1992); Young, *Inclusion and Democracy*, 271.
20. Here I follow Henry Shue, *Basic Rights: Subsistence, Affluence, and U.S. Foreign Policy* (Princeton, NJ: Princeton University Press, 1996).
21. Ibid., 21–22.
22. John Stuart Mill, "Considerations on Representative Government," in *Utilitarianism, on Liberty, and Considerations on Representative Government*, ed. H. B. Acton (Cambridge, UK: Cambridge University Press, 1972), 275.
23. Shue, *Basic Rights*, 84.
24. Jack Donnelly, "Human Rights and Asian Values: A Defense of 'Western Individualism,'" in *The East Asian Challenge for Human Rights*, ed. Joanne R. Bauer and Daniel A. Bell (Cambridge, UK: Cambridge University Press, 1999).
25. E.g., Charles Taylor, "What's Wrong with Negative Freedom?" in *Contemporary Political Philosophy: An Anthology*, ed. Robert E. Goodin and Philip Pettit (Oxford: Blackwell, 1997).
26. E.g., Winfried Brugger, "The Image of the Person in the Human Rights Concept," *Human Rights Quarterly* 18, no. 3 (1996), 594-611; Martha C. Nussbaum, "Human Functioning and Social Justice: In Defense of Aristotelian Essentialism," *Political Theory* 20, no. 2 (1992), 202–46; John Rawls, *A Theory of Justice* (Cambridge, MA: Harvard University Press, 1971).
27. E.g., Benjamin Barber, *Strong Democracy: Participatory Politics for a New Age* (Berkeley: University of California Press, 1984); Michael J. Sandel, *Liberalism and the Limits of Justice*, 2nd ed. (Cambridge, UK: Cambridge University Press, 1998).
28. Gould, "Feminism and Democratic Community Revisited," 409.
29. Peter Jones, *Rights* (Basingstoke, UK: Macmillan, 1994), 210–11.
30. Ibid., 211.
31. Will Kymlicka, *Multicultural Citizenship: A Liberal Theory of Minority Rights* (Oxford: Clarendon Press, 1995), 26.
32. Gould, *Rethinking Democracy*, 208.
33. Jürgen Habermas, "Why Europe Needs a Constitution," *New Left Review* 11 (2001).
34. Shue, *Basic Rights*, 16; cf. R.J. Vincent, *Human Rights and International Relations* (Cambridge, UK: Cambridge University Press, 1986).
35. Shue, *Basic Rights*, 159–60.
36. Thomas W. Pogge, "Cosmopolitanism and Sovereignty," *Ethics* 103, no. 1 (1992), 48–75; cf. Thomas W. Pogge, "Human Flourishing and Unusual Justice," *Social Philosophy and Policy* 16, no. 1 (1999): 333–61.
37. Shue, *Basic Rights*, 13.
38. Thomas W. Pogge, "The International Significance of Human Rights," *The Journal of Ethics* 4, no. 1 (2000): 52.
39. Ibid.
40. Pogge, "Human Flourishing," 344. Pogge notes that this view can yield an apparently paradoxical but still plausible result: "your physical integrity, but not that of your black colleague, [might be] sufficiently well protected … even if you are in fact assaulted while she is not" (344-45).
41. Cited in Skinner, *Liberty before Liberalism*, 86.
42. Cf. Pogge, "Human Flourishing," 351ff.
43. Lawrence S. Finkelstein, "What Is Global Governance?," *Global Governace* 1, no. 3 (1995): 368.
44. James N. Rosenau, "Governance, Order, and Change in World Politics," in *Governance without Government: Order and Change in World Politics*, ed. James N. Rosenau and Ernst-Otto Czempiel (Cambridge, UK: Cambridge University Press, 1992), 15.

45. See Gould, "Feminism and Democratic Community Revisited."
46. For an overview see Susan Moller Okin, "Gender, the Public, and the Private," in *Political Theory Today*, ed. David Held (Stanford, CA: Stanford University Press, 1991).
47. For an overview of recent arguments against this view of property rights see Will Kymlicka, *Contemporary Political Philosophy: An Introduction*, 2nd ed. (Oxford: Clarendon Press, 2002), chap. 4; against property rights entailing corporate government rights see Robert Dahl, *A Preface to Economic Democracy* (Berkeley: University of California Press, 1985), 82ff.
48. Thomas Paine, "Agrarian Justice," in *The Writings of Thomas Paine*, ed. Moncure Daniel Conway (New York: G.P. Putnam's Sons, 1894), 337.
49. See Iris Marion Young, "Communication and the Other: Beyond Deliberative Democracy," in *Democracy and Difference: Contesting the Boundaries of the Political*, ed. Seyla Benhabib (Princeton, NJ: Princeton University Press, 1996).
50. Cf. Brian Barry, "Statism and Nationalism: A Cosmopolitan Critique," in *Global Justice: Nomos XLI*, ed. Ian Shapiro and Lea Brilmayer (New York: New York University Press, 1999); Hillel Steiner, "Three Just Taxes," in *Arguing for Basic Income: Ethical Foundations for a Radical Reform*, ed. Philippe van Parijs (London: Verso, 1992).
51. Goodhart, "Origins and Universality."
52. Claude Lefort, "Politics and Human Rights," in *The Political Forms of Modern Society: Bureaucracy, Democracy, Totalitarianism*, ed. John B. Thompson (Cambridge, UK: Polity Press, 1986), 260.
53. Norberto Bobbio, *The Age of Rights*, trans. Allan Cameron (Cambridge, UK: Polity Press, 1996), 12.
54. Rosemary Foot, "Human Rights, Democracy, and Development: The Debate in East Asia," *Democratization* 4, no. 2 (1997), 139-53.
55. Philippe van Parijs, *Real Freedom for All: What (If Anything) Can Justify Capitalism?* (Oxford: Oxford University Press, 1995), 228ff.
56. Michael Freeman, "The Perils of Democratization: Nationalism, Markets, and Human Rights," *Human Rights Review* 2, no. 1 (2000): 34–35.
57. Fareed Zakaria, "The Rise of Illiberal Democracy," *Foreign Affairs* 76, no. 6 (1997): 22.
58. Ibid.
59. The classic example is Joseph A. Schumpeter, *Capitalism, Socialism, and Democracy* (New York: Harper & Row, 1942).
60. Freeman, "Perils of Democratization," 37; cf. Ronald Dworkin, *Freedom's Law: The Moral Reading of the American Constitution* (Cambridge, MA: Harvard University Press, 1996).
61. Sheldon Leader, "Three Faces of Toleration in a Democracy," *The Journal of Political Philosophy* 4, no. 1 (1996), 45-67; cf. Dworkin, *Freedom's Law*, who talks about "egalitarian" justifications, a term more congenial to my purposes.
62. Robert Dahl, *A Preface to Democratic Theory* (Chicago: University of Chicago Press, 1956), 36.
63. Leader, "Three Faces of Toleration," 50.
64. Cf. Ronald Dworkin, "Rights as Trumps," in *Theories of Rights*, ed. Jeremy Waldron (Oxford: Oxford University Press, 1984).
65. Ian Shapiro, *Democratic Justice* (New Haven, CT: Yale University Press, 1999), 5.
66. John Markoff, "Who Will Construct the Global Order?", in Bruce William Morrison, ed., *Transnational Democracy in Critical and Comparative Perspective: Democracy's Range Reconsidered* (London: Ashgate Publishing, 2004), 13.
67. John Markoff, "Globalization and the Future of Democracy," *Journal of World-Systems Research* 5, no. 2 (1999): 280.
68. Markoff, "Who Will Construct the Global Order?" 14.

Chapter 8

1. Archon Fung and Erik Olin Wright, "Deepening Democracy: Innovations in Empowered Participatory Governance," *Politics and Society* 29, no. 1 (2001): 17; cf. John Burnheim, *Is Democracy Possible? The Alternative to Electoral Politics* (Berkeley: University of California Press, 1985).
2. Thomas W. Pogge, "The International Significance of Human Rights," *The Journal of Ethics* 4, no. 1 (2000), 45–69.
3. See the discussion in the previous chapter and ibid.

4. Henry Shue, *Basic Rights: Subsistence, Affluence, and U.S. Foreign Policy* (Princeton, NJ: Princeton University Press, 1996), 60, 159–60.

5. Peter Jones, "Human Rights, Group Rights, and People's Rights," *Human Rights Quarterly* 21, no. 1 (1999): 104.

6. Cf. Amartya Sen, *Development as Freedom* (New York: Alfred A. Knopf, 1999); Amartya Sen, "Freedoms and Needs: Why Political Rights Are Primary, Even in the Face of Dire Economic Need," *The New Republic* 213, no. 4.121 and 4.122 (1994).

7. Cf. William E. Connolly, "Democracy and Territoriality," *Millennium: Journal of International Studies* 20, no. 3 (1991), 463–84.

8. See also Frederick G. Whelan, "Prologue: Democratic Theory and the Boundary Problem," in *Liberal Democracy: Nomos XXV*, ed. J. Roland Pennock and R.W. Chapman (New York: New York University Press, 1983).

9. Archon Fung, "Accountable Autonomy: Toward Empowered Deliberation in Chicago Schools and Policing," *Politics and Society* 29, no. 1 (2001), 73–103.

10. Amy Gutmann and Dennis Thompson, *Democracy and Disagreement* (Cambridge, MA: Harvard University Press, 1996); Jo Lenaghan, "Involving the Public in Rationing Decisions. The Experience of Citizens' Juries," *Health Policy* 49, no. 1–2 (1999), 45–61.

11. David Price, "Choices without Reasons: Citizens' Juries and Policy Evaluation," *Journal of Medical Ethics* 26, no. 4 (2000), 272–76.

12. See Carole Pateman, "Democratizing Citizenship: Some Advantages of a Basic Income," *Politics and Society* 32, no. 1 (2004), 89–105.

13. Carole Pateman, "Freedom and Democratization: Why Basic Income Is to Be Preferred to Basic Capital," in *The Ethics of Stakeholding*, ed. Keith Dowling, Jurgen de Wispelaere, and Stuart White (New York: Palgrave, 2003); Robert E. Goodin, "Towards a Minimally Presumptuous Social Welfare Policy," in *Arguing for Basic Income: Ethical Foundations for a Radical Reform*, ed. Philippe van Parijs (London: Verso, 1992).

14. See Fung and Wright, "Deepening Democracy." for a discussion of institutional design requirements for local institutions of this type; see James S. Fishkin, *Democracy and Deliberation: New Directions for Democratic Reform* (New Haven, CT: Yale University Press, 1991), for a discussion of how these goals might be achieved beyond the local level.

15. Frank I. Michelman, "How Can the People Ever Make the Laws? A Critique of Deliberative Democracy," in *Deliberative Democracy: Essays on Reason and Politics*, ed. James Bohman and William Rehg (Cambridge, MA: MIT Press, 1997); David Estlund, "Beyond Fairness and Deliberation: The Epistemic Dimension of Democratic Authority," in *Deliberative Democracy: Essays on Reason and Politics*, ed. James Bohman and William Rehg (Cambridge, MA: MIT Press, 1997).

16. See Giandomenico Majone, "Europe's 'Democratic Deficit': The Question of Standards," *European Law Journal* 4, no. 1 (1998), 5–28.

17. Christian Hunold and B. Guy Peters, "Bureaucratic Discretion and Deliberative Democracy," in *Transformation in Governance: New Directions in Government and Politics*, ed. Matti Mälkiä, Ari-Veikko Anttiroiko, and Reijo Savolainen (Hershey, PA: Idea Group Publishing, 2004).

18. Marion Sawer, *Sisters in Suits: Women's Public Policy in Australia* (Sydney, Australia: Allen & Unwin, 1990).

19. Ibid., 228ff. Unfortunately a change in government spelled the end of the WBP; see Marion Sawer and Lani Russell, "The Rise and Fall of the Australian Women's Bureau," *Australian Journal of Politics and History* 45, no. 3 (1999), 362–75.

20. San Francisco Commission on the Status of Women, *Guidelines for a Gender Analysis: Human Rights with a Gender Perspective* [website] (City and County of San Francisco, 2000 [cited May 21, 2003]); available from http://www.sfgov.org/site/cosw_page.asp?id=10854.

21. Charles Sabel, Archon Fung, and Bradley Karkkainen, *Beyond Backyard Environmentalism: How Communities Are Quietly Refashioning Environmental Regulation* [Web page] (Boston Review, 2003 [cited May 30, 2003]); available from http://bostonreview.mit.edu/BR24.5/sabel.html.; Craig W. Thomas, "Habitat Conservation Planning: Certainly Empowered, Somewhat Deliberative, Questionably Democratic," *Politics and Society* 29, no. 1 (2001), 105–30.

22. Council on Economic Priorities Accreditation Agency (CEPAA), "Guidance Document for Social Accountability 8000" (New York: CEPAA, 1999).

23. Labor Rights in China et al., *No Illusions: Against the Global Cosmetic SA8000* (1999 [cited May 28, 2003]); available from www.ellipson.com/sa8000/pdf_files/noillusions.pdf.

24. Francesca Klug, Keith Starmer, and Stuart Weir, *The Three Pillars of Liberty: Political Rights and Freedoms in the United Kingdom* (New York: Routledge, 1996); David Beetham, "Key Principles and Indices for a Democratic Audit," in *Defining and Measuring Democracy*, ed. David Beetham (Thousand Oaks, CA: Sage, 1994) ; David Beetham, "The Idea of Democratic Audit in Comparative Perspective," *Parliamentary Affairs* 52, no. 4 (1999), 567–81.
25. Beetham, "Democratic Audit in Comparative Perspective," 568–69.
26. Ibid.: 579.
27. Iris Marion Young, *Inclusion and Democracy* (Oxford: Oxford University Press, 2000).
28. Burnheim, *Is Democracy Possible?*
29. Anne Phillips, *Engendering Democracy* (University Park, PA: Pennsylvania State University Press, 1991); Young, *Inclusion and Democracy*.
30. Registrar of the European Court of Human Rights, *The European Court of Human Rights: Historical Background, Organization and Procedure* [Web page document] (Council of Europe, 2003 [cited May 30, 2003]); available from http://www.echr.coe.int/Eng/EDocs/Historical-Background.htm.
31. Simon Hix, *The Political System of the European Union* (New York: Palgrave, 1999), 103ff.
32. Eyal Benvenisti, "Margin of Appreciation, Consensus, and Universal Standards," *International Law and Politics* 31, no. 4 (1999), 843–54.
33. Thomas W. Pogge, "Achieving Democracy," *Ethics and International Affairs* 15, no. 1 (2001), 3–23.
34. Esref Aksu and Joseph A. Camilleri, eds., *Democratizing Global Governance* (New York: Palgrave Macmillan, 2002); David Held, *Democracy and the Global Order: From the Modern State to Cosmopolitan Governance* (Stanford, CA: Stanford University Press, 1995).
35. Robin Round, "Time for Tobin," *The New Internationalist* 320 (2000), 16–17; Ruben P. Mendez, "Financing the United Nations and the International Public Sector: Problems and Reform," *Global Governance* 3, no. 3 (1997), 283–310.
36. Round, "Time for Tobin"; Stephen Kobrin, "Electronic Cash and the End of National Markets," *Foreign Policy* 107 (1997), 65–77.
37. James N. Rosenau, "Governance and Democracy in a Globalizing World," In *Re-Imagining Political Community: Studies in Cosmopolitan Democracy*, ed. Daniele Archibugi, David Held, and Martin Köhler (Cambridge, UK: Polity Press, 1998), 49.

Chapter 9

1. Thomas Risse and Kathryn Sikkink, "The Socialization of International Human Rights Norms into Domestic Practices: Introductions," in *The Power of Human Rights: International Norms and Domestic Change*, ed. Thomas Risse, Stephen C. Ropp, and Kathryn Sikkink (Cambridge, UK: Cambridge University Press, 1999); cf. Thomas Risse, "The Power of Norms Versus the Norms of Power: Transnational Civil Society and Human Rights," in *The Third Force: The Rise of Transnational Civil Society*, ed. Ann M. Florini (Tokyo/Washington: Japan Center for International Exchange/ Carnegie Endowment for International Peace, 2000).
2. Daniel C. Thomas, *The Helsinki Effect: International Norms, Human Rights, and the Demise of Communism* (Princeton, NJ: Princeton University Press, 2001).
3. Margaret E. Keck and Kathryn Sikkink, *Activists Beyond Borders: Advocacy Networks in International Politics* (Ithaca, NY: Cornell University Press, 1998); Kathryn Sikkink, "Transnational Politics, International Relations Theory, and Human Rights," *PS: Political Science and Politics* 31, no. 3 (1998), 517–20; Kathryn Sikkink, "Human Rights, Principled Issue-Networks, and Sovereignty in Latin America," *International Organization* 47, no. 3 (1993), 411–41.
4. John Markoff, "Globalization and the Future of Democracy," *Journal of World-Systems Research* 5, no. 2 (1999): 297.
5. Sanjeev Khagram, James V. Riker, and Kathryn Sikkink, "From Santiago to Seattle: Transnational Advocacy Groups Restructuring World Politics," in *Restructuring World Politics: Transnational Social Movements, Networks, and Norms*, ed. Sanjeev Khagram, James V. Riker, and Kathryn Sikkink (Minneapolis: University of Minnesota Press, 2002), 7–8.
6. Risse, "The Power of Norms," 185ff.
7. Khagram, Riker, and Sikkink, "From Santiago to Seattle," 15; cf. Chetan Kumar, "Transnational Networks and Campaigns for Democracy," in *The Third Force: The Rise of Transnational Civil*

Society, ed. Ann M. Florini (Tokyo/Washington, D.C.: Japan Center for International Exchange/ Carnegie Endowment for International Peace, 2000).

8. Sanjeev Khagram, "Restructuring the Global Politics of Development: The Case of India's Narmada Valley Dams," in *Restructuring World Politics: Transnational Social Movements, Networks, and Norms*, ed. Sanjeev Khagram, James V. Riker, and Kathryn Sikkink (Minneapolis: University of Minnesota Press, 2002).

9. Paul J. Nelson, "Agendas, Accountability, and Legitimacy among Transnational Networks Lobbying the World Bank," in *Restructuring World Politics: Transnational Social Movements, Networks, and Norms*, ed. Sanjeev Khagram, James V. Riker, and Kathryn Sikkink (Minneapolis: University of Minnesota Press, 2002).

10. Richard Falk, "Global Civil Society and the Democratic Prospect," in *Global Democracy: Key Debates*, ed. Barry Holden (New York: Routledge, 2000), 171.

11. See Vladimir Tismaneanu, *Reinventing Politics: Eastern Europe from Stalin to Havel* (New York: Free Press, 1992).

12. See, e.g., George J. Andreopoulos and Richard Pierre Claude, eds., *Human Rights Education for the Twenty-First Century* (Philadelphia: University of Pennsylvania Press, 1997).

13. David Ransom, "Fair Trade: Small Change, Big Difference," *The New Internationalist* 322 (2000), 9–12.

14. Cf. William P. Kreml and Charles W. Kegley, Jr., "A Global Political Party: The Next Step," *Alternatives* 21, no. 1 (1996).

15. See Susan Mendus, "Human Rights in Political Theory," *Political Studies* 48, special issue "Human Rights in the Study of Politics," ed. David Beetham (1995), 10–24.

16. Cf. Matthew J. Gibney, "Introduction," in *Globalizing Rights: The Oxford Amnesty Lectures 1999*, ed. Matthew J. Gibney (Oxford: Oxford University Press, 2003).

17. Norman Geras, *The Contract of Mutual Indifference: Political Philosophy after the Holocaust* (New York: Verso, 1998), 26.

18. Ibid., 28ff.

19. Ibid., 60.

20. Ralph Nader and Lori Wallach, "GATT, NAFTA, and the Subversion of the Democratic Process," in *The Case Against the Global Economy*, ed. Jerry Mander and Edward Goldsmith (San Francisco: Sierra Club Books, 1996).

21. Ibid.

22. Constantine Michalopoulos, "Developing Countries' Participation in the World Trade Organization," in *Policy Research Working Paper* (Washington, DC: 1998).

23. Krishna Kumar, ed., *GATT, WTO, and Indian Agriculture* (Delhi: Farm Digest Publications, 1996).

24. Nader and Wallach, "GATT, NAFTA, and Democracy."

25. Miles Wolpin, "Fair Labor Standards, Economic Well-Being, and Human Rights as Costs of 'Free Trade,'" *International Journal of Peace Studies* 2, no. 1 (1997), 65–96; Nader and Wallach, "GATT, NAFTA, and Democracy."

26. Joseph Kahn, "Global Trade Forum Reflects a Burst of Conflict and Hope," *The New York Times*, November 28, 1999, 1.

27. David E. Sanger, "The Shipwreck in Seattle: White House Miscalculation Led to Talks without a Focus," *The New York Times*, December 2, 1999, 26.

28. See Thomas W. Pogge, "Creating Supra-National Institutions Democratically: Reflections on the European Union's "Democratic Deficit"," *The Journal of Political Philosophy* 5, no. 2 (1997), 163–82.

29. Geoff Tansey, "Trade, Intellectual Property, Food and Biodiversity: Key Issues and Options for the 1999 Review of Article 27.3(B) of the Trips Agreement" (London: Quaker Peace and Service, 1999), 3.

30. Ibid.; Bhagirath Lal Das, *The WTO Agreements: Deficiencies, Imbalances, and Required Changes* (New York: Zed Books, 1998). On *sui generis* systems and related challenges see also Biswajit Dhar, "*Sui Generis* Systems for Plant Variety Protection: Options under Trips" (Geneva: Quaker United Nations Office, 2002).

31. Bhagirath Lal Das, *An Introduction to the WTO Agreements* (New York: Zed Books, 1998), 116–17.

32. Geoff Tansey, "Patenting Our Food Future: Intellectual Property Rights and the Global Food System," *Social Policy and Administration* 36, no. 6 (2002): 579.

33. Dhar, "*Sui Generis* Systems," 18.

34. Tansey, "Trade, Intellectual Property, Food and Biodiversity," 21.
35. Fellowes A. Mwaisela, "WTO and Sustainable Seed Multiplication Programmes in Tanzania," *Development* 43, no. 2 (2000): 83; cf. Tansey, "Trade, Intellectual Property, Food and Biodiversity," 10–11.
36. Dhar, "Sui Generis Systems," 26.
37. Carlos M. Correa, "Traditional Knowledge and Intellectual Property: Issues and Options Surrounding the Protection of Traditional Knowledge" (Geneva: Quaker United Nations Office, 2001), 7.
38. Ibid.
39. Dhar, "*Sui Generis* Systems," 6.
40. Correa, "Traditional Knowledge and Intellectual Property," 6. Modifications made through traditional practices are typically not codified—not published or made available according to Western research standards. Patents give corporations proprietary control over alterations developed by farmers, who are charged for using seeds they in effect developed.
41. Dhar, "*Sui Generis* Systems," 13.
42. Tansey, "Patenting Our Food Future," 586.
43. See Kumar, ed., *GATT, WTO, and Indian Agriculture.*
44. Cited in Tansey, "Patenting Our Food Future," 576.
45. Tansey, "Trade, Intellectual Property, Food and Biodiversity," 18–19.
46. Correa, "Traditional Knowledge and Intellectual Property," 26.
47. See Das, *The WTO Agreements: Deficiencies, Imbalances, and Required Changes.*
48. Audrey R. Chapman, "The Human Rights Implications of Intellectual Property Protection," *Journal of International Economic Law* 5, no. 4 (2002): 868.
49. See Ernst-Ulrich Petersmann, "Time for a United Nations 'Global Compact' for Integrating Human Rights into the Law of Worldwide Organizations: Lessons from European Integration," *European Journal of International Law* 13, no. 3 (2002): 635; Robert Howse and Makau Mutua, "Protecting Human Rights in a Global Economy: Challenges for the World Trade Organization" (Montreal: International Centre for Human Rights and Democratic Development, 2000), 8. Curiously, the scrupulous concerns states often raise about sovereignty in objecting to human rights obligations are rarely mentioned in connection with their obligations under the WTO; Chapman, "The Human Rights Implications of Intellectual Property Protection," 866.
50. Petersmann, "Time for a Global Compact," 622. Contrast this with regional accords, especially in Europe, where democracy and human rights are key, operative principles; ibid., 623.
51. UN High Commissioner for Human Rights, "The Impact of the Agreement on Trade-Related Aspects of Intellectual Property Rights on Human Rights" (Geneva: Commission on Human Rights, 2001), 7.
52. Ernst-Ulrich Petersmann, "Human Rights and International Economic Law in the 21st Century: The Need to Clarify Their Interrelationships," *Journal of International Economic Law* 4, no. 1 (2001): 23.
53. Tansey, "Patenting Our Food Future," 583.
54. Petersmann, "Time for a Global Compact," 624.
55. Chapman, "The Human Rights Implications of Intellectual Property Protection," 867.
56. UN High Commissioner for Human Rights, "Globalization and Its Impact on the Full Enjoyment of Human Rights," (Geneva: Commission on Human Rights, 2002), para. 46.
57. Ibid.; UN High Commissioner for Human Rights, "Impact of Trips on Human Rights."
58. Richard B. Freeman, "Are Your Wages Set in Bejing?," *Journal of Economic Perspectives* 9, no. 3 (1995), 15–32.
59. Glenn Firebaugh, "Empirics of World Income Inequality," *The American Journal of Sociology* 104, no. 6 (1999), 1597-1630; Vincent A. Mahler, David K. Jesuit, and Douglas D. Roscoe, "Exploring the Impact of Trade and Investment on Income Inequality: A Cross-National Sectoral Analysis of the Developed Countries," *Comparative Political Studies* 32, no. 3 (1999), 363–95.
60. Mahler, Jesuit, and Roscoe, "Impact of Trade and Investment on Inequality."
61. Firebaugh, "Empirics of World Income Inequality."
62. David R. Cameron, "The Expansion of the Public Economy: A Comparative Analysis," *American Political Science Review* 72, no. 4 (1978), 1243–61; Peter J. Katzenstein, *Small States and World Markets: Industrial Policy in Europe* (Ithaca, NY: Cornell University Press, 1985); Dani Rodrik, "Why Do More Open Economies Have Bigger Governments?" in *NBER Working Papers Series* (Cambridge, MA: 1996).

63. John Gerard Ruggie, "International Regimes, Transactions, and Change: Embedded Liberalism in the Postwar Economic Order," *International Organization* 36, no. 2 (1982), 379–415.
64. Ronald Rogowski, *Commerce and Coalitions: How Trade Affects Domestic Political Alignments* (Princeton, NJ: Princeton University Press, 1989); Wolfgang F. Stolper and Paul A. Samuelson, "Protection and Real Wages," *The Review of Economic Studies* 9, no. 1 (1941), 58–73.
65. Dani Rodrik, "Sense and Nonsense in the Globalization Debate," *Foreign Policy* 107 (1997), 65–77.
66. E.g., Katzenstein, *Small States*.
67. Nita Rudra, "Openness, Welfare Spending, and Inequality in the Developing World," *International Studies Quarterly* 48, 3 (2004), 683–709. The picture is much less clear in developed countries; see C. Mesa-Lago, *Changing Social Security in Latin America: Toward Alleviating the Social Costs of Economic Reform* (Boulder, CO: Lynne Rienner, 1994); Nita Rudra, "Globalization and the Decline of the Welfare State in Less Developed Countries," *International Organization* 56, no. 2 (2002), 411–45.
68. UN High Commissioner for Human Rights, "Globalization and Human Rights," para. 35.

Conclusion

1. John Williamson, "What Should the World Bank Think About the Washington Consensus? " *The World Bank Research Observer* 15, no. 2 (2000): 252–53; Richard Falk, *Predatory Globalization: A Critique* (Cambridge, UK: Polity, 1999), 2; David Held, *Globalisation: The Dangers and the Answers* [article] (openDemocracy, 2004 [cited 11 June 2004]); available from http://www.opendemocracy.net/content/articles/PDF/1918.pdf.
2. See Joseph E. Stiglitz, *Globalization and Its Discontents* (New York: W.W. Norton, 2002).
3. Cf. Falk, *Predatory Globalization*, 2ff.
4. Benjamin Constant, "On the Liberty of the Ancients, Compared with That of the Moderns," in *Political Writings*, ed. Biancamaria Fontana (Cambridge, UK: Cambridge University Press, 1988), 323.

Index